THE DYNAMICS OF BUSINESS BEHAVIOR

THE DYNAMICS OF BUSINESS BEHAVIOR

AN EVIDENCE-BASED APPROACH TO MANAGING ORGANIZATIONAL CHANGE

BEIREM BEN BARRAH
PHILIP JORDANOV

WILEY

Published by John Wiley & Sons, Inc., Hoboken, New Jersey.
Published simultaneously in Canada.

For general information on our other products and services or for technical support, please contact our Customer Care Department within the United States at (800) 762-2974, outside the United States at (317) 572-3993 or fax (317) 572-4002.

Wiley also publishes its books in a variety of electronic formats. Some content that appears in print may not be available in electronic formats. For more information about Wiley products, visit our web site at www.wiley.com.

Library of Congress Cataloging-in-Publication Data is Available:

ISBN 9781394196562 (cloth)
ISBN 9781394196579 (ePub)
ISBN 9781394196586 (ePDF)

Cover Design: Wiley
Cover Image: © putracetol_std/Shutterstock

SKY10067142_021524

To the ones who raised us between cultures,
teaching us the nuances of human behavior.

Contents

Foreword

OUR PATHS CROSSED about a year ago through a social media platform. Beirem and Philip, two young entrepreneurs and experts in the field of behavioral science, inspired me to explore how behavioral science can make us better as the change management team at Johnson & Johnson. More importantly, we shared our joint belief that change management holds elements of art and science.

The change management organization within Johnson & Johnson supports complex and global transformations initiated by our global functions and/or business. The portfolio of initiatives consists of a combination of digital, technology, process, and cultural transformations and are project or systemic by nature. Through our human-centric model, the change management team always works within and for the business, delivering end-user and customer outcomes.

But is change management more an art or a science?

In different ways, this question comes up in conversations I have with people about change management. To grasp: what is change management, why does it matter, who drives it, what activities does it involve, how does it work, and how can we ultimately influence and change actions people take?

What about the art? Over centuries, art has been used as a means of expression and a vehicle for social commentary. Artists throughout history have used their creative works to shed light on societal issues, challenge norms, and advocate for change. Art extends this idea by intentionally harnessing artistic endeavors to raise awareness, provoke thought, and drive action around pressing global challenges. An artist creates art using conscious skills and creative imagination.

An example is the "Inside Out Project." This global participatory art project was initiated by French artist JR. It involves people taking large-scale black-and-white portraits (pictures) of themselves and pasting them in public spaces to help individuals and communities to make a statement. Through their "Actions," communities around the world have sparked collaborations and conversations about topics that matter to them. Since 2011, over 500,000 people across 152 countries have participated in the Inside Out Project. Thanks to participants' portrait donations, the project has reached all the continents, with over 2,500 actions created.

These actions have a range of topics: diversity, community, feminism, racism, climate change, education, children's rights, and art are just a few of them. This is an impactful example where creativity, skills, and imagination are used to raise awareness about common issues people around the globe face and to mobilize groups to stand up for these issues by actions. This is also what we do in change management.

The art side of change management does something similar. It involves the creative and human-centric aspects of guiding individuals and organizations through periods of transition. Just as artists use their creativity to convey emotions and provoke thought, change management professionals can employ artistic approaches to inspire, engage, and navigate change in ways that resonate deeply with people, providing meaning about the current and future state. Think about storytelling at different levels and in different ways, or visual maps to help people understand why to change, what it means, and how it works, and more specifically what it means for an individual.

Embracing the art side of change management means that you as a practitioner tap into the emotional and creative dimensions of individuals and ultimately teams and groups, fostering a more holistic approach to navigating change. This approach recognizes that change is not just a rational process but mostly a deeply human experience that can be enriched through room for (artistic) expression, different perspectives, purpose, meaning, and engagement.

What about the science? Is there any science to change? Sometimes we tend to believe there isn't because there is no one recipe we can use as practitioners or those leading change. Neither can we accurately predict or plan the outcomes of our interventions.

Could we say, "The science side of change management involves understanding the psychological, neurological, and behavioral aspects that influence how individuals and organizations respond to change"? By drawing on scientific principles and research, wouldn't it be impactful if change management practitioners could develop strategies that are evidence-based and tailored to the way the human mind and behavior work? My strong belief is that this is essential and will strengthen the art side of your change management interventions. This will enhance the predictability of the outcomes. This will make the conversation about the what, why, and how of change management with stakeholders more robust and help you as practitioner or leader in change to assess your interventions to learn.

This book brings together both the art and the behavioral science of change management. You will embark on a voyage that brings together the art of change—where creativity, meaning, and imagination are leveraged—with behavioral science, unlocking the secrets to transforming our responses to change on both personal and professional levels.

As the book dives into this synergy of disciplines, it uncovers the profound impact neuroscience has on our ability to adapt, learn, and embrace change. The human brain, an intricate web of connections and synapses, is a marvelous instrument that holds the key to our resilience and transformative potential. With a profound understanding of how our brains process and react to change, we can chart a course that steers us toward growth and success.

So is change management an art or a science? I strongly believe it is both, with you as a leader of change or a practitioner as the unique orchestrator. By understanding and applying behavioral science, you will be able to make more impactful interventions and embed behavioral science in everything you do daily. In all this art and science, it is you as a change "artist" who will always make the difference. The unique personal "toolbox" of characteristics, experience, intuition, creativity, and imagination, combined with your knowledge of behavioral science, will make the impact a transformation requires.

Enjoy *The Dynamics of Business Behavior* and allow yourself to study the (behavioral) science, learn about certain interventions and why they make the impact they make, and apply your new learnings.

Let's continue to evolve the change management practice by exploring the breadth and depth of the science and art of change management!

—**Bas Zwart**

—Global Leader, Change Management,
Johnson & Johnson

Preface

I AM FRUSTRATED and disappointed. Behavioral science entered the public imagination almost 15 years ago, perhaps starting with Thaler and Sunstein's *Nudge*,[1] and gaining more traction and credibility with Kahneman's *Thinking, Fast and Slow*[2] 12 years ago.

When those books appeared, I had been working in the fields of leadership development, and change, for nearly three decades. While I would like to think I produced more concrete and sustainable moments for clients than most, in my quiet moments I had doubts. I always suspected that we could do much better.

In private conversations with peers, I would ask, "What percentage of what we teach clients in our programs do we think they use in their work as leaders?"

The answers we whispered to each other (away from clients' ears) hovered around 25% percent. Academic research on "training transfer" suggests that it may be worse, sometimes as low as 10%![3]

Every change practitioner reading this book will have had their share of such disappointments: the workshops where participants leave inspired and committed but do little differently the following week; the carefully crafted vision and value statements that appear beautifully on walls, but rarely in leader behavior as they walk the halls. I'm of course talking about the intention-action gap, the gap between thinking and doing, the gap between mind and behavior. In change, behaviors matter most. (Has anyone ever lost weight by thinking about losing weight?)

Yet the change practitioners, coaches, leadership consultants, and organizational development (OD) consultants that I know are passionately committed to making a difference to their clients.

What to do?

In 2011, I wrote *The Science of Organizational Change*, my first book. In it, I tried to adapt findings on choice architecture, cognitive biases, nudges, and decision science into a book on change management. While the book remains a change best-seller, it is fair to say that the treatment of behavioral science was far too abstract—there were no change "use cases" to point at. The work of pioneers in the field, such as the UK's Nudge Unit, was aimed at public health and civic behaviors, not commercial enterprises, not organizational change.

Things haven't changed much. At IBM, a company I left just a few months ago, I tried to introduce behavioral science into a client proposal. My change colleagues insisted we use ADKAR (debunked in one of my other books).

Why? "The client uses ADKAR!" Despite our passion for making a real difference (behaviorally) to clients, our conservatism as a firm and our unwillingness to challenge clients' thinking meant we proposed a same-old, same-old approach to change.

In 2023, as someone who still travels the conference circuit, I can say with some authority that very few change experts have integrated the best behavioral science tools into their methodologies. And, because there are behavioral science boutiques popping up every month that are bringing behavioral science into leading businesses, the change management expert unschooled in behavioral science risks getting left behind.

The Dynamics of Business Behavior is a huge step in the right direction and the best book to date on behavioral science and organizational change. It is a book aimed squarely at change professionals, and the managers who lead change day in and day out at their companies. Philip and Beirem have written a book that explicitly tries to link behavioral science and organizational change management. They start with an excellent conceptual treatment that, as a bonus, includes another new area, evidence-based change management.

They then get practical in a way that I could not in 2011, offering use cases in areas such as Planning and Risk Management, Communications, Leadership, Engagement, Measurement, and Learning and Development. In each area, they offer case studies from business pioneers (such as Microsoft and ING) and insights from fellow behavioral scientists (such as Katie Milkman) breaking new ground in the field.

Between the lines, the careful reader will find other tools rarely found in orthodox change methodologies, for example, Large Group Interventions (or Whole System in the Room) or habit change methods (implementation triggers).

I do not recommend that you read this book; I recommend that you study it. Make notes in the margins and return to it often. If you are courageous enough to try what it suggests, I believe that the results you produce for clients will follow.

For the change community, this book promises to help us make our passion for change a behavioral reality.

—**Paul Gibbons**

Author of *The Science of Organizational Change*,
Impact, and *Change Myths*

Acknowledgments

IT'S REMARKABLE HOW many people are involved in creating a book like this, and we are deeply, deeply grateful to all of you. Words cannot fully express this, but let's make an attempt.

Maarten Bronkhorst, the hero linchpin who got us in touch with most of the interviewees. Peter van Gorsel, the trusted advisor who was always there if we had any questions. The brilliant people on Neurofied's team who helped us develop the foundational knowledge in these areas over the years and for their patience with us during the writing process. The many wonderful clients who trusted us over the years, gave us the opportunity to turn these ideas into real-life experiments, and continue to teach us invaluable lessons. Onwards!

Wiley, thank you for asking us to write this. Without you offering us this opportunity, there would only be Capability and Motivation but no book. Kezia Endsley, you are an amazing editor and at least as good a communicator. Sally Baker, thank you for spotting us in Amsterdam all the way from New York. And Deborah Schindlar, we appreciate you for guiding us through the Wiley publication process. A special thanks to Bas Zwart (and the extended J&J team) for your continued trust, proactive attitude, positive energy, and eloquent foreword.

We also raise our glass to all the people we interviewed. Thank you for trusting us, contributing your views, ideas, and real-life examples. These insightful conversations have leveled our thinking on this topic and your words have brought this book to life. In order of the interviews, here's to Thomas Mulder, Floor Huizer, Judith Peters, Wies Wagenaar, Kati Terza, Michael Hallsworth, Kiki van den Berg, Martin Sitalsing, Bas Kersten, Inca van Uuden, Gwen Burbidge, Natasja van Rens, Raymond van Hattem, Dominique Dingjan, Jeroen van der Brugge, Kenneth Kirindongo, Maarten van Beek, Tessa Peetoom, Pieter Versteeg, Marjon Kaper, Michiel van Meer, Wieke Scholten, Roger van Lier, Julia Wittlin, Diana Chiang, Tijs Besieux, Kristel Buitink, Barbara Lammers, David Hulsenbek, Marco Mullers, Clim Parren, Gerard Penning, Nadine Beister, and Meike Salvadó-de Reede.

Finally, none of this would have been possible without our families and especially our parents. You made us into who we are. You helped us navigate this, at times confusing, world. You gave us the strength, mindset, and discipline to embrace big projects like this. And you gave us the confidence to be ourselves, whether that be in the Netherlands, Tunisia, or Bulgaria. Thank you Ingrid and Salem. Thank you Straschimir and Karin. And the same goes for the continued support and love of our brothers and sisters, Ramy, Timo, Katja, and Mina. Finally, Luna and Lisanne, thank you for enduring us during this intensive writing process. We'll be more fun in the upcoming period, we promise.

Introduction

How CAN WE leverage behavioral psychology and neuroscience for organizational change? This book is about humanizing change management for managers, executives, project managers, and change professionals in areas like HR, L&D, and DEI. It combines scientific research, management consulting experience, and insights from 40-plus interviews with industry leaders and scientists to provide you with a behaviorally informed toolkit to drive positive and lasting change with step-by-step guides on 18 evidence-based interventions.

Behavioral science can, and should, significantly improve the success rate of organizational change initiatives while making it more human-centric. This bold claim is the core hypothesis behind our quest for knowledge. Why do so many organizational change initiatives fail? Why are so many employees disengaged? And what can you do to leverage scientific insights for better answers to these and other questions?

This book is not an all-encompassing approach to change management and is not intended to replace existing change management theories or practices. Neither does it claim to provide plug-and-play solutions to complex organizational challenges. Rather, it will provide you with the knowledge, tools, and strategies to identify behavioral challenges and tackle them with evidence-based interventions for positive and sustained change.

This book combines three main components to ensure practical value: behavioral insights, evidence-based interventions, and insights from industry leaders. The behavioral insights help you understand why things happen and what drives this behavior. The 18 evidence-based interventions—the core of this book—are tools that help you solve behavioral challenges, and each comes with a detailed, step-by-step guide to enable you to enhance your change management skills across the discussed six change areas.

But the leap from academic insights to organizational reality is often more complex and dynamic, with outcomes influenced by countless variables, including the organization's culture, the sector it operates in, structure and governance nuances, and the people involved. To ensure that the book's content is not only scientifically robust but also broadly applicable within an organizational context, we interviewed more than 40 leaders across a diverse array of sectors, including telecom, finance, retail, consultancy, the public sector, energy, tech, construction, mobility, recruitment, facilities, and healthcare. Their insights on change approaches, challenges, and interventions help bridge the gap between theory and practice, and navigate the complex dynamics of business behavior.

Who Is This Book For?

This is a book for managers and executives who are responsible for driving change across the organization. These people go under many flags but some of the most common names include change management, people and organization, human resources, organizational design, internal communications, and learning and development. This book will be just as valuable for managers of teams undergoing changes, regardless of whether they're in HR, tech, sales, support, or any other department.

Whatever your role, we assume that you continuously drive change in your organization, both directly through planning, implementing, or reinforcing change initiatives, and indirectly by, for example, role modeling and contributing to your organizational culture. Your ability to effectively drive organizational change depends on your ability to deal with situations as they arise. Often there is a large behavioral component and, as a manager or executive, you strongly benefit from a better intuitive grasp on the behavioral drivers behind change, as well as evidence-based tools to deal with recurring challenges.

We also wrote this book with two other audiences in mind, both of whom we consider our colleagues. The first is the broader organizational change management community, whether that is in the public or private sector, freelance, or at a large consulting firm. With your knowledge and experience in managing organizational change comes a strong intuition, and we aim to provide you with a more in-depth understanding of behavioral science. This will empower you to better understand and explain *why* some approach is more likely to drive the results you need. And from experience in working with a variety of organizational change management (OCM) teams, we know that many of you will benefit from the evidence-based interventions.

And of course, we wrote this book to give back to the behavioral science community that is the giant upon whose shoulders we stand. Experienced behavioral scientists who want to learn how to apply their expertise in an organizational context should find many actionable pointers. And young, aspiring behavioral scientists who are exploring career opportunities should find inspiration for use cases and examples of skill-building exercises. For other behavioral practitioners in the field, we salute you and hope you find this helpful in optimizing your approach and expanding your toolkit.

Why Behavioral Science Matters in Change Management

It's worth asking why the field of change management that has its own tried and tested methods and frameworks needs to be enhanced with behavioral science in the first place. We would argue that it's not about viewing behavioral science as an optional add-on to change management; rather, it's about recognizing it as a fundamental part of the process. This perspective holds across many of the challenges we face today.

Let's look at climate change as an example. Hard sciences provide clear guidelines on how to tackle this global issue. Yet the real challenge lies not in the scientific recommendations but in motivating individuals to adapt their behaviors in line with these solutions. The same is true in the medical field. Even though professionals know how to handle diseases like obesity, the real struggle is to incite changes in health behaviors.

In organizational change, a similar argument applies. No matter how well-structured or comprehensive a change plan is, it's still set to fail if individuals in organizations don't adapt their behaviors. Here's where behavioral science steps in. It helps us not only to identify but also to understand and influence human behavior for better outcomes.

In the last 15 years, applying behavioral science beyond academia has started to show real-world results, both in business and in society. One example of how a small behavioral science intervention can have a big impact comes from the public sector. To address long-term retirement saving, the UK government introduced automatic enrollment in workplace pensions, implemented between October 2012 and February 2018.[1] This policy mandated employers to automatically enroll eligible employees into a qualifying pension scheme and make minimum contributions. Employees aged 22 or over and under the state pension age earning over £10,000 annually became part of this scheme.

This behavioral intervention resulted in the number of eligible employees participating in a workplace pension rising from 55% in 2012 to 87% by the end of 2019. Moreover, the annual total amount saved in pension funds stood at £90.4 billion in 2018, an increase of £7 billion from 2017.

These types of behavioral interventions have shown a big impact in the private sector too. A satisfying example could be seen in Facebook's response to Apple's iOS privacy changes, which led to a significant shift in user behavior and a substantial financial impact on Facebook.[2] In 2021, Apple introduced the App Tracking Transparency (ATT) feature on its iOS operating system, enabling users to opt out of being tracked when using apps. This behavioral shift drastically reduced the ability of advertisers like Facebook to target specific demographics, resulting in a predicted $10 billion decrease in Facebook's ad revenue for the year. By simply giving users the choice of whether to be tracked, Apple initiated a minor shift in online behavior with major business impact. We explore these interventions further in Chapter 2.

As seen in these examples, behavioral science offers potent tools for change, but it's not a cure-all. Small behavioral interventions alone won't solve massive organizational issues. However, this book's essence isn't about seeking a silver bullet. We focus on a mix of intervention strategies—from minor tweaks to systemic changes—and tailoring them to your context.

The Challenges of Applying Science

In the daily grind of getting things done, we often forget that many of the problems we encounter have already been solved by others. This is where scientific insights could and should make organizations more human-centric by imbuing organizational processes with scientific insights.

Science is such an essential asset for societies that its core institutions are generally funded by the state. Their mission is to develop a network of scientists who help us solve the unsolvable questions. If much of the most important research is in the public domain, why don't we—meaning corporate professionals—all fully leverage this? As it turns out, there are many reasons. There is too little time. There is too much information. It is hard to ask the right questions. The information is too fragmented. General models do not apply to unique problems. We need action, not theory. Key info is behind a paywall. And so on.

In addition, behavioral science has its own challenges. There is no one truth like in physics. Neither is there a commonly agreed-upon overarching theoretical model. Not all research is reliable (or can be replicated). Behavior is extremely context-specific, so the value of models depends heavily on the user's experience and expertise. It is equally important to be aware of these challenges and to know they can be solved, or at the very least significantly improved.

That is why the practical interventions in this book are not proposed as plug-and-play solutions to managing change. Instead, you learn how to test, evaluate, tailor, and implement them step-by-step to find out whether they work for your organization and its unique context. This is what *behaviorally informed change management* is about. Let's build this concept from the ground up.

Behaviorally Informed Change Management

We start with **change** itself, the process of moving from one state to another. In the same vein, **organizational change** refers to the process of changing the state of an organization, such as its culture, internal processes, or the underlying technologies or infrastructure it uses to operate. **Organizational change management (OCM)** is the process of guiding this organizational change to a successful resolution, a big part of which has to do with people. You can view OCM as a framework and toolkit to drive organizational change forward, and for the purposes of this book, change management and OCM will be used interchangeably.

As you can probably imagine, this involves a lot. OCM activities can range from the executives' strategic restructuring plan to the managers' tactical shift in team responsibilities all the way to changes in the frontline employees' operational daily workflow. Large organizations often have dedicated change management teams responsible for driving a coherent, effective, and lasting change strategy while empowering all stakeholders.

Then we get to the **behaviorally informed** side of things. Think about data-informed decision-making, considered the holy grail by many organizations, especially in tech, where data is abundant. In essence, it simply means making decisions based on data. Similarly, behaviorally informed means "informed by behavioral science." Here, you make decisions grounded in an understanding of human behavior and what is driving it.

As an organization, why would you want to make your approach behaviorally informed? Since people are at the core of (almost) any business, making things more human-centric tends to drive better results and higher employee engagement. And personally, would you rather work for an organization that improves its processes based on financial results only or also takes into account the psychological impact of changes on its people?

So let's bring it all together: **behaviorally informed change management** is a methodology that successfully drives organizational change informed by insights from behavioral psychology and neuroscience. It is a framework that helps managers and executives approach organizational change in a human-centric way and a toolkit with evidence-based change interventions that can drive effective and lasting change.

The Academic, Practitioner, and Entrepreneur

How did we end up doing this? It turns out we both ended up with the same mission from opposite directions. Beirem Ben Barrah is an entrepreneur at heart who voraciously reads books on business, psychology, and technology. In 2018, he founded Neurofied with the mission to harness behavioral psychology to address business challenges. Meanwhile, Philip Jordanov, a behavioral scientist trained in cognitive psychology and neuroscience, kept asking himself whether the insights he learned in college and in the brain imaging labs would ever be actually applied in the real world. Ever since we met, we've been chasing the vision of translating academic insights on human behavior into actionable solutions for real-world problems. Philip has since become a cofounder, and we've built a team of behavioral scientists and a network of industry specialists we trust and admire for their unique qualities.

Since that time, Neurofied has trained thousands of professionals and collaborated with over 100 management, HR, growth, and innovation teams, applying behavioral psychology and neuroscience insights to tackle issues in business and society. We've helped organizations like Johnson & Johnson, KPMG, Deloitte, Novo Nordisk, ABN AMRO, and the Dutch government with behaviorally informed change in areas like business transformation, leadership development, sustainability, HR, and DEI. Throughout our journey, we have designed, tested, and implemented dozens of evidence-based interventions to support these organizations in achieving effective and sustained behavioral change. These projects in our daily work life are one source for the content of this book. (See Figure I.1.)

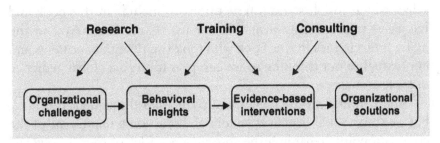

Figure I.1   Neurofied's process for applying behavioral science.

We see ourselves not just as entrepreneurs, academics, or practitioners, but as ambassadors of behavioral science, striving to democratize its understanding and application. To achieve this, we've produced resources including a blog with 100-plus articles on applying behavioral science and a YouTube channel that offers free online courses and detailed intervention guides. You can find these and other resources at neurofied.com. This book is a major advancement in our mission, representing our biggest effort yet to democratize behavioral science and bring its potential to a broader professional audience.

In writing a book like this, one always has to make tradeoffs, and the best books we read make these decisions explicit. We aim to choose pragmatism over theory and simplification over complexity. The idea is to leverage academic rigor to make change processes more suitable for the ever-faster speed of industry. The other side of the coin is the actual change out there in organizations, happening every day. Even though we have years of experience in consulting and training management, HR, and innovation teams, it's still different from leading this change "from the inside." So how do we truly make sure the information in this book is actually relevant for you, the reader?

Unique Insights from 40-Plus Interviews

To ensure the behavioral insights and interventions are relevant for a wide range of organizations, we reached out to industry leaders, government officials, and behavioral scientists. This way, we could offer a variety of perspectives, organizational contexts, and field examples that give life to the tools in this book. It also helped us select which insights and interventions to include in this book and has been tremendously insightful for us. Again, thank you to the many interviewees in this book who took the time to educate us and contextualize our thinking so we can pass it on to a global audience of professionals.

You will find all the names and companies throughout this book but we think you'll benefit from a brief discussion around some of the core data points regarding the interviewees. Out of the 41 "official" interviewees, two are from the public sector, five are specialized behavioral experts, and the other 34 are organizational professionals. Of this last group, almost all interviewees represent large enterprises, but we also included three people from small and medium-sized businesses (SMB) and one scale-up. They include many of the largest organizations in the Netherlands and beyond, such as the three biggest Dutch banks (ING, Rabobank, and ABN AMRO), healthcare titans like Novo Nordisk and Johnson & Johnson, and organizations you're unlikely to know but that have a global impact, such as the maritime dredging giant Van Oord.

We were pleasantly surprised to see that the interviewees represented a total of 15 sectors and 34 organizations! Six interviewees are active in finance, five in mobility and transport, four in consultancy, and three each in the energy, healthcare, public, retail, and technology sectors. Other sectors represented range from chemicals and construction to telecom and maritime dredging. This was perhaps the most important element for us to have diversity in, because we want the ideas in this book to be relevant for and tailored to any organization, not just one specific kind. Behavior underlies all change, whether that's at the office, in the air, or across the warehouses.

Let's look at the roles and level of seniority that the organizational interviewees represent. Among them were 23 HR professionals, seven change specialists, and a few other related roles. At the time of writing, almost half of the interviewees were executives, 26% were directors, and the remaining quarter was quite evenly divided between vice presidents (VPs), managers, and frontline employees. We're aware of the potential bias here, since HR and executives are heavily represented, so we spent a lot of time making sure to select the insights from these interviews that are relevant for all audiences.

Finally, let's look at the geographical reach of the interviewees. The majority of our interviewees are based in the Netherlands, but that does not mean they do not represent a larger group. About half of the interviewees were responsible for the Netherlands, whereas 7 had roles whose responsibility carried over to (parts of) Europe and 12 interviewees had roles with global responsibility. Since this book has a global audience, we tried our best to make the insights and interventions as broadly applicable as possible, and without all of these interviews that would have been much harder. You will find the interviews insights in this book to capture the fascinating dynamics of business behavior through first-hand experience.

How to Read This Book

We wrote this book in the hope that you can use it as a field guide that is insightful enough to keep close to your desk and come back to throughout projects. It consists of two parts.

In Part I, Chapter 1 discusses the history and fundamentals of OCM as well as recurring challenges mentioned by interviewees. It will provide relevant context, but if you're an experienced change professional, you're free to skip this. Chapter 2 explores the value of behavioral science as a lens, tool, and approach. You learn the relevant behavioral insights and frameworks that are revisited throughout this book. If you're a seasoned behavioral scientist who knows all the concepts, you're free to move on.

Chapter 3 introduces you to the idea of behaviorally informed change management (BICM). It builds on the foundation of and merges the previous chapters. It showcases its value in use cases ranging from managing change fatigue and mergers and acquisitions (M&A) to diversity, equity, and inclusion (DEI), and building resilience. This chapter makes the case for BICM, whereas Chapter 4 introduces you to the tools of this craft: evidence-based change interventions (EBCIs). This brings you to real life, where behavioral insights are pragmatically implemented in organizations. Once you see the shared underlying framework of interventions and know what makes them evidence-based, you're ready for the part of this book in which we turn this theory into pragmatic step-by-step interventions.

Part II is all about applying behavioral science and neuropsychology insights into six change areas that any change professional will recognize. Each subsequent chapter looks into the current approach and recurring challenges of one change area and provides behavioral insights and evidence-based interventions you can directly start experimenting with. Chapter 5 is about planning and risk management, Chapter 6 is on narrative and communication, Chapter 7 is on leadership support, Chapter 8 is on stakeholder engagement, Chapter 9 is on measuring change, and Chapter 10 is on learning and development. There will be step-by-step guides on implementing or facilitating the interventions, and we chose this book setup so you can quickly revisit relevant areas, insights, or interventions.

At the end of this book, you'll have an understanding of how to apply behavioral science to organizational change management initiatives. You will have the knowledge, tools, and strategies required to identify behavioral challenges, implement evidence-based solutions, and drive positive, lasting, and human-centric change. We hope that the book provides you with inspiration, insights, and actionable next steps.

PART

I

Bridging Two Disciplines

1

Managing Organizational Change

WHAT IS ORGANIZATIONAL change management? How did it evolve over time? Which models and frameworks have impacted the field most? How does organizational change come about? What is the current standard approach to organizational change management (OCM)? What are recurring challenges when driving organizational change? These are some of the questions we answer in this chapter before embarking on the journey of applying insights from behavioral psychology and neuroscience to organizational change management.

A History of Organizational Change Management (OCM)

This is a simplified and nonexhaustive history, but it should provide you with context on how the field was formed, both through research and in practice.

Pre-1960s: "What Do You Mean Change Management?"

You could reasonably argue that change has always inspired people to manage the change. Think of the formation and organization of

15

towns, armies, kingdoms, or religions throughout history. These are no small projects and require a group of people to stand behind a common vision, take on a form of shared identity, and coordinate their behavior. Yet on Wikipedia, the history of change management barely starts until the 1960s, when theorists and practitioners began to lay the groundwork for the field of change management that we know today.

By now, there is a plethora of change models one can ascribe to, so let's explore some of the most influential ones over time. It's worth emphasizing that almost every interviewee mentioned how they do not simply copy the original model but use it as a jump-off point for creating a tailored approach that suits their organizational context.

The first formation of such a formal change process is ascribed to Kurt Lewin, a German-American pioneer in the fields of social, organizational, and applied psychology. He developed change management tools such as Force Field Analysis and Action Research while laying the foundation for the well-known three-step Unfreeze-Change-Refreeze model.[1] While these models are historically significant because they form the foundation upon which many subsequent approaches and models have been built, they hold relatively little practical value when it comes to managing continuous change in today's fast-paced, globally connected world. In over 40 interviews, Kurt Lewin was mentioned only once, and that was to state that his method is mostly outdated.

The 1960s and 1970s: "Can We Structure This Process?"

In the 1960s, two important developments made organizational change management more human-centric. First, as it became clear that people's pain of losing things like their old job, team, or way of working correlates to pain from other kinds of grieving, new models were introduced. For example, the Kübler-Ross Change Curve identifies the emotional impact of each phase of the change, which allows for dealing with these emotions more proactively.[2] This is also where organizations started paying more attention to how employees engage with the change. Since then, the Kübler-Ross Curve has been partly debunked. Criticism highlights its limitations, such as presupposing change as negative and not distinguishing between intended and unintended changes. Change managers should exercise caution when using this model for managing change because it may not be universally applicable and can oversimplify employee reactions. However, this is still a useful tool for illustrating the range of emotions people can experience based on change and demonstrate the importance of acknowledging grief, as mentioned by four interviewees.

The second big development was the introduction of Everett Roger's Diffusion of Innovation theory,[3] which aims to explain how, why, and how fast new ideas and technology spread. It introduced terminology still at the core of business (early adopters, early/late majority, and laggards), but more importantly, it put people at the core of change thinking. It emphasized the importance of understanding change in the context of time, communication channels, and its impact on people. It also strengthened the connection between innovation and OCM. Only one interviewee explicitly referred to this model, but we found that this way of thinking was regularly reflected in sentences like "We found it's best to focus on the roughly 70% in the middle who can go either way instead of the roughly 15% of people who will resist until everyone else changes." One could also argue that change champion or agent networks are a way of building and leveraging a group of early adopters.

The 1980s and 1990s: "What's with the Resistance?"

In the 1980s, the large consulting firms started rebranding their reengineering services to *change management*, which helped legitimize the field, attracting more talent in both industry and academic institutions. In 1980, Bob Waterman, Tom Peters, and Julien Phillips published another influential change management model: McKinsey's 7-S model.[4] It took a more holistic approach by analyzing seven aspects of the organization and their interactions with each other: strategy, structure, systems, shared values, style, staff, and skills. If any of the seven components are not aligned with or does not support the others, you know where to start improving things. Interestingly, in our interviews, this model was mentioned only once, but McKinsey's other, more recent influence model to change[5] was mentioned more often.

Then the 1990s started, the golden decade of organizational change management in terms of publications. Peter Senge (Stanford & MIT) published *The Fifth Discipline* in 1990,[6] a masterpiece on the learning organization that became a cornerstone in the field of organizational development (OD). He leveraged management, systems thinking, and psychological knowledge to reimagine how organizations could evolve. According to Senge, to effectively drive organizational change, there must be 1) a compelling case, 2) time to change, 3) support during the process, and 4) proactive prevention of potential critical barriers. Personally, we were especially impressed with Peter's case for the value of harnessing the power of mental models (more on this in Chapter 2).

The following year, William Bridges (Harvard) published *Managing Transitions*,[7] a book on the importance of dealing not only with the change but also with what he calls *transitions*, the psychological or human side of the change. The transition process consists of three phases: letting go, the neutral zone, and a new beginning. The idea of letting go builds on the grief-based methods we saw before, and the neutral zone is this tricky phase where you haven't quite let go of the old ways, nor have you really adopted the new ways. Things are up in the air, and although this makes it hard to perceive progress and might be demotivating, it is the perfect opportunity to try new things and drive innovation. This book is one of our personal favorites, and we still use Bridges's transition model daily.

Two years later, Daryl Conner published *Managing at the Speed of Change*,[8] which added a few key ideas to the field of OCM. The book suggested that people and organizations have a range of the amount and speed of change they can tolerate and that leaders are responsible for managing this. Conner also proposed a set of eight patterns in organizational change processes, which provide a general direction. These are broad themes like the "nature" and "process" of change, "roles played during change," and "resistance" and "commitment" to it. There are also pointers on how to drive the resilience of your organization, a theme that resurfaced in McKinsey's 2022 survey[9] as the top priority for CEOs.

In 1995, *Harvard Business Review* published John Kotter's seminal article, "Leading Change,"[10] which became the bedrock of the change management industry we've seen in the past two decades.

Kotter's eight steps to change model proposes that organizational change follows a series of eight sequential phases and identifies the actions needed and pitfalls for each phase. The structure of urgency-coalition-vision-communication-empowerment-quick wins-consolidation-institutionalization has been widely implemented, and to this day most change management frameworks draw inspiration from Kotter's approach. This was one of the most mentioned models during our interviews.

In the words of Thomas Mulder, the CHRO of VodafoneZiggo, a Dutch company that provides fixed, mobile, and integrated communication and entertainment services to consumers and businesses, "Kotter's model is useful but only for a singular change. It does not address how you manage an organizational or cultural change that puts the changes in the DNA of the organization or culture. A lot of change models lack this element. That is why purpose and congruence are key: saying what you think and then embodying it in the organizational culture and everything you do."

Start of the 21st Century: "How Do We Deal with This Barrage of Change?"

The 2001 book *Beyond Change Management* by Dean Anderson and Linda Ackerman[11] became a staple in literature for the organizational development field. Their approach goes beyond overcoming resistance and supporting implementation but actually providing the kinds of support that is required for all change to be successful. They described the goal of OD as transforming organizations to a new state through a systematic change effort by using behavioral science knowledge and skill. Instead of top-down change management, they chose a multidimensional approach that addresses change at four levels: organizational, team, relational, and personal. They also coined the Drivers of Change model we describe later in this chapter.

Since then, the world has become increasingly globalized and digitized, two developments that strongly impact the field of change management. Global organizations require more skill and knowledge in OD and OCM to effectively develop and scale their operations. Digitalization has further connected the world, and the field of software development has given rise to many new project management methodologies such as Agile, Lean Startup, and Design Thinking. The amount of data we can leverage has skyrocketed and is slowly becoming a key part of most organizations' decision-making process. All of these things have a place in effective and human-centric change management, as we explore throughout this book.

The Evolution of OCM

The evolution of organizational change management we just sketched can be broken down into four phases.

1. Up until around the 1960s, OCM as a team was essentially nonexistent in most organizations and change was driven by authority because people weren't used to speaking up and most were comfortable with the notion that the boss knows best.

2. The 1960s and 1970s were marked by a focus on structuring the OCM process and a growing awareness of the central role of people.

3. The 1980s and 1990s were about identifying and overcoming resistance while ensuring OCM becomes more of a core capability for organizations.

4. The first two decades of the 21st century could be characterized by the rise of information technology, enabling fast-paced corporate experimentation and learning.

> We believe that the most likely contender for the next phase of OCM's evolution is the integration of brain and behavior insights to make it more effective and human-centric.

It seems to be a fundamental truth that organizational change management both depends on and impacts people the most. You can implement the most advanced performance management system out there, but if people do not adopt the tool (i.e., adapt their mindset and behavior to the new situation), it is more likely to result in reduced productivity and employee engagement than better performance. Since everyone in the organization, from the janitor to the CEO, is a person, this theme is likely to resurface time and time again.

Another reason is that scientific and technological advances are enabling behavioral science and neuroscience to develop at a much higher pace than in the previous decades. What's more, there is a growing amount of evidence that small nudges can really make a difference when it comes to changing behavior at scale. There will be plenty of examples throughout the book of small nudges that, especially when combined and compounded using a coherent strategy, can have a big impact on our behavior. And you can harness these invisible forces to promote sustainable and healthy behaviors in organizations. Surely, understanding more about how people think, decide, and act should be reflected in how organizations function.

And indeed, we see the early waves of behaviorally informed teams and departments come into existence. Think of roles such as behavioral risk managers, behavioral designers, and chief behavioral officers. These professionals come from a variety of backgrounds, but it'd be hard to do this without a strong understanding of what makes people tick. On the academic side, there are now master's degree programs in areas like behavioral and neuro-economics, brain and cognition in society, and applied cognitive science. If both supply (students) and demand (job functions) are growing, we can safely say that society's current bet is on behavioral and neuroscience becoming more prevalent across organizations. And to us, the most obvious candidate for a behaviorally informed transformation is change management—the facilitator of change throughout the rest of the organization.

The Drivers of Change

So how does organizational change come about? Instead of reinventing the wheel, we believe that Anderson and Ackerman's Drivers of Change model is an excellent foundation to build upon. (See Figure 1.1.) To briefly reiterate, the goal of this chapter is to provide context for those who are relatively new to organizational change management. If you or your organization uses another model and you don't want the confusion, that's completely fine and you're free to skip this section.

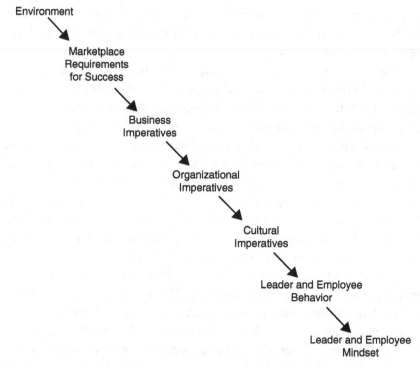

Environment

Marketplace
Requirements
for Success

Business
Imperatives

Organizational
Imperatives

Cultural
Imperatives

Leader and Employee
Behavior

Leader and Employee
Mindset

Figure 1.1   Anderson and Ackerson's Drivers of Change model.

But for those who haven't looked into this, let's see how the Drivers of Change model helps clarify how organizational change happens.

It describes seven drivers of change: environment, marketplace, business, organization, culture, behavior, and mindset. When a change in the **environment** happens (let's say changing demographics, as in the case of globalization, or new government regulations, as in the case of COVID-19), it can change the requirements for success in the **marketplace**. This in turn can force the **business** to make strategic changes to meet customer demand, which often means that the **organization** has to change their structure, systems, processes, technology, resources, skills, or staffing. If this change is large enough, it can trigger the additional need for **cultural** change, described as a collective way of being, working, and relating in the company. An organizational culture is best expressed by the collective behaviors, decisions, and attitudes of people, so naturally cultural change requires **behavioral** change among the leaders and employees. Finally, behavioral change usually requires a shift in **mindset,** which describes the worldview, assumptions, beliefs, or mental models that cause people to behave and act as they do.

Anderson and Ackerman argued that many of the challenges with transformation are a result of leaders not effectively attending to the cultural, behavioral, and mindset components of transformation. We believe the time has come for insights from behavioral and neuroscience to deepen managers' understanding of all three of these components, as you will read about in the next chapter and beyond.

It is undoubtedly true that change is already happening at all levels of the organization. On the organizational level, it is very rare nowadays to see an organization that has only one strategic priority and is not running at least a transformational change involving many separate initiatives. On the departmental and team levels, there are often multiple transitional and developmental changes going on at once and they often relate to one another. If organizations work with strong OKRs, this might be information available to all employees, but usually very few people, if any, have the full picture of what's going on across departments. On the individual level, change takes a more abstract form, but it is still a constant. Apart from training and development, people's mindset and behavior are strongly affected by their environment and experiences, making them change their mind and behavior all the time, albeit in small ways.

The Audio Technician

As you can see in the Drivers of Change model, organizational change does not happen in a vacuum. This makes it unlikely that change will be successfully managed by a small group of people in a separate room. That's why we believe that despite the official title, the role of a change manager should mainly be to *facilitate* instead of *manage.* Let's explore this idea through the lens of a metaphor. Think of organizations as a concert hall. If the orchestra is changing from one song to the next, who represents the change manager? At first glance, it might seem like the change manager is the conductor, but zoom out and you will see that the orchestra is not all there is. The musicians are playing for the audience and both of them are hosted by support crews ranging from catering and audio technicians to hosts and security. There is no one right way to view a metaphor, but we found it useful to think of change managers as the audio technicians. Hear us out.

The audience is clearly the organization's customer. If they enjoy themselves, it's probably considered a great concert. The musicians are then the employees, especially those on the frontline or in product teams, given that they directly affect the customer experience. It's tempting to think of the conductors as change managers but we believe this role equates to *change leaders*, the corporate managers and executives who are in many ways role-modeling the behaviors they'd like to see in their employees.

So the role of a change manager seems to us more like that of the audio technician. They work with multiple orchestras (teams) and conductors (leaders) but always to improve the experience of the audience (customers) by improving the quality of sound. Audio technicians also don't need to know as much about the individual instruments and musicians, but given their experience with previous concerts (organizational change projects), they know how all the instruments add up to the overall sound and can make technical tweaks to optimize the quality. They are also responsible for predicting where the potential points of failure in the sound system are and how to prevent them—or worst case, solve them. If the entire sound system is set up correctly and harmoniously, the sound can theoretically be perfect, but whether it is good music is still up to the conductor and the musicians.

The Success Rate of Organizational Change Projects

So how are we doing when it comes to managing change in organizations? The success rate of organizational change initiatives has long been a topic of debate and concern among practitioners. There is a common belief that most change initiatives fail, with estimates of failure rates around 70%. This belief has been echoed by prominent voices in change management like John Kotter. However, according to Paul Gibbons, author of the book *The Science of Organizational Change*,[12] this claim is not very helpful and not necessarily true.

Both change and the success rate of change are situational and highly context-dependent. Success rates depend on various factors, such as the type of change initiative, the organization's culture and structure, the level of employee engagement, and the overall economic climate. Therefore, it is essential to assess the type of change initiative you are undertaking and set realistic expectations based on the context, complexity, and potential obstacles.

In his book, Gibbons included a short review of 49 organizational change studies and their success rates, from strategy deployment (58% median success rate) to mergers and acquisitions (33% median success rate), all the way to culture change (19% median success rate). Although the sample size is small, these statistics show that expectations about success and failure should be tailored to the type of change you're dealing with. For example, change initiatives aimed at changing an organization's culture are more challenging and may have lower success rates than those aimed at deploying a new strategy.

It is worth noting that these median success rates should not be taken as gospel because they are based on generalizations and may not apply to all organizations or specific change initiatives. However, they do provide a useful starting point for understanding the potential success rates of different types of organizational change initiatives.

In the following chapters, we explore how incorporating insights from behavioral psychology and neuroscience can help improve the success rates of organizational change initiatives. By leveraging these insights, organizations can design more effective and tailored change interventions that address the specific needs of their employees, culture, and context. To provide some structure in applying behavioral insights to change management, let's find out more about the six change areas in which we found these evidence-based change interventions to be particularly useful.

Six Change Areas

Most organizational change projects, especially transformations, have a variety of parallel projects hidden inside them—from planning the change and engaging key stakeholders all the way to measuring progress and supporting the professional development of people. To simplify the ideas in this book, we chose six areas that any change manager will recognize in which evidence-based change interventions can add value. In Chapter 3, we consider the interventions in each area. For

Table 1.1   Six change areas for applying behavioral science.

Change Area	Description
Planning and Risk Management	How to plan the change and balance risk with innovation
Narrative and Communication	How to structure your change narrative and communicate
Leadership Support	How leaders can effectively drive and support change
Measuring Change	How to set good metrics and measure true progress
Stakeholder Engagement	How to engage stakeholders in a human-centric way
Learning and Development	How to facilitate continuous learning and development

now, we briefly highlight them. Table 1.1 lists the six change areas and includes short descriptions.

You might have more experience or knowledge in one area or another, but if you're in the profession of driving organizational change, you will recognize each one. That brings us to the next question: is there some kind of hierarchy of importance within these six change areas? This is a somewhat subjective question and, as always, depends on the context such as the organizational culture, the phase of the change, and the kind of challenges you encounter. Nonetheless, there seem to be some dependencies, so allow us to tentatively break down how these change areas relate to one another.

Connecting the Change Areas

In 2024, it still seems unlikely that organizations will be able to function fully autonomously within the next few decades. This means humans will still be at the heart of organization, that is, leadership support and stakeholder engagement at the top of the hierarchy. Other elements—like planning and risk management, narrative and communication, measuring change, and even learning and development—are essentially tools people can use to solve problems and take advantage of opportunities they encounter. In the long run, this might change as developments in artificial intelligence and robotics could enable sophisticated AI-driven systems to automate and streamline many of the tasks that are now in the domain of the average change manager. But that's tomorrow; today is today.

Let's start with leadership support. Top-down changes, as their name suggests, usually originate from leadership and therefore are strongly supported. Whether bottom-up approaches are just as supported depends on many things, including the organizational culture, whether you find suitable sponsors (business leaders), and how well you enable them to help you and their people. Good change facilitators actively guide leaders in how they can support the change and remind them throughout the change of what the value will be for them and their people. Strong leadership support creates a strong foundation for successful change by setting the priorities, tone, and direction while ensuring adequate resources for it to be implemented effectively. Change leaders and facilitators can then use this foundation to engage stakeholders, make plans, assess risks, create a narrative and communicate, measure change progress, make data-driven optimizations, and drive suitable forms of L&D (learning and development).

Stakeholder engagement is in many ways the true heart of change management. As we discussed, collective change stems from individual (often behavioral) change. In conventional change management, stakeholder engagement often refers to ensuring buy-in and collaboration, but as highlighted in many interviews, the biggest value of stakeholder engagement is in co-creation. The earlier you can involve stakeholders, the better. If you co-create the change effectively, it will lead to more effective planning and risk management. Stakeholders can also help you shape the narrative and are both the audience of and ideally contributors to change-related communications. Measuring change effectiveness involves stakeholder engagement in itself, whether it is qualitative (e.g., interviews) or quantitative (e.g., engagement surveys). And the same goes for L&D. The best L&D programs are often co-created with stakeholders because they are the ones whose behavior is involved. It is also worth mentioning that change champion (or agent) networks—one of the most common ways to grow internal change capabilities—are essentially supercharged stakeholders that will help you manage each of the other change areas more effectively.

The four "tools" among the change areas are less directly related, except for the area of planning and risk management, because it directs the use of the other change areas, thereby creating a kind of coherence. A good planning involves balancing all of the mentioned change areas, and quality risk management helps find the right balance between promoting the risk-taking behavior required for innovation and mitigating the chances of high-impact mistakes or failures. Although narrative and communication are not as directly related to the other areas, it might be just as vital. Without the mechanisms to ensure the change is widely understood and accepted, driving lasting change at scale is next to impossible. Measuring change is about tracking the progress and impact of your change initiatives, thereby identifying potential areas of threat or opportunities. Often the result is a change in the project planning to rebalance the activities in any of these change areas. And finally there is L&D, which is about empowering people with the mindset, skills, knowledge, or tools that they need in order to thrive in the new environment. Given the pace with which the world is speeding up, the L&D format is likely to change considerably (e.g., generative AI, virtual/augmented reality, and massive open online courses), but its importance will only grow as people need to keep up with a continuously changing world.

Recognizing Who Is Responsible

In Chapters 5–10 we go much deeper into each of these change areas, but let's consider one final note here. Not every one of these change areas will be in the domain of a single change professional, and who focuses on which areas differs per organization, based on their governance. During our interviews, Jeroen van der Brugge, at the time organizational development director at Facilicom Group, a Dutch company that provides facility management services, explained how different roles focus on different areas. His team (OD) focused on leadership support, stakeholder engagement, and narrative and communication. HR was mainly responsible for measuring change and L&D, whereas planning and risk management fell under the guidance of a project manager. We have also seen cases where narrative and communication fall directly under the responsibility of (internal) communications or the change managers. In some organizations, such as Microsoft, measuring change is arranged by the technology or data analysis department and in others, such as dsm-firmenich, mandatory training (e.g., safety) is part of risk management as opposed to the L&D department.

This reiterates the fundamental truth that organizations need to find their own unique approach to driving change. It's very useful to draw inspiration from models and other organizations' blueprints, but this far from replaces the need to tailor it to the structure, systems, and culture of your own organization.

Recurring Challenges in Change Management

During our interviews, we also asked for and found a broad range of recurring challenges in managing organizational change. Let's explore some of the interesting findings.

Change Fatigue or Continuous Change

The leading recurring challenge mentioned by interviewees was change fatigue and continuous change. *Change fatigue* refers to the overwhelming exhaustion, disengagement, and stress experienced by individuals and organizations due to continuous or poorly managed change. Most people inherently seek stability, predictability, and order, but the alarming rate at which many organizations are changing nowadays tends to create a chaotic and at times overwhelming environment, contributing to change fatigue. This concept is closely related to change saturation, so let's explore both concepts after we discuss why this is such a particularly thorny issue for organizations nowadays.

When COVID-19 happened, organizations had to change radically, resulting in a variety of change initiatives such as future of work and resilience. A combination of impactful movements, including Black Lives Matter, #MeToo, and LGBTQ advocacy, has rapidly shown organizations worldwide why it is important to get their diversity, equity, and inclusion (DEI) affairs in order. The Russia-Ukraine conflict continues to have a global impact ranging from volatile oil and gas prices all the way to political tensions causing organizations to withdraw from either country. Meanwhile, the digital natives known as Gen Z are entering the workforce, bringing with them new cultural values and workplace demands, resulting in phenomena such as "quiet quitting" and even "loud leaving." Since the release of ChatGPT in 2022, organizations' urgency to leverage new generative AI technologies has skyrocketed as well. On top of all this, there might be geographically bound challenges such as the shortage of talent in the local job market. These are mostly unrelated events or trends, yet they all impact how organizations are supposed to be running their daily operations. The point is that our global society is speeding up, and the market, governments, and their own people expect organizations to keep up. So how does this change overload affect us?

Change saturation refers to the situation that arises when the number and the intensity of changes exceed the capacity of your people to adopt them. This causes a kind of continuous turmoil where it is hard to prioritize, implement, and reinforce projects because people are simply at full capacity in terms of dealing with all the changes. Progress tends to slow, bottlenecks become more apparent, and project outcomes begin to suffer. As a change manager or leader, you have to gauge the level of change saturation so you can proactively prevent and mitigate the situation as soon as it arises. Ideally, reduce the amount of parallel changes implemented to open up people's energy, bandwidth, and time, but at the very least do not introduce new changes at this time or it might evolve into change fatigue.

Change fatigue is often a result of neglecting the signs of change saturation. By now the changes are so overwhelming that chaos turns into disengagement. Some of the signs include a lack of interest or an apathy toward the change, negativity and cynicism regarding the approach or its likelihood of success, and higher levels of stress or even burnout. Engagement or pulse surveys, absence rates, and turnover rates can also be indicators of fatigue among stakeholders. Change saturation and fatigue are more of a spectrum than a black-and-white distinction, but once you see any of these signs you want to seriously consider reducing the number and intensity of changes as soon as possible. People are at the core of your organization, and when a significant part of them withdraws, a variety of other problems start appearing. Change fatigue will be revisited as well as strategies to mitigate it.

Reinforcing Change

The second clearly identifiable challenge in OCM is reinforcing change, mentioned by 27%. This can refer to the third phase of the simple prepare-implement-reinforce model of change or to the activities within this phase to make the change stick. Let's explore what interviewees mentioned on this topic for more context. Inca van Uuden, HR director at Essent—a Dutch energy company that provides electricity, gas, and energy services to consumers and businesses—explained that "starting is easy but consistently reinforcing change is hard. You have to keep people engaged throughout the change and prevent an isolated strategy that 'they' will have to execute." She also hints at the importance of co-creation in driving engagement and ultimately lasting change (a topic we explore in Chapter 6).

Kati Terza, global transformation and change manager at Royal HaskoningDHV, an independent international engineering and project management company, gave a practical example of the importance of reinforcing change: "If you have a CRM system successfully implemented but after few months there is low adoption among users and, for instance, not every account manager fills out specific data, did you really use the system to its full potential and so achieve what you set out to do as an organization?"

Michiel van Meer, chief people officer at Aon Nederland & ASC EMEA, a leading advisor in the field of risk, pension, and health solutions, explains how the focus of change teams is essential: "Everyone gets energized from planning the change, but focus on execution and reflection is harder to keep. Do you keep mitigating risks? Do you make small changes to facilitate adoption? This helps give people a sense of belonging and if you don't do it, it might leave. Sustained focus also helps in creating momentum for continuous learning. Celebrate the wins and highlight the improvements."

Clim Parren, who was chief people officer at Aegon Nederland until the Dutch market was merged with a.s.r. in July 2023, emphasized the importance of "keeping the focus and attention over time." The Dutch-based multinational life insurance, pensions, and asset management company focused their cultural change project—with a life cycle spanning over three years—on purpose and behaviors. Their change manager reported to the management team at Aegon Netherland every four weeks and for them, this worked very well.

Floor Huizer, transformation director at ABN AMRO, a Dutch bank for retail, corporate, and private banking clients, hinted at the mindset you need in order to successfully reinforce change: "It's hard to drive lasting change. Attention slackens. Priorities shift. We often start great initiatives but it's hard to maintain focus and a sustained attention to reinforcing the change. It's about coupling perseverance with deliberate attention." This reminds us of what psychologist Angela Duckworth calls *grit*, a combination of passion and perseverance.

Implementing Change

The next recurring challenge, actually implementing the change, is similar to the previous one but this time it can refer to both the second phase and all the activities and dynamics within it. It was interesting to notice that in practice, this often came down to issues regarding time. Is time spent on the right things? Do stakeholders have enough time? Do they prioritize change management activities? Does the OCM team get involved early or late? Let's walk through some of what interviewees mentioned regarding challenges in implementing organizational or cultural change.

According to Inca van Uuden, HR director at Essent: "Too little time is spent on actually making people feel the change. How does a new purpose change the average bookkeeper?" Another contentious issue in effectively implementing organizational change has to do with stakeholders not having (enough) time. In the words of Kati Terza, global transformation and change manager at Royal HaskoningDHV: "Some stakeholders want to change but it is nearly impossible for them. The consulting business requires a high billability rate, leaving very little time for internal transformation. This also has to do with the change capacity of an organization as people are just overwhelmed by the many changes they have to face continuously."

Making Time for Reflection

Another increasing challenge in today's fast-paced business landscape, reflection, has emerged as a key component for organizations aiming for sustainable change. Often, in the hustle and bustle of continuous innovation and development, pausing for reflection gets sidelined. But it's exactly in these pauses that organizations get the chance to assess the impact of changes, gather learnings from experiences, and guide future decision-making.

Pieter Versteeg, CHRO at Sodexo, as well as one HR vice president we spoke to, have both offered insights into the need for reflection, especially in large and complex organizations. Sodexo, a multinational food services and facilities management company, deals with a vast and varied clientele, requiring constant adaptation and innovation to meet diverse needs and expectations. The VP HR is from one of the world's largest food retail groups, a global network of supermarkets and e-commerce sites that must similarly keep pace with rapid changes in consumer behavior, supply chain dynamics, and technological innovation.

In such environments, transformative changes are frequent and often occur on a grand scale. They range from overhauling entire business processes to adapting to new technology trends or adjusting to shifts in market behavior. It then makes perfect sense for both of them to put emphasis on making time for reflection. Their organizations are not just implementing changes; they are constantly shaping and reshaping themselves in response to an ever-changing external landscape. However, the catch is in the fast pace of this landscape. Amidst constant change, organizations like Sodexo face the challenge of balancing the need to move quickly with the necessity for reflection. Finding time to pause, evaluate, and learn from the implemented changes is no small task in their respective environments. And yet, as both executives assert, reflection should be a number one priority when it comes to continuous change.

Seeing this challenge, leaders are pushing for a shift in organizational culture. Clim Parren, chief people officer at Aegon, underlines the importance of empowering individuals to embrace change, encouraging room to experiment, learn from mistakes, and carve out time for reflection. Likewise, Kiki van den Berg, global director of human resources at Rabobank, a Dutch multinational banking and financial services company, stresses the importance of learning agility among change leaders, the ability to reflect, seek feedback, and learn from errors. As such, even as the pace of change quickens, the practice of reflection should remain at the heart of change management.

Prioritizing Change Management

On the broader topic of time, another question is whether business managers should prioritize change management or whether being "too busy" is a reason to postpone or ignore the demands of change management. Maarten van Beek (global HR director at ING Retail), Michiel van Meer (chief people officer at Aon Nederland & ASC EMEA), Kristel Buitink (VP HR at CEVA Logistics), and Bas Zwart (global leader of change management at Johnson & Johnson) all mentioned something along the lines of "every manager is a change agent." Here is how Bas Zwart elaborated on this point: "Change management is a key responsibility, not a nice-to-have. Caring for your people should be at the core of a leader and even if a business leader doesn't think about it consciously, they still usually work on change management but they might not be aware of it."

But how can we expect stakeholders to make change management a priority if the organization doesn't? In the words of David Hulsenbek, CHRO at Salta Group, a private educational organization,

"Change management is a bit neglected in most organizations and honestly also in ours. That is because you need to spend a lot of extra attention on communicating to everyone what exactly you're doing. People often have the idea that a change has to be very big in order to involve change management but that's not the case. I believe change management should be involved more often and earlier. Right now, it's more of a tool than an approach or way of working for us. Change management should be an integral part of any approach to move things forward, and not a separate action element. I often ask people, 'How are we going to communicate this to stakeholders?' This forces you to pay attention to what you're doing and why."

From the perspective of an on-the-ground change manager such as Kati Terza from Royal HaskoningDHV, it becomes even clearer why this is important: "What's difficult is to get involved early on. The change maturity in our organization is not that high since we started just two years ago with an official change management role but we are getting there. There is a big advantage in being involved in the planning or initiation phase to do that risk assessment, but it's hard to get a spot at the project table. If a solution is already designed and we're just implementing the plans, we cannot ensure that the solution suits the purpose from the people's perspectives." We can also validate this from our own experience; more than one client told us at the start of a project how we had to "jump on a running train" without room to question whether the entire plan itself was a sound idea with a high chance of success.

Balancing Short-Term and Long-Term Change

There is another challenge that executives especially face when it comes to change management: balancing short-term and long-term change. Thomas Mulder, the CHRO at VodafoneZiggo, put it beautifully: "The balance between short- and long-term [change] is hard. Short-term is pragmatic, data-driven, and focuses on immediate results. Real lasting change requires seeing the underlying complex systems and processes in the org. These are long-term change projects that take a long time and it's hard to build a business case around them because they are high risk. These initiatives are usually postponed in favor of a quick win focus."

Kenneth Kirindongo, VP HR at Shell, a British-Dutch multinational oil and gas company, also spoke of how an organizational culture affects elements such as the speed of execution: "Shell is good at long-term projects such as installing a pipeline for 30 years, but nowadays you have to go faster. We also acquire and collaborate with smaller, more lean organizations and they often ask why things are going so slowly. We're getting better but it's definitely a challenge. That is why we focus a lot on experimentation, to pivot or pursue? Speed is key."

Balancing the short- and long-term is especially challenging when there is much going on such as in scale-ups. Gwen Burbidge was the CHRO of WeTransfer, a Dutch cloud-based computer file transfer service, when it went through a turbulent period in which many things quickly followed each other: COVID hit, which required a business shift; they prepared for going public; they went from IPO to IPNO (if only delayed); and they got a new CEO with a new profile and priorities. In her own words, "It's tough to stay on course. How long will a strategy be viable? When to shift? When to keep going? It might be too reactive, but it's also what this world requires. People want to work in a dynamic environment but they do not want their work to become too dynamic. Change is fun if you control it yourself, not if you're at the 'whim' of it."

Conclusion

Throughout this chapter, we traced the history of organizational change management, revealing its evolution from a simple, hierarchical approach to the nuanced, people-centric discipline we see today. We examined how the field has adapted and grown in response to new challenges and opportunities, and which drivers shape organizational change. We touched on the often low success rates of change initiatives, pointing toward the importance of understanding and addressing this issue. You now know the six change areas we use in this book and how they collectively make or break an organizational change.

In the face of recurring challenges such as change fatigue and implementing or reinforcing change, the leaders we interviewed emphasized the need for adaptive, informed change management practices. Behavioral science can play a key role here. In the next chapter, you see how you can make behavioral science work for you.

2

Think Like a Behavioral Scientist

LET'S ZOOM OUT for a moment first to see the bigger picture of why behavioral science (BeSci) is worth exploring. We're circling through the universe on a giant rock with over eight billion people. What makes us different from a colony of eight billion ants that works in perfect harmony toward a common goal? Each of us has a unique inner world and conscious mind with which we can make individual decisions. This can be clearly seen in history where most historical tribes and kingdoms have been regularly at war in order to gain territory, resources, prestige, or whatever else drove the decision-makers.

In modern, relatively peaceful times with a few notable exceptions, you can still see the same pattern in most walks of life. Whether we're talking about business, politics, technology, or science, many of the problems we encounter are created because different groups of people are lobbying for opposing courses of action. Of course, they each believe theirs is the right approach because they each have a different set of mental models about how the world works. What if we could understand how these mental models are shaped and how they, along with other forces, drive our behavior? This is the quest of behavioral science.

In this chapter, we explore the fundamental insight from behavioral psychology and neuroscience that you need in order to leverage the interventions throughout the rest of the book. You'll learn about the use cases of behavioral science that relate specifically to change initiatives. You get to see how BeSci can function as a lens (mindset), tool (frameworks), and approach (methodology), depending on where you are in the process of applying BeSci to solve your organizational challenges.

A Brief History of Behavioral Science

Let's review some historical background on the rise of behavioral science in organizations.

The 1950s to 1970s: The Academic Foundation

Where some principles of behavioral science can be traced back to 19th-century economic thinkers like David Ricardo, John Stuart Mill, and perhaps most importantly the "father of economics," Adam Smith, many scholars like to start this narrative in the mid-20th century. In the 1950s, Herbert Simon, a prominent psychologist and economist, began challenging the traditional economic theory that assumes humans always act rationally to maximize their benefits. His groundbreaking work in cognitive psychology led to the development of the concept of "bounded rationality,"[1] which suggests something we now take for granted: that people's decision-making abilities are limited by their knowledge, environment, and cognitive abilities. Simon's work laid the groundwork for what we now call behavioral science.

The 1980s to 1990s: The Early Years

The term "behavioral economics" came into widespread use in the 1980s. In 1979, psychologists Daniel Kahneman and Amos Tversky introduced prospect theory,[2] challenging traditional economic theories with the idea that people often make irrational decisions based on potential losses or gains. This theory, combined with Richard Thaler's work on anomalies in economic behavior, set the stage for the future of behavioral economics. In his work on "mental accounting,"[3] Thaler (a professor of behavioral science and economics at the University of Chicago Booth School of Business) highlighted how people irrationally divide their money into different mental categories, affecting their spending behavior.

These insights offered a new way to understand and predict human decision-making, paving the way for the application of behavioral science in a range of sectors. By the close of the 1990s, thanks to the pioneering work of these researchers, behavioral science had significantly evolved, setting the stage for the impactful role it would later play beyond academia.

The 2000s: Going Mainstream

The 2000s marked a pivotal point for behavioral economics. In 2002, Daniel Kahneman won the Nobel Prize in Economics for his work on prospect theory, propelling the field into the mainstream. This achievement, unique in that Kahneman is a psychologist, triggered a surge in interest in behavioral economics, not just from academia but also from the general public. In 2008, Richard Thaler and Cass Sunstein published *Nudge: Improving Decisions About Health, Wealth, and Happiness*,[4] a groundbreaking book that made behavioral economics accessible to the masses. Importantly, it demonstrated how these theories could be applied to public policy and business practices, making it influential in the private sector. This decade also saw the UK government setting up the Behavioral Insights Team, also known as the *Nudge Unit*, which applied behavioral economics in public policy. These developments gave behavioral economics greater legitimacy and paved the way for its adoption in business and policy spheres.

The 2010s: Integration into Business Practices

The 2010s marked a significant shift in the field of behavioral economics, witnessing its transition from a specialized academic field to a significant part of popular culture. The publication of Daniel Kahneman's influential book *Thinking, Fast and Slow*[5] in 2011 sparked widespread interest, introducing a broader audience to the field's key concepts and principles. Even though some of the research cited has been subject to debate in terms of its enduring relevance, the book undeniably had a profound impact on the field's visibility. The decade further cemented its standing in 2017 when Richard Thaler received the Nobel Prize in Economics, the second awarded to a behavioral economist.

This era also became a period of democratizing knowledge, with figures like Dan Ariely and Rory Sutherland using platforms like TED Talks to inspire millions and bring behavioral economics into the public eye. The real-world applications of the field's theories, explained in such accessible formats, fueled a surge of interest, resulting in a new generation of enthusiasts ready to dedicate their careers to furthering the field. Such public communication strategies, while not necessarily advancing academic literature directly, played an integral role in popularizing the field and inspiring its application to real-world situations. Consequently, the 2010s were instrumental in transforming behavioral economics from an academic specialty into a domain of significant societal relevance.

The 2020s: The Era of Behavioral Science

In the 2020s, the reach and influence of behavioral science saw a massive expansion, transcending the realms of academia and gaining momentum in both the public and private sector. The term "behavioral economics," which had been predominantly used to describe the field, became somewhat confined to the realm of academics who were mainly focused on debunking the notion of human rationality. As we moved beyond the sole aim of challenging economic assumptions, the more comprehensive term "behavioral science" became the go-to description for professionals in the industry. This term captured the expanded nature of the field, which had grown to draw on psychology, sociology, anthropology, and evolutionary biology in its quest to understand why people behave as they do.

The growing appreciation of behavioral science's potential was evident in the increasing adoption of its principles by businesses, governments, and organizations globally. Major banks and corporations began to incorporate behavioral science units within their organizational structures, and governments worldwide established their own behavioral insights teams. While traditional economic models continued to be influenced by behavioral ideas, the real revolution was in the growing recognition that behavioral science offered an invaluable tool for understanding and influencing human behavior. This era also witnessed an essential shift toward accessibility and diversity in the field. Digital platforms began to play a role in making dense academic research in behavioral science more comprehensible and accessible to a global audience. Internationally, consultancies started doing remarkable work in applying behavioral science principles in non-Western countries.

The field, historically dominated by men, saw an influx of brilliant female researchers who have been leading the way with groundbreaking work. Figures like Angela Duckworth, Maya Shankar, Katie Milkman, and Wendy Wood are just a few of the women who have not only contributed substantially to the field but have also served as inspirational figures for young women aspiring to make their mark in the world of behavioral science. Thus, as the 2020s unfolded, behavioral science morphed into a global, inclusive, and practical field that has significantly impacted a diverse range of areas.

BeSci Explained

At its core, behavioral science is about studying the behavior of individuals and groups, and the underlying psychological and social drivers. The practitioners of this field called behavioral scientists analyze how people interact, think, and act in response to the environment. The environment here refers to a wide variety of things that can change in the external world, impacting us and often causing us to react. Examples range from physical space to digital platforms to social interactions.

This is where it becomes evident that BeSci is a multidisciplinary approach. Psychology is the foundation; it helps us understand how the human mind tends to think, decide, and act. Neuroscience is a logical next layer; it studies our nervous system (including the brain), which is essentially the infrastructure upon which our thoughts, decisions, and behavior are manifested. Biology and physiology allow us to look even deeper into what makes up the human body and are essential building blocks for neuroscience. Whenever we're talking about the interaction between people, it draws on insights from sociology. When it touches on large groups of people, especially in a historical sense, anthropology is a rich source of inspiration. And all of these disciplines are, in turn, inspired by other fields of study such as history, economics, political science, education, and even public health.

In the context of organizations, the overarching discipline is work and organizational psychology. This field studies people's mental state and behavior in the workplace to facilitate an environment that promotes productivity and well-being. In other words, it aims to make organizations more human-centric. When we look at the departmental level, the most valuable scientific disciplines differ based on who you ask. Marketing and sales (or growth) departments are relying more and more on insights from behavioral economics in order to gain a competitive advantage. The role of the HR department tends to be less competitive, but still, HR professionals often draw inspiration from behavioral, cognitive, and social psychology in order to design effective processes and policies in areas such as compensation, benefits, and performance management. Learning and development professionals can also benefit from all the psychological fields mentioned above and especially developmental psychology, essentially the study of how we learn and how our minds develop. There is much more going on, but this simplified view should give you a better intuitive feel for which teams can benefit from what kinds of scientific insights.

Use Cases of BeSci

Behavioral science has become renowned for its impact in the public sector, including policy, healthcare, and sustainability, but also established profound influence in the private sector as well over the past 15 years. The following exploration focuses on some of the principal use cases in the private sector, based on our interactions with numerous industry professionals: business strategy, marketing, product and user experience, financial services, human resources, and organizational change.

Business Strategy

The foundations of a solid business strategy often lie in a solid understanding of human motivation and behavior. After all, business is, in the end, all about people. Behavioral science offers insights to anticipate potential roadblocks and biases. This empowers businesses to devise more effective strategies, calibrating risk management and decision-making processes.

Businesses, now armed with these insights, find themselves better equipped to tackle strategic challenges like entering new markets, acquiring other businesses, and even designing and launching innovative products or services. In the past ten years, behavioral science applied to strategy has become its own subdiscipline, called—you guessed it—behavioral strategy.

Marketing and Consumer Behavior

At its core, marketing is the science and art of understanding and influencing consumer behavior, making behavioral science a natural ally. Behavioral science can help marketers better understand their customers' preferences, decision-making processes, and shopping behaviors. Whether it's designing more effective advertisements, enhancing the customer journey, or developing products that truly meet customer needs, behavioral science insights play a pivotal role. More and more businesses are leveraging these insights to devise marketing strategies that truly resonate with their target audiences, leading to increased customer loyalty and, ultimately, revenue growth. Subfields like neuromarketing and consumer neuroscience have gained popularity in this sphere.

Product Design and User Experience

Product design and user experience (UX) are increasingly driven by insights from behavioral science. By understanding how users interact with a product and what drives their behaviors, companies can create products that are more intuitive, engaging, and satisfying to use. Whether it's simplifying a user interface, optimizing a product's features, or even designing a product packaging, behavioral science can inform decisions that enhance the user's overall experience. Consequently, products designed with behavioral science in mind often enjoy greater user satisfaction and success in the market. Clim Parren, former chief people officer at Aegon, noted that their in-house customer journey experts continuously improve the journey of clients who apply for their financial products, especially the more complex products. They focus on areas like expectation management, simplifying complex tasks, and supporting customer decision-making.

Finance and Risk Management

Behavioral science, when applied to finance and risk management—known collectively as behavioral finance—extends its reach to consumer protection and fostering financial resilience. Contrary to traditional economic theories, which consider people as rational actors always maximizing self-interest, behavioral science recognizes the influence of cognitive biases, emotions, and other nonrational factors on human decision-making. This insight enables businesses and policymakers to better predict and manage financial behaviors, and design effective, consumer-friendly financial products.

Behavioral finance is also leveraged in consumer protection, designing interventions against predatory lending practices, misleading advertising, and other harmful behaviors that are facilitated by our cognitive limitations and pitfalls. It aids in creating financial literacy programs that help individuals make more informed financial decisions. Moreover, by understanding behavioral barriers that inhibit financial resilience—such as saving, investing, or obtaining insurance—interventions can be designed to encourage financially secure behaviors.

Wies Wagenaar, who leads the Center of Expertise for Behaviour, Ethics, and Learning at ABN AMRO, adds an essential layer to our understanding of behavioral science in the financial sector: "My ultimate dream is that since a bank has such a systemic impact on the economy and society, we utilize this influence to not just enrich the already wealthy but to empower those who need it the most. This, in turn, provides individuals more freedom from financial worries, thereby contributing positively to society at large."

Wagenaar and her team have designed an approach that uncovers the underlying drivers and promoters of specific behaviors in the bank. They employ behavioral interventions focused on mitigating cognitive biases and empowering stakeholders to create ethical financial products and services that serve broader social goals. By doing so, they're illustrating how behavioral science can extend its reach beyond mere consumer protection, enabling financial institutions to be proactive agents of social change.

Human Resources

In the realm of human resources (HR), the incorporation of behavioral science has led to interesting outcomes as well. Our interviews highlighted the importance of behavioral science in fostering "organizational insight (people, teams, culture)" across diverse HR contexts. This involves recognizing habitual behavior, enhancing cross-silo collaboration, measuring employee engagement, and conducting behavioral root cause analyses. The applications of behavioral science in HR have also extended to recruitment, learning and development (L&D), performance management, employer branding, and overcoming resistance to change. Significantly, the understanding and integration of behavioral science are increasingly viewed as a core HR competency. This empowers HR professionals to, for example, debias hiring and promotion processes, understand the role of grit and attention in employee performance, and leverage data analysis for insights—thus facilitating more nuanced, effective strategies in managing and developing human capital. In the words of Thomas Mulder, CHRO at VodafoneZiggo, "Behavioral and neuroscience are just as important for HR as pension legislation and performance management."

Another thing that we consistently heard from executives and senior leaders we interviewed was their need to "get a feel for the temperature across the organization." For a CHRO or HR director at a large organization with tens of thousands of employees, it's impossible to interact with everyone and learn how they feel, what their days are like, and what's occupying their mind for both time- and space-based reasons. Yet they are the "people leaders" and in order to make decisions that optimally benefit everyone, this information is essential. This is where a lot of interviewees felt that behavioral scientists can make a difference: by leveraging both quantitative and qualitative research methods that provide people, cultural, and organizational insights.

Organizational Change

The application of behavioral science to the field of organizational change presents a promising but relatively underutilized opportunity. Behavioral science can offer evidence-based interventions to facilitate change management, a complex process that often encounters resistance. As such, understanding and addressing the behavioral aspects that drive resistance can significantly enhance the effectiveness of change initiatives.

Organizational change, whether it's restructuring, cultural shifts, technology adoption, or strategy realignment, involves altering established patterns of behavior. By incorporating behavioral insights, change managers can design interventions that account for cognitive biases and behavioral barriers, thereby guiding employees toward desired behavioral changes in a human-centric way. This book aims to shed light on this topic and guide you through practical application.

Mindset: BeSci as a Lens

One of the most intangible yet worthwhile reasons for learning the fundamentals of BeSci is its value as a lens through which to view the world. Whatever you spend attention on, you become better at. Spending attention on studying BeSci helps you build a strong mental model of how people tend to think, decide, and act in a variety of scenarios. In fact, even the concept of a mental model itself is a psychological concept, better understood once you study BeSci. From a simplified scientific perspective, a mental model is someone's representation of how something works.

You have a mental model of a dog, a car, a company, the organization you work at, perhaps inflation, and even the world (that is, your world). Your mental models are unlikely to be the exact same as those of your friends and colleagues. Concrete and everyday objects or entities like "dogs" or "cars" are more likely to overlap with others' mental models, whereas complex concepts like "inflation" or "the world" are more likely to vary between people based on their unique experiences and knowledge. To oversimplify but get the point across: Someone with 30 years of experience in sales might see an organization primarily as a commercial system, whereas a seasoned HR professional might view it mainly as a vehicle for unlocking the potential of the people who work there.

> One of the main advantages of mental models is that once you're familiar with them, you can see and use them to explain, predict, or approach things, far beyond the discipline in which you initially learned it.

For example, *compounding* may be a mathematical concept you learned in economics but once you understand how a small, consistent periodic increase (say 1% monthly interest on $10,000) becomes an exponentially growing curve, you'll see that the same mental model can be applied in a variety of situations. If you like your job 1% less every week, it doesn't take long before it becomes unbearable. But if you focus on improving the value you add to clients with 1% every month, you're harnessing the same principle for improved results over the long-term.

There are many useful mental models in this book, but this is just the tip of the iceberg in terms of what behavioral science can mean for professionals. Consider the words of Charlie Munger, Warren Buffett's partner at Berkshire Hathaway: "You can't really know anything if you just remember isolated facts and try and bang 'em back. If the facts don't hang together on a latticework of theory, you don't have them in a usable form. You've got to have models in your head. And you've got to array your experience—both vicarious and direct—on this lattice-work of models."[6] The beauty of this era is that information is freely flowing and you could essentially learn any mental model, but not every model. Time is the constraint, so pick the ones that will be most valuable to you both personally and professionally. This book aims to provide you with the latticework of theory and models, as well as practical step-by-step guides on how to get started.

Rather than using behavioral science solely as a tool for specific interventions, it can be more beneficial when applied as a broader lens within organizations. This wider perspective enables a more profound understanding of how behaviors shape change, enhancing the effectiveness of change management strategies.

Especially during complex organizational transitions, cultural shifts, or structural reforms, the lens of behavioral science can be invaluable in identifying the underlying factors driving these changes. Moreover, it's not confined to "behavioral" issues but can be integrated across all organizational activities, because most business goals rely on certain behaviors occurring (or not). You could go as far as saying that all business is behavioral. Therefore the lens of behavioral science should be integrated into an organization's core activities, rather than being treated as an optional specialist tool.

Applying the lens of behavioral science effectively requires a good understanding of its fundamental mental models. The next sections describe a few essential concepts that not only explain human behavior, but also provide actionable insights for designing impactful interventions during change management.

Bounded Rationality and Dual Processing Theories

A cornerstone of understanding behavioral science begins with the idea of bounded rationality, coined by Hebert Simon, whom we discussed earlier in this chapter. Simply put, this means that the human brain, while magnificent, has limitations when it comes to judgment and decision-making. Our cognitive abilities like attention span, memory, and information processing are not infinite. We can't always make perfectly rational decisions because our cognitive resources are finite.

Daniel Kahneman, the renowned psychologist we saw in the history of BeSci, proposed a framework to understand this dynamic in a more detailed way in his book *Thinking, Fast and Slow*. He introduced two systems of thinking—System 1, which is fast, instinctive, and automatic, and System 2, which is slow, deliberate, and needs conscious effort (see Figure 2.1).

To simplify for a moment, think of System 1 as intuitive thinking and System 2 as reflective thinking. How much is 2+2? If 4 immediately comes to mind, that's System 1. Now how much is 14 * 19? You probably have to do some conscious calculations in order to find this number. That's System 2.

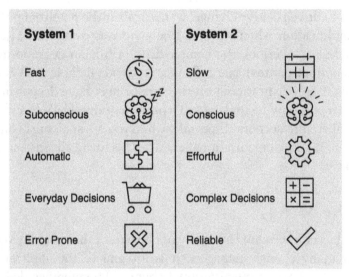

Figure 2.1   Kahneman's System 1 and System 2.

When dealing with organizational change, understanding the dynamic between these two modes of thinking can be helpful. An efficient change manager can design interventions that tailor to both systems. For example, a catchy narrative could appeal more to System 1 thinking, while a comprehensive training program would also deeply engage System 2 thinking. While Systems 1 and 2 are often mistakenly viewed as separate processes, they work together to drive our decisions and behavior. Understanding and leveraging this dual process can help you design change interventions that are more effective and easier to adopt.

Some scholars and practitioners took the ideas of bounded rationality and dual systems thinking further, arguing that humans are, in fact, irrational most of the time. However, it is important to be cautious about labeling human behavior as irrational. This caution was the central argument in Michael Hallsworth's 2023 article "Let's Talk Less About 'Irrationality.'"[7]

Hallsworth, the managing director at the Behavioral Insights Team (BIT), a global social purpose company of over 200 professionals across many offices around the world that creates and applies behavioral insights to drive positive change, warns against the potential pitfalls of oversimplification when we brand behaviors as irrational. The term can lead us to overlook the complexities of human decision-making and the unique context that influences individual choices. A decision that might appear irrational on the surface may have deeper motivations that can only be understood when the individual's specific context is taken into account. Especially when you are applying behavioral science to manage organizational change, this nuanced lens becomes a must have.

Cognitive Biases

While the term *cognitive biases* may not be part of the everyday vocabulary for many change managers, it is integral to the application of behavioral science in organizational change. Therefore we dedicate a substantial portion of this book to providing a comprehensive understanding of cognitive biases and their impact on change management. Once you see these patterns of human behavior and decision-making, it becomes that much easier to find the appropriate evidence-based interventions. We cover both elements.

Before we delve into the realm of cognitive biases, it's important to distinguish them from heuristics and to understand the interaction between System 1 and System 2 thinking. Recall that System 1 relies on heuristics or mental shortcuts that help us make decisions quickly and efficiently under uncertainty. Cognitive biases represent systematic patterns or blind spots in our thinking that emerge primarily from our reliance on System 1. These biases can skew our decision-making process, leading to potentially suboptimal outcomes. Even though heuristics, due to their simplifying nature, can sometimes result in biases, it's important to note that they are not inherently negative. They serve as our brain's efficient approach to dealing with complex information and uncertainty. Behavioral scientists have mapped over 200 biases and heuristics; in this book, we focus on the ones that are most relevant for change managers and leaders to know.

For example, let's consider a well-researched cognitive bias that fundamentally influences how different stakeholders perceive change initiatives and act upon them: *loss aversion*. This bias refers to the tendency of individuals to prefer avoiding losses over acquiring equivalent gains, meaning the psychological impact of potential losses is typically much stronger than the potential benefits. For employees, this may translate into a focus on potential job losses, changes in job roles, or fear of unfamiliar work processes, instead of recognizing the potential gains, such as skill development, improved work processes, or long-term job security. It explains why employees may resist changes even when they're designed to benefit the organization and, by extension, their long-term employment.

Management, on the other hand, might be hesitant about potential short-term financial losses, disruptions in workflow, or decreases in productivity during the transition period. This could overshadow the potential long-term benefits, such as improved efficiency, cost savings, or increased market competitiveness. External stakeholders, like customers or investors, may also demonstrate loss aversion. Customers may worry about potential decreases in product or service quality, changes in pricing, or loss of familiar interfaces or personnel. Investors might focus on short-term financial risks, potential market instability, or temporary dips in stock prices, instead of long-term profitability and growth potential. Loss aversion really is one of those biases that, when you know how to look for it, is everywhere.

Another example is *confirmation bias*, our tendency to interpret new evidence as confirmation of our existing beliefs and to discount evidence that says otherwise. This "only seeing what we want to see and hearing what we want to hear" can become a real barrier to change. Employees may selectively focus on information that confirms their fears about change, ignoring communications about the potential benefits. Similarly, managers might subconsciously favor data or opinions that confirm their fears about the short-term downsides of change, ignoring evidence of long-term benefits. External stakeholders are not immune to confirmation bias either. Customers, for example, might gravitate toward reviews that confirm their fears about a decline in service or product quality following the change, while ignoring positive testimonials. Confirmation bias is something that is quite easy to spot in others, but often impossible to catch in ourselves.

The final example we discuss in this chapter is the *anchoring effect*. Anchoring is a persistent cognitive bias that affects our decision-making processes, often causing us to rely too heavily on an initial piece of information (the "anchor") when making decisions. For example, a variety of studies have shown that people who have to decide on numbers are heavily influenced by the number(s) that they processed just before the decision, even when this anchor was clearly unrelated. When asked to write down the last two numbers of their Social Security number, those with high anchors estimated the value of objects to be significantly higher than those with low anchors.

One prevalent case of anchoring in organizations is the departmental budget allocation process where everyone is aware that when they do not spend their budget, the likelihood is high that it will be cut next year. This often leads to spending resources that perhaps could have been better allocated elsewhere as departments feel the Sword of Damocles above their heads that whispers, "Once given away, you shall never get it back." In the context of organizational change, anchoring can also lead to biased resource allocation as leaders unconsciously base their decisions on historical data or past experiences rather than objectively assessing the current situation and future needs. You see anchoring in action in multiple chapters.

While there is some form of hierarchy between the many cognitive biases known to researchers, understanding some of the most prevalent ones in the context of organizational change is much more important than cramming lists of biases into your mind. Moreover, Michael Hallsworth, the managing director at BIT, rightly points out in his publication "A Manifesto for Applying Behavioural Science"[8] that our understanding of behavioral science must evolve beyond merely compiling lists of cognitive biases. Simply put, behavioral science is not a laundry list of biases but a dynamic field with practical implications for how we understand human behavior. When we reduce behavioral science to a catalog of biases, we risk overlooking the broader, interconnected patterns of human behavior that guide decision-making processes.

We strongly agree with this view, but in our experience there is a knowledge gap in the field of change management. Unlike their counterparts in marketing, design, and policymaking, many change managers are not familiar with the concept of cognitive biases and their impact on organizational behavior and change. Without a basic understanding of these biases and their implications, the application of behavioral science's lens, tools, and approach becomes an uphill battle.

That's why we chose to give cognitive biases a prominent role in this book. In Part II, each of the chapters has a section on some of the biases and heuristics that play a role in that change area. Our aim is not just to provide another list of biases but to foster a foundational understanding of cognitive biases and their implications in change management. However, awareness of cognitive biases alone won't provide solutions.

> The primary focus of this book is on evidence-based interventions and practical strategies to address organizational change challenges.

Through the course of the book, we hope to empower change managers with the tools to understand, anticipate, and leverage cognitive biases and evidence-based interventions in their quest for successful organizational transformation.

Interventions, Nudges, and Choice Architecture

As stated, behavioral scientists should not put all their time in composing lists of biases, but rather in designing evidence-based solutions, or *interventions*. These are carefully designed strategies that help individuals overcome barriers, including cognitive biases, and support them in positive, sustained behavioral change. These interventions, which form the core of our approach in this book, can range from subtle nudges to larger systemic changes.

Nudges, a term popularized by Richard Thaler and Cass Sunstein, represent a specific type of intervention that gently guides individuals toward a particular decision or behavior, without restricting their options. They're like a friendly elbow poke, coaxing individuals in a certain direction, yet leaving the freedom to choose. In the introduction, we discussed two exceptional examples of nudges—the auto-enrollment in workplace pensions in the UK and Apple's App Tracking Transparency (ATT) feature that enables users to opt out of being tracked when using apps.

Both of these nudges use the *default effect*, a powerful psychological principle that leverages people's tendency to stick with preset options. Given the many decisions each of us makes in one day, this is a clever shortcut our brain uses to conserve energy. The UK's auto-enrollment into pensions made participation the default, significantly boosting retirement savings. Similarly, Apple's ATT nudged users toward privacy, with the default option being non-tracking. In both instances, individuals retained full autonomy over their decisions, yet the default effect guided them toward outcomes more beneficial to themselves.

The effectiveness of nudges is significantly influenced by their context—the surrounding environment in which decisions are made. This context is referred to as *choice architecture*, another cornerstone of behavioral science interventions. Choice architecture involves designing the ways in which choices are presented to individuals and understanding the subsequent impact of this presentation on decision-making. To illustrate, the order in which food is displayed in a buffet can significantly alter what and how much people eat. Placing healthier options at the start of a buffet line, where plates are empty, can nudge individuals toward making healthier choices. This seemingly simple decision of arrangement reflects the power of choice architecture.

In this book, the interventions we discuss harness these principles of nudging and choice architecture. They recognize the importance of context, the nuances of individual and collective behavior, and the value of both small nudges and larger systemic changes in achieving organizational change. However, since the design of these interventions can become complex and academic quite fast, we may at times simplify the underlying science to ensure that this book remains practical and readily applicable.

Understanding these and other mental models from BeSci and beyond will strengthen your intuitive understanding of why people act and make decisions the way they do. They will also help you facilitate effective and lasting human-centric change without relying on coercion. Imagine for a moment that all your colleagues would be aware of these mental models. Would this not help in cultivating a more mindful culture that promotes productivity and excellence without compromising on employee well-being, satisfaction, and engagement? One step smaller: what if everyone in HR would know them? Or even just the organizational change management and transformation teams?

There is no need for everyone to be a behavioral expert but learning these basics is, from our experience with hundreds of professionals, a fun and insightful process that helps facilitate further organizational changes.

For executives and senior leaders, there is an even bigger imperative to know the basics of BeSci. You might already have developed a strong intuitive grasp of what drives people and how to deal effectively with things like communication and management built over decades of experience, but when the time comes to make decisions and policies that affect thousands of people, it obviously helps to have a better understanding of the things that tend to make people more or less engaged, productive, or innovative. We don't aim to pretend that BeSci is a panacea because nothing is in the complex, ever-changing system of organizing people, but we do believe it can transform the way you spend countless hours at work. Additionally, it becomes increasingly complex to know what your people are experiencing and struggling with on a daily basis as organizations become larger. BeSci and behavioral scientists can help you get a better feel for the "temperature" of your organization.

Frameworks: BeSci as a Tool

The second main benefit from studying the fundamentals of BeSci is using the frameworks. Whereas mental models help you make sound decisions by giving you a better understanding of what is going on around you, frameworks help you apply your knowledge to drive results. The frameworks you learn by heart will also become mental models over time, allowing you to use them across a wide variety of contexts. There are countless BeSci frameworks that can help you become a better change manager or leader, many more than we can or should cover in this book. So what are the models and frameworks worth learning to get a head start? We compiled the following list based on the frameworks we keep coming back to during client projects and throughout this book:

- **COM-B:** A method developed by Susan Michie, Lou Atkins, and Robert West[9] that helps people understand behavior by analyzing its three interacting components: capability, opportunity, and motivation (see Figure 2.2). *Capability* refers to the physical

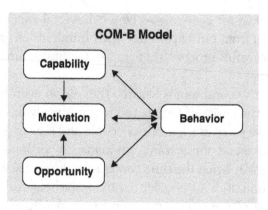

Figure 2.2   COM-B.

and psychological capacity to perform the behavior, *opportunity* refers to the external factors that enable or inhibit the behavior, and *motivation* refers to the internal factors that drive or demotivate the behavior. To drive behavior, make sure people are able to, want to, and have a reason to. By identifying and addressing these components, change managers can develop more effective interventions to modify behavior. You see this model in action in Chapter 4 when we discuss the topic of behavioral change in more depth.

- **MINDSPACE:** A framework developed by BIT[10] that outlines nine behavioral insights that can be used to nudge behavior change. The nine insights are messenger, incentives, norms, defaults, salience, priming, affect, commitment, and ego. By leveraging these insights, change managers can create nudges that help people make better decisions without restricting their freedom of choice. We come back to this model in Chapter 6.

- **Systems Mapping:** A tool for visualizing and understanding the complex interrelationships between people, processes, and systems in an organization. By mapping these relationships, change managers can identify key leverage points for behavior change and design interventions that target the root causes of behavior. Systems mapping is used in Chapters 5 and 8. Two resources we found particularly useful are Donella Meadows's book *Thinking in Systems*[11] and Daniel Kim's short book *Introduction to Systems Thinking.*[12]

Methodology: BeSci as an Approach

One of the most compelling attributes of BeSci is its application as an approach to solving organizational challenges. Like any other scientific discipline, BeSci employs an empirical methodology that hinges on evidence-based, metric-driven, and behaviorally informed strategies. This systematic approach to change can profoundly impact organizational growth and development. Let's take a deeper dive into how this works.

BeSci relies heavily on the scientific method, which involves developing hypotheses based on observations, conducting experiments to test these hypotheses, analyzing the results, and forming conclusions. In the context of BeSci, the scientific method can be used to understand and alter human behaviors in an organization. It's not just about studying the patterns; it's about influencing them for the better. The empirical method allows BeSci to operate in an evidence-based manner. This means that interventions and strategies aren't based on conjecture or gut feelings. Instead, they are founded on well-documented research findings and facts. By taking this evidence-based approach, organizational change managers can make informed decisions that stand the best chance of achieving the desired results.

> Working in a metric-driven way is another cornerstone of BeSci. By quantifying behaviors and their impacts, organizations can monitor progress and gauge the effectiveness of their interventions. These metrics provide an objective measure of whether the implemented changes are moving the organization toward its goals or if further adjustments are needed.

The behaviorally informed aspect of BeSci ensures that the strategies used to bring about change are grounded in an understanding of human behavior. By leveraging behavioral insights, change managers can develop interventions that align with the way people naturally think and behave. This increases the likelihood of the interventions being adopted and maintained over time.

When we asked Kenneth Kirindongo, the VP of HR at Shell we met earlier, about the value of behavioral science for him and his unit, he shared this: "I have benefited especially from the systemic approach that behavioral scientists choose. Where an HR professional often thinks from the perspective of process or key stakeholders, a behavioral scientist tends to help not only in choosing the right methodology but also in adapting the steps to your unique context and ensuring that it actually solves the problem you want to tackle." He also mentioned how the behavioral scientists he worked with tended to have good data and analytical skills, which made for better decisions and more effective approaches to problem-solving.

One of the key benefits of using the scientific method in behavioral science is the ability to factor in two essential elements: context and heterogeneity:

- The **context** in which an intervention is implemented often matters more than the intervention itself. Whether the organizational culture, the physical environment, or the societal norms prevailing in a particular setting, understanding and shaping the context can significantly enhance the efficacy of behavior change strategies. In many ways, shaping the context to facilitate new behaviors is the core of applied behavioral science.
- **Heterogeneity** acknowledges that not all individuals or groups respond to change in the same way. What works for one group might not work for another, and recognizing this is crucial. For example, the factors motivating change in a sales team may not be the same as those driving a tech team. By tailoring strategies to individual groups and contexts, lasting and impactful change can be realized.

Applying the scientific method in BeSci doesn't mean there is a single approach or methodology; there are many. However, the fundamental principles of the scientific method remain constant. One method we often use is derived from Matt Wallaert's four-stage model: Behavioral Strategy, Behavioral Insights, Behavioral Design, and Behavioral Change.[13] This model incorporates the principles of BeSci into a holistic and practical process. It helps define the desired behavioral outcome (strategy), identify the factors influencing current behaviors (insights), design interventions to encourage new behaviors (design), and assess the impact of these interventions to optimize them over time (change).

> You don't have to memorize these models and methods, nor should they replace your existing change management strategies. This book is designed to help you integrate behavioral science into your organizational change efforts seamlessly. The principles of the scientific method and its evidence-based, metric-driven, and behaviorally informed foundations are embedded into every strategy, tool, and intervention we discuss. That said, by understanding behavioral science as an approach and method, you can significantly improve your capacity to bring about meaningful and sustained organizational change, by seeing the bigger picture.

Conclusion

Throughout this chapter, we walked through the progression of behavioral science, exploring its journey from its initial birth to the interdisciplinary science it is today. Along the way, we identified several key use cases of BeSci across different sectors, ranging from business strategy to product design and, of course, change management. Our discussions with industry leaders reiterated the practicality of behavioral science in different aspects of their daily work.

We covered some key mental models such as bounded rationality and Systems 1 and 2 thinking, and added some initial tools like COM-B and MINDSPACE to our toolkit, which we start applying more in later chapters. Next to applying behavioral science as a lens and tool, we also looked into how it can be leveraged as an approach to solving organizational challenges. In the next chapter, we zoom in further to the essence of this book: applying behavioral science to organizational change management or, as we call it, *behaviorally informed change management*.

3

Behaviorally Informed Change Management

How MANY ORGANIZATIONS have you heard say something like "experimentation is in our DNA" or "innovation is woven into our corporate fabric"? The idea of having a certain quality ingrained within the foundations of your organization sounds great and is very popular, but it has one major flaw: it simply takes too long to get there, especially in today's world of increasing uncertainty and complexity. Genetic evolution often takes thousands if not millions of years to result in adaptive characteristics. Think about it: giraffes didn't grow their necks overnight when they ran out of low-hanging fruit. Some primates, however, discovered a more efficient strategy.

During the ice age, and other extreme examples of acute change in nature, many organisms relied solely on their DNA to adapt and quickly exited the gene pool. However, primates used their ability to rapidly learn from their experience and update their individual and group behavior accordingly. These early "culture changes" required their brains and nerve centers to physically rewire themselves in response to rapidly changing environments.

One of the main reasons we wrote this book is because we argue for a similar approach when it comes to organizational change. Instead of waiting for your organization's very DNA to change, leverage your collective ability to rapidly experiment, learn, and adapt. Just like primates used the adaptability of their nerve center (which literally rewires itself in response to experience), organizations need to have the right leadership skills, clear communication, resilience, collaboration, and performance monitoring in place to effectively navigate change. Behaviorally informed change management is one way to go about developing these capabilities.

What Is Behaviorally Informed Change Management?

Behaviorally informed change management combines insights from behavioral science and neuropsychology to open up a wealth of new tools and perspectives for managing change. The underlying idea is quite straightforward. As Gerard Penning, former CHRO at ABN AMRO, only half-jokingly put it, "Understanding human psychology must be a prerequisite for all change management, otherwise you're set up for immediate failure."

We like to refer to applying behavioral sciences to organizational change using the term *behaviorally informed change management* (BICM). To provide a concrete understanding of real-world applications in BICM, this chapter delves into its utilization in addressing various change-related challenges such as cultural integration; diversity, equity, and inclusion (DEI); resilience; and change fatigue. Through exploring these use cases, you'll learn how BICM can be a potent force in tackling tough organizational challenges, and how a deep understanding of human behavior can shape change initiatives for the better.

After setting this groundwork, the next chapter introduces you to evidence-based interventions, strategies, and approaches that are derived from scientifically validated research and have been proven to be effective in influencing behaviors. Coupled with this, we outline an underlying framework that provides a structured approach for applying BICM systematically. This combination will empower you with the necessary tools to design and implement change initiatives that are both scientifically sound and human-centric. An interesting entry point to start exploring BICM is where behavior science and organizational change overlap perhaps most strongly: cultural change.

BICM (behaviorally informed change management) combines organizational change management with behavioral psychology and neuroscience. Its objective is to drive organizational change in a human-centric and design-led manner, using evidence-based interventions that can spur impactful and enduring changes.

Cultural Change as Behavioral Change

The BICM approach is particularly valuable in areas where human behavior is pivotal, such as cultural change. As discussed in Chapter 1, cultural change is the most challenging form of organizational change to implement successfully, with a median success rate below 20 percent. Why is this? The crux could lie in the multifaceted nature of "culture" within an organization. Scholars, practitioners, and leaders have proposed numerous definitions of organizational culture and cultural change, which often revolve around shared values, beliefs, behaviors, and attitudes within a company. This range of definitions underscores the intricate nature of culture and the difficulty in pinning it down. Given the scope of this book, we do not go into a detailed review of organizational culture covering various academic definitions. Instead, we look at culture through the lens of behavioral science, and let our interviewees shine light on how they experience their unique organizational cultures.

Culture plays a crucial role in organizations and has to be taken into account one way or another. In fact, different interviewees thought very differently of culture. Most ascribed to the "culture as a mediating factor" philosophy and found it to be an enabler of change. Dominique Dingjan is the CHRO at Olympia, a 50-year old Dutch recruitment company focused on providing people with meaningful work. When we showed her the change areas for the second part of this book, she remarked, "It seems to me like people and culture is missing. It takes a long time to change it but if you can get the culture moving, the other areas will follow surprisingly well." Thomas Mulder, the CHRO of VodafoneZiggo, also viewed culture as missing: "A transformation that misses one component is a risk. One time, we had a series of operational issues that caused problems in our network due to insufficient testing. The tech team did a root cause analysis, which pointed to processes, systems, and procedures. This can be seen as planning or risk management but culture is overarching. There is a culture where risk is neglected in this example. How can we get beyond that and build more trust?"

Although we were tempted, this book does not have culture as a separate chapter because it plays a key role in every chapter. For us, culture is indistinguishable from the other change areas because it permeates them. Our thinking is actually very well encapsulated by the words of Floor Huizer, the transformation director you met in Chapter 1. When we asked her whether she thought culture should be one of the change areas, she replied, "Culture, to me, is overarching. The way in which you implement these change areas should result in a cultural change. It should be the product of a new way of looking at or dealing with, let's say risk management or engaging colleagues." She went on to explain how ABN AMRO is executing their new strategy and divided the program into 23 strategic themes. In between "Mergers and Acquisition" and "Digital Products" was the theme "Culture and People Transformation," which she was asked to be in charge of. "I pushed back because how can culture be a part of this 23-part list? It's the only thing that cuts through everything else! Viewing it as one part of these kinds of lists presumes that just a few people are going to do something that's going to change the culture. But it's a collective thing. The tough thing about culture is that people often see it as a job to be done, not as an outcome or something you change by changing how you do other things."

From a behavioral perspective, organizational culture can be perceived as the behavior, attitudes, and decisions of individuals and groups in the organization, accumulated over time. For instance, if sustainability is a common consideration in decision-making across the organization, it implies that the culture is highly focused on environmental consciousness. If the organization aims to drive a culture more attuned to sustainability, interventions that offer clarity on how they will incite actual behavioral change are the most likely to yield long-lasting effects. The many different definitions of organizational culture, and the absence of a definitive one, might contribute to the difficulties encountered when discussing culture, let alone attempting to change it. We are aware that we do not do the rich discussion about organizational culture and its implications justice with such a brief account, but since this book is written for the practitioner, we have to apply a practical lens.

During our discussion with Gerard Penning, the former CHRO of ABN AMRO, he offered an insightful description of organizational culture as "what people are doing when you're not looking." This statement resonates with the behavioral science viewpoint and underpins our approach in this book. At the risk of sounding reductive, we embark on this journey with a bold working hypothesis: **Cultural change is fundamentally about behavioral change**. More specifically, it is behavioral change at scale.

What do leaders mean when they want to make their culture more innovative, quality-focused, or inclusive? It sure seems like in nearly all cases, they would like to see different results and hope to achieve this by collectively adopting new (or sometimes old) behaviors. There is a lot of insightful research on how organizations can foster curiosity and creativity in their teams to drive innovation, and the same goes for instilling a consistent focus on quality or inclusion. What all of these cultural changes have in common is that they are about driving behavioral change at scale. You just have to choose the right interventions for the right scale (i.e. personal, team, department, organization). This hypothesis will shape our exploration of BICM as a practical lens, tool, and approach for organizational change.

Use Cases of Behaviorally Informed Change Management

While cultural change is the most pronounced area of application for BICM due to its inherent strong tie to behavior, almost all forms of organizational change are deeply interwoven with aspects of human behavior. Each change area presents a unique set of challenges and opportunities that can be better understood and addressed using a behaviorally informed approach.

In the second part of this book, we explore six distinct change areas in detail: Planning and Risk Management, Narrative and Communication, Leadership Support, Stakeholder Engagement, Measuring Change, and Learning and Development. We demonstrate how BICM can be effectively applied in each of these areas by analyzing organizational challenges, providing relevant behavioral insights, and dissecting evidence-based interventions into step-by-step protocols, allowing you to see their mechanics and potential impact. Most importantly, you will be equipped to start experimenting with these interventions yourself!

Before we delve into the specifics, let's take a step back and go over some recurring challenges in change management. We asked the experienced leaders and change managers we interviewed which issues or themes kept resurfacing in driving organizational change. These challenges feature a potent behavioral dimension that enhances our comprehension of where and how BICM can deliver value. In exploring these challenges together, we hope to provide you with a robust understanding of the potential of BICM in facilitating effective and sustained organizational change.

Change Fatigue

The common challenge of change fatigue, as discussed in Chapter 1, highlights the physical exhaustion, disengagement, and stress that individuals and organizations may endure amid perpetual or poorly executed change initiatives. Left unchecked, change fatigue can result in high rates of burnout and turnover at scale.

In such an environment, organizations often struggle with distinguishing change saturation and change fatigue. Change saturation arises when the sheer volume and intensity of changes surpass an organization's capacity to absorb them, making prioritizing, implementing, and reinforcing initiatives difficult, and often leading to slower progress and suboptimal project outcomes. On the other hand, change fatigue usually manifests when signs of change saturation are overlooked. This often results in employees experiencing an overwhelming sense of apathy toward change, increased negativity, stress, and even burnout.

Gerard Penning, former CHRO of ABN AMRO, offered an insightful perspective on this phenomenon, emphasizing that fatigue is never completely avoidable. He doesn't like using the term "change fatigue" because it sounds to him like just another way to describe a very basic human experience: we all get tired. A fatigued employee is, per definition, more prone to frustration and often clings to the past rather than embracing new ways of doing things. In his words, "It's really just fatigue. If you're tired, you get more easily frustrated (e.g., with boss, friends, at home). . . . A tired person grabs back to the past." This can again be explained by our brain's tendency to conserve energy, especially when the energy tank is low. It is mainly the role of leaders to ensure people are not pushed beyond their limits (over longer periods of time) because fatigue will inevitably set in and results will suffer. Overextension is never a long-term strategy.

This notion of change fatigue is also acknowledged by the Municipality of Amsterdam, where Roger van Lier acts as the interim P&O director. The organization understands the impact of fatigue, which has been heightened due to numerous recent changes. Instead of placing sole emphasis on outcomes, they strive to balance the scope of change with the capacity of their employees to handle it without risking fatigue. One of their key challenges here is identifying a way to measure change fatigue objectively.

Existing resources such as Prosci's Change Saturation Model[1] provide some guidance on this subject. Built around observable signs of change fatigue like apathy, stress, and resistance, the model advocates for a combination of employee feedback, satisfaction surveys, resource allocation assessments, and comparative observations to detect fatigue. However, this approach is not without limitations.

An inherent problem, not just in Prosci's model but in various other tools employed across organizations—such as engagement surveys—is their reliance on self-reported data. This introduces an element of subjectivity, which could lead to inconsistent and less reliable assessments. Observable symptoms of fatigue might vary between and within employees, making change fatigue hard to identify concretely.

Furthermore, the self-reported data is sensitive to—you guessed it—various biases. Employees might consciously or unconsciously underreport their fatigue levels due to a multitude of (often partly subconscious) personal and professional pressures, such as fear of being perceived as less committed or resilient. This issue isn't exclusive to change management. It's a broader problem that touches many aspects of organizational research and practice, highlighting how hard it is to gauge the psychological and emotional states of individuals in a workplace setting.

At the heart of these challenges lies a significant gap in our understanding and management of change fatigue within organizations. This gap underscores the need for more rigorous research, innovative solutions, and, perhaps most importantly, scalable interventions that can more effectively identify and address change fatigue.

To counteract such fatigue, organizations like the recently merged dsm-firmenich—a leading innovator in nutrition, health, and beauty, under the leadership of VP of Learning and Development Marco Mullers—champion a growth mindset or "learning agility." This prompts their employees to see every change as a learning opportunity and a chance to grow, thus challenging traditional legacy models they previously utilized. We explore the effectiveness of growth mindset and learning agility interventions in managing change fatigue in Chapter 8. Chapter 10 also provides insight into how Mullers and his team is on a (successful) mission to make learning fun, indirectly affecting our ability to deal with change in a variety of ways.

Mergers and Acquisitions and the Role of Culture

Changes like mergers and acquisitions (M&A) can have a significant impact on organizational culture, making them tougher and more complex than they might appear at first sight. We discussed this topic at length with Judith Peters, HR director of PLUS, a Dutch supermarket chain that has more than 550 stores, to revisit the complexities of understanding, shaping, and integrating different cultures during big changes.

PLUS and COOP are two leading supermarket chains in the Netherlands that embarked on a significant change initiative, merging their operations to create a stronger, more resilient organization with enhanced IT and supply chain capabilities. The integration of COOP and PLUS supermarkets makes them the third largest supermarket chain in the Netherlands and is obviously a complex and challenging process, requiring meticulous planning and execution, as well as a deep understanding of the two companies' cultures, values, and ways of working.

There is often a substantial difference between an acquisition and a merger of two companies. A takeover entails one company absorbing the other, with the acquiring company having more say with regard to new processes and structures. In contrast, a fusion requires both companies to collaborate on decisions about the new organization's structure, processes, and policies. The fusion process is more challenging, as it demands greater attention to creating balance and equality between the two organizations and their employees.

One of the main challenges here is integrating the organizational cultures, which strongly influences the success of the merger. This calls for a behaviorally informed approach. In the case of COOP and PLUS, research into the work cultures of both companies revealed shared values and beliefs, emphasizing the importance of strong interpersonal work relationships and high-performance drive. This shared culture facilitated a smoother integration process, as employees from both companies were more likely to be receptive to the changes.

Effective communication plays a crucial role in change initiatives, especially when dealing with organizational culture. Clear and timely communication can alleviate employee concerns about job security, changes in work environment, and other aspects of the integration. In addition, leadership must exhibit a united front to foster confidence in the new organization's direction. We discuss evidence-based interventions for communication and leadership in Chapters 6 and 7, respectively.

Mergers and acquisitions not only bring together different business operations and strategies but also present unique challenges in integrating the organizational cultures of the merging entities. We discussed this with Tessa Peetoom, global director of DEI at ALD | LeasePlan. (LeasePlan is a Dutch multinational fleet management and driver mobility company, an international company specializing in automobile leasing and fleet management. They underwent a merger with ALD in May 2023.)

One of the critical steps taken during the merger was conducting a culture check-in with ALD and LeasePlan employees. This assessment revealed both similarities and differences between the two organizations. Both companies had positive cultures focused on entrepreneurship, independent thinking, and inclusivity. However, the French ALD was found to focus more on local action and less on central alignment, while the Dutch LeasePlan was more focused on strong central steering and consensus-based decision-making, or as we call it in the Netherlands, *polderen* (the polder model is a way to cooperate despite differences, inspired by Dutch economic and social policymaking in the 1980s and 1990s). To successfully integrate the two cultures, Peetoom emphasized the importance of creating shared agreements about the ways of working, values, and cultural norms. The culture check-in played a crucial role in identifying the best aspects of both cultures and blending them into a new organization based on shared values.

Another intriguing perspective in this use case comes from the HR director we interviewed at a global optical retailer, which was acquired by a multinational corporation that designs, manufactures, and distributes eyewear. Her experience highlighted the human and behavioral aspects of such transitions. The acquisition necessitated selling part of the business and adjusting operations to comply with EU laws, which introduced challenges. These ranged from handling the transition over time to reorganizing the organization and redefining processes like performance reviews.

The HR director emphasized the importance of understanding what people need and want, especially when it comes to defining new processes and compensation agreements. Though this can be challenging in a large corporation, it remains a crucial aspect of the change process. Her insights underline the need for clarity of purpose and adaptability. In her own words, "It is not about stoically following a predefined purpose but about adapting it to align with the changing circumstances and needs of the people."

In conclusion, whether it's the merger of two supermarket chains, LeasePlan's fusion with ALD, or the acquisition of an optical retailer by an eyewear manufacturer and distributor, each case illustrates the multifaceted and complex nature of change in M&A scenarios. Integrating organizational cultures is just one aspect of this change (often called post-merger integration). Attending to the behavioral aspects is equally critical for successful transitions. A common thread through all these cases is the importance of open communication, understanding, and empathy—attributes that are further explored in the upcoming chapters on communication and leadership.

Diversity, Equity, and Inclusion

Another organizational change area that could benefit from a behaviorally informed approach entails promoting diversity and cultivating an inclusive workplace culture. The field of diversity, equity, and inclusion (DEI) is an important cultural, human-centric development that's clearly visible across a wide variety of industries and organizations. We briefly define diversity, equity, and inclusion because these terms recur throughout our discussion:

- **Diversity:** Diversity refers to the presence of varied attributes among individuals within an organization or, as we saw in the previous chapter, heterogeneity. It encompasses multiple dimensions, including race, ethnicity, gender, age, religion, disability, and sexual orientation. It also extends to diversity of thought, experiences, and skills. It is about recognizing, respecting, and valuing differences in the workplace.
- **Equity:** Equity involves ensuring fair treatment, access, opportunity, and advancement for all individuals in the organization. It is not about treating everyone equally, but about acknowledging their unique circumstances and addressing systemic barriers that prevent the full participation of certain groups. Equity seeks to level the playing field.
- **Inclusion:** Inclusion refers to the fostering of a sense of belonging by creating an environment where individuals feel valued, respected, and involved. It is about making sure everyone has an equal opportunity to be part of and contribute to the organization's goals.

Bringing it all together, in the context of organizational change, DEI encompasses efforts to establish a diverse workforce, create equitable systems, and foster an inclusive environment where every individual feels valued and can thrive.

The idea of providing equal opportunities and treatment to people regardless of their background is far from new, but historically it's been hard to drive continuous and lasting change in this area. On a societal level, it is beautiful to see the advances in human rights spread across the globe, albeit slowly, and heartbreaking to see the many challenges surrounding immigration and economics. We believe the decision-makers regarding these issues, often rooted mainly in economics and politics, could benefit from a behaviorally informed approach. There has been much headway in this area, with a growing number of governments setting up behavioral insights units, but there is still a lot of room to improve. So let's return to the workplace—how can the strong rise in DEI's strategic importance be explained?

As organizations grow, they tend to get more complex and require more specialists. Each of these organizations needs people to fill these roles, and there seems to be more and more competition on the job market, especially for top talent and niche specialists. Apart from investing in L&D (mainly talent and leadership development programs) to educate people and grow them into these roles, organizations needed to find ways to broaden their talent pool. Combine this with globalization, digital communication, viral social media posts affecting organization's reputations, and the growing independence of employees who make decisions based on their values instead of their paycheck, and you can imagine why organizations make it a strategic imperative to ensure that they are diverse, inclusive, and equitable.

What this means is contextual: it differs for each organization and probably most departments and teams. A wide variety of DEI interventions are in use across organizations, so this is one of the things we asked for during most of our interviews: how do you approach DEI? The strategies and initiatives the interviewees shared reflect their unique organizational contexts, revealing an interesting web of approaches.

For instance, several organizations emphasize the importance of strategic planning and risk management in their DEI efforts. They undertake comprehensive company-wide DEI scans to understand the current status of diversity and inclusion in their environment. Regular surveys and focus groups are also employed to gather insights and feedback, while yearly health scans are conducted to maintain accountability. These are often backed by global policies designed to foster a culture of inclusivity.

In the realm of communications, organizations are increasingly redefining their narratives to embed DEI into their core identities. This may involve revisiting and adapting cultural values, creating diverse and inclusive narratives, or even drafting comprehensive vision documents or DEI statements. Some organizations also optimize their communications with a DEI lens and launch targeted DEI campaigns to amplify their message.

The DEI insights and strategies we discussed with our interviewees deserve an entire book dedicated to discussing evidence-based interventions for DEI, akin to Joan Williams's *Bias Interrupted*.[2] However, in the scope of this book, we provide more context and bring clarity to some of the most commonly encountered DEI challenges and initiatives by our interviewees.

Kati Terza, global transformation and change manager at Royal HaskoningDHV, emphasizes the importance of DEI initiatives, stating they are vital to the organization's overall health. A cornerstone of their strategy involves training managers to appreciate and value the diverse perspectives and experiences of their colleagues. This not only contributes to the successful implementation of DEI initiatives but also creates an environment that fosters growth and innovation.

While there may not be a linear relationship between an organization's ability to navigate change and its embracement of diversity, there is certainly an interaction. A company's willingness to engage with the challenges and rewards of diversity can potentially enhance its approach to change, cultivating a more flexible and adaptive organizational culture.

At Dura Vermeer, a Dutch family-owned construction company that has been operating since 1855, DEI is considered a strategic priority, with a practical and goal-oriented approach driven by the organization's HR director, Natasja van Rens. The company consciously fosters a pool of diverse young talent, ensuring a balanced succession planning pipeline. This intentional emphasis on nurturing diversity not only contributes to the organization's innovative strength in the present, but it also promises a vibrant and inclusive future leadership.

From a BeSci perspective, setting explicit DEI targets has proven a productive strategy in the right contexts. It's important to note, though, that these targets should never just aim to tick boxes, but to foster an environment that actively prioritizes genuine inclusion. Dura Vermeer's approach of cultivating a diverse talent pool is an example of a thoughtful implementation, demonstrating a long-term vision that aligns with scientific evidence. These targets, revisited and reassessed periodically, serve as a blueprint for an organizational culture where diversity becomes embedded in everyday operations and decision-making processes.

Shell, the oil and gas company we met in Chapters 1 and 2, also places DEI at the forefront of its strategy and made it a strategic imperative. They are optimizing their recruitment, talent management, and engagement processes to facilitate DEI as well as organizing monthly meetings and having action committees focused on topics such as neurodiversity, LGBTQ+, and cultural background. These initiatives play a critical role in the complex, matrixed organizational context of Shell, as described by Kenneth Kirindongo, the VP of HR we spoke to. Apart from their key focus on environmental concerns, their high-priority initiatives include developing a learner mindset and fostering collaboration, both topics that we explore in other chapters.

Finally, revisiting the LeasePlan/ALD merger, Tessa Peetoom provides an insightful perspective on how behavioral science (BeSci) can be integrated in the DEI strategy. In her view, understanding human behavior—particularly how people perceive and experience change—is critical in enhancing DEI measures. To this end, she takes an approach that combines both qualitative and quantitative behavioral data. By focusing on root cause analysis and maintaining a suite of key metrics (which we discuss in depth in Chapter 9), Peetoom can tailor DEI initiatives based on evidence. This method allows for iterative changes in governance, performance measurement, peer review, and more, as informed by the data. This fusion of BeSci, data, and DEI is a vivid example of behaviorally informed change management in action.

Organizational and Individual Resilience

Resilience is another construct that has gained popularity as a vital capability to navigate unpredictable challenges. As we heard from our interviewees, and in line with findings from behavioral science and psychology, resilience is not just about surviving adversity. It's a multifaceted trait that equips individuals and organizations with the capacity to adapt, recover, and even thrive amidst disruptions and change. We often symbolize resilience as bamboo, since it has properties that allow it to bend considerably without breaking. It also tends to return to its original form (straight up) and grows very fast!

Building resilience is a dynamic process that cultivates critical skills such as self-regulation, goal-setting, and problem-solving at an individual level. At the organizational level, resilience is fostered by nurturing a culture of resourcefulness, flexibility, and collective learning. Floor Huizer, transformation director at ABN AMRO, underscores this viewpoint by highlighting the role of appreciative inquiry in change management. Appreciative inquiry is a model for analysis, decision-making, and creating strategic change that is particularly well suited to enhancing resilience. Coined by David Cooperrider and Suresh Srivastva in their 1987 paper,[3] appreciative inquiry involves a shift from a problem-oriented perspective to a strengths-based approach.

The appreciative inquiry approach operates on a 4D model—Discover, Dream, Design, and Destiny. *Discover* focuses on identifying what works well in an organization. *Dream* encourages envisioning what the organization might become by building on these positive aspects. *Design* involves creating strategies to make this dream a reality, and *Destiny* is about implementing these strategies in a way that empowers every member of the organization to contribute. Huizer's approach emphasizes leveraging the potential of appreciative inquiry to identify and enhance an organization's strengths and successes.

Gwen Burbidge, the former CHRO at WeTransfer, underscores the importance of distinguishing between individual and organizational resilience. She highlights a potential bias where organizations, in a bid to build resilience, may inadvertently favor certain personality types over others. For example, extroverts, who are often more expressive, may sometimes be perceived as more resilient than introverts. Leaders who are (subconsciously and perhaps temporarily) influenced by this bias might accidentally overemphasize resilience at the expense of diversity, sabotaging their own goal of building resilience.

Another misinterpretation of resilience Burbidge poses is that it could potentially cast those grappling with workplace stresses as deficient, creating a harmful, culturally tainted perception. This discussion emphasizes the need for a nuanced understanding of resilience within diverse cultural contexts, which can provide insights into disparities in burnout rates among countries and enhance the effectiveness of DEI initiatives.

Reflecting on these thoughts, it becomes clear that leaders should see resilience more like an all-encompassing quality rather than a fixed trait exclusive to certain personalities. Furthermore, Huizer's emphasis on appreciative inquiry underscores the power of leveraging existing strengths to enhance organizational resilience. We embrace this expanded view of resilience: an unwavering determination to overcome setbacks and an agility to tackle obstacles promptly. In the context of this book, we look at resilience as the unwavering resolve to move past setbacks and the agility to overcome hurdles quickly. These are traits that can be developed by anyone who is willing to learn.

These industry insights into resilience have demonstrated its nuance and complexity, its essential role in change management, and some potential pitfalls. Our interviewees have prompted us to explore evidence-based interventions like growth mindset, to bolster resilience. In Chapter 8, we translate these insights into practical strategies, offering strategies for fostering resilience in the realm of change management that you can start experimenting with.

Conclusion

In this chapter, we laid out the concept of behaviorally informed change management (BICM) and its application in a variety of organizational change challenges. We used organizational culture and cultural change as principal use case for applying BICM, and discovered that cultural change is fundamentally about understanding and adapting behaviors, thereby benefiting directly from behavioral insights.

We also looked at other practical BICM use cases based on the interview insights with organizational leaders, such as change fatigue management, mergers and acquisitions, DEI initiatives, and resilience building. Their expertise on how they intuitively apply behavioral science principles to solve the toughest change challenges demonstrates the importance of behavior in driving lasting organizational change. You've seen what BICM as a field can do for organizations. Now let's open the toolkit that will enable you to start experimenting with applying behavioral science to drive change. The next chapter is about evidence-based change interventions, and afterward you'll start seeing the interventions in action for each of the change areas!

4

Evidence-Based Change
Interventions

IN ORGANIZATIONAL CHANGE, countless elements intertwine and evolve simultaneously, making it challenging to pinpoint the impact of specific strategies. The vast number of factors at play, just to name a few, include organizational culture, leadership style, stakeholder perception, market dynamics, and technological advances. Some of these factors are somewhat controllable, and some are beyond even the most skilled leader's control. This interplay makes each change initiative unique, demanding a tailored approach rather than a one-size-fits-all solution.

Central to the complexity of organizational change is the role of human behavior. Often seen as an obstacle, it can (and should!) be viewed as a powerful factor that, when effectively harnessed, can provide a competitive edge in successful change. Human behavior, driven by a web of conscious and subconscious factors, is almost never linear or predictable. As any experienced manager can attest, people may not always seem fully rational or logical, but their actions can significantly influence change outcomes. Acknowledging that each organization, team, and individual employee adds a layer of complexity, it's not weird that behavior is so often seen as an obstacle, not an opportunity, in managing change. But it's exactly here that behaviorally informed change management (BICM), as elaborated in the last chapter, comes into play. By applying the lens, tools, and approach of behavioral science to change management, BICM enables organizations to proactively address the human side of change.

What Are Evidence-Based Change Interventions?

The application of the BICM approach in practice is facilitated by what we term *evidence-based change interventions* (EBCIs—we'll try to keep abbreviations to a minimum from here on out, we promise!). These are not just theoretical constructs but involve strategies or actions grounded in scientific research and verified in real-world contexts. Built with several components, EBCIs are geared toward mitigating change management challenges. Each of these interventions is based on unique working mechanisms underpinned by robust evidence. Their key role lies in bringing behavioral science to change management, providing a toolkit to address the human element, which is so often seen as complex and unpredictable.

EBCIs can be applied to address a wide range of change management challenges. Whether it's planning and managing risk, narrative and communication, securing leadership support, engaging stakeholders, measuring change, or fostering learning and development, EBCIs offer reliable tools that can help you navigate the complexities inherent in organizational change (without having to reeducate yourself into becoming a behavioral scientist!). Some EBCIs are complex and benefit greatly from collaborating with behavioral specialists, but many can be turned into simple and practical step-by-step processes that you and your colleagues can experiment with yourself. That said, EBCIs aren't magical solutions to complex problems. Instead, they are designed to offer a proven way to increase the success rate of various aspects of your change initiatives.

In the chapters that follow, we introduce you to a number of these evidence-based interventions, providing you with practical tools to enhance your change management efforts. But before we talk specifics, let's make sure we understand what these interventions are and why they matter.

What Is an Intervention and What Makes It Evidence-Based?

In the context of organizational change management, an *intervention* refers to a deliberate, structured, and planned set of actions that aim to alter the status quo. These actions could be aimed at shifting organizational culture, improving processes, or enhancing individual and team performance. Interventions come in handy when managing change because they provide a structured way to navigate the often chaotic process of change. And although you might not think of them as interventions, as a change manager you are undoubtedly already designing and implementing a ton of them. They are in many ways simply the "how" to achieve your "what."

Change management and interventions are not exclusive to commercial organizations. We spoke with Martin Sitalsing, the police chief of Mid Netherlands, who shared his experience with the effectiveness of different types of changes and interventions in this unique public organization: "Top-down changes are almost never successful, and if they are they are usually culture interventions. Interventions that focus on norm enforcement such as promoting a key figure to an unusual position are, in my experience, very effective. For example, promoting someone with a strong digital background but no formal police training to a leadership position can send a powerful message."

This approach strongly aligns with behavioral science findings on normative behavior. Behavioral science consistently indicates that social norms—our perceptions of what others think is normal and acceptable—affect our behaviors. By making unexpected promotions or changes, organizations can signal a shift in what's valued and expected. The act of promoting an employee on its own does not immediately shift organizational norms as new norms are established over time, but it does contribute to an environment in which the new norm is more likely to be established/adopted over time. In short, by actively and visibly changing norms such as in this example, organizations can drive significant shifts in behavior.

It's worth noting that the interventions discussed in this book come in various shapes and sizes. While there are countless ways to categorize these interventions, to keep things simple and focused in this book, we primarily concentrate on two broad categories:

- **Debative Interventions:** The primary goal of these interventions is to engage stakeholders in constructive discussions and actively seek different viewpoints to identify potential biases, recognize hurdles to successful change, and pinpoint opportunities. By fostering open dialogue, these interventions excel at bolstering stakeholder and leadership engagement, cultivating psychological safety, and amplifying effective communication.
- **Analytical Interventions:** These interventions employ a behaviorally informed approach to leverage data and metrics, providing a more objective and debiased view of change initiatives that informs decision-making along the way. This category of interventions is exceptionally useful in areas such as stakeholder engagement, resource allocation, and measuring change effectiveness.

Now let's consider what makes an intervention evidence-based. In the most rigorous sense, "evidence-based" refers to approaches that are firmly grounded in scientific research and have been validated through real-world testing. This might make you think of extensive literature reviews in scientific databases or randomized controlled trials (more on this in Chapter 9). However, we acknowledge that very few change managers have the time or resources to delve into academic journals on a regular basis.

This is why it's important to note that there are different levels and types of evidence that can be used to inform interventions. These can range from subjective and personal experience to systematic observations, to best-practices shared by industry peers, or insights gleaned from professional development workshops. In this book, we strive to provide a comprehensive, balanced view by drawing from a variety of evidence sources. These include peer-reviewed scientific journals, case studies, published books in the field of behavioral science, and interviews with experts. Each of these sources provides a different level and type of evidence, contributing to a robust and pragmatic understanding of evidence-based change interventions.

The Role of Evidence in Selecting Effective Interventions

While a strong evidence base is a fundamental criterion in selecting change interventions, it's important to remember that lacking extensive scientific backing doesn't automatically render a tool ineffective. There is often more to consider when evaluating the usefulness of an intervention in a specific context.

Take, for example, the Myers-Briggs Type Indicator (MBTI)[1] and the Insights Discovery system.[2] These tools, which categorize individuals based on different personality traits, are used extensively in organizations for promoting cultural change. They can be particularly valuable in enhancing team building, fostering mutual understanding among team members, and boosting employee engagement. In this way, they contribute to shaping a more collaborative and understanding organizational culture.

However, these tools aren't without criticism. They lack rigorous scientific support in terms of their reliability and replicability. For instance, a significant proportion of individuals receive different personality types when they retake the MBTI test. Consequently, while these tools may have some positive effects, their impacts are not necessarily predictable or consistent across different settings or over time. This lack of predictability may limit their effectiveness in bringing about the desired cultural change, especially at scale.

In contrast, consider the "Big Five," "OCEAN," or "Five-Factor Model" of personality.[3] This model encompasses five core personality traits: Openness to experience (inventive/curious versus consistent/cautious), Conscientiousness (efficient/organized versus easy-going/careless), Extraversion (outgoing/energetic versus solitary/reserved), Agreeableness (friendly/compassionate versus challenging/detached), and Neuroticism (sensitive/nervous versus secure/confident).

> Supported by robust scientific evidence, the Big Five model provides a more reliable and valid evidence-based intervention for assessing personality than either the MBTI or Insights Discovery.

The Big Five Model can be employed as an evidence-based intervention to facilitate various types of organizational change. For instance, it can be used to improve recruitment and selection processes, design better team structures, and enhance leadership development programs. Understanding an individual's Big Five personality traits can provide insights into their work style, leadership approach, and how they interact with colleagues. This understanding can then be used to align individuals and teams more effectively with organizational goals, enhancing the likelihood of successful change. On the other hand, to be able to effectively utilize the Big Five Model, you have to allocate enough resources (often including trained psychologists) to conduct the intervention rigorously and interpret the results in a valid way.

So, while tools like MBTI and Insights Discovery can offer some benefits, when it comes to predictable, reliable outcomes, interventions grounded in a stronger evidence base, like the Big Five, can be more likely to contribute positively and predictably to the change you're trying to achieve. The flipside is that, in order to gain maximum validity, you have to compromise on speed and resources. This is a tradeoff you see throughout the book and that can be navigated based on your organization's values, priorities, and limitations.

Experimentation, Testing, and Iteration

EBCIs carry significant potential for driving positive change in organizations, but as stated earlier, their application isn't a one-size-fits-all solution. We cannot underscore enough the importance of experimenting, testing, and iterating with these interventions before scaling and implementing them throughout an organization. This process allows for the necessary adjustments to be made to ensure the intervention fits your unique organizational context.

In our discussions with Tijs Besieux, an independent researcher at Harvard and a behavioral change advisor, he highlighted the importance of piloting new interventions in a controlled environment before full-scale implementation. He shared a telling example from his work with financial institutions, a sector characterized by stringent regulation and high stakes. In one project, Besieux and his team designed an intervention aimed at encouraging more reflective decision-making within a bank. The intervention was a meeting tool that prompted stakeholders to pause for reflection at critical moments to enhance decision quality. The pilot phase was well received by the organization's senior leaders and showed promising results. However, when the intervention was scaled across the organization, the positive effects were less pronounced than expected.

This scenario underscores the importance of testing and iteration, even for interventions that are evidence-based and have proven successful in pilot settings. It also brings to light a phenomenon known as the *Hawthorne effect*. This effect occurs when individuals alter their behavior due to the awareness of being observed, which can often manifest as improved performance or altered behavior during the testing phase. Such an effect can inflate the perceived success of an intervention during pilot phases. However, this heightened performance often diminishes when the observation is no longer present or when the intervention is rolled out more broadly, leading to less impactful results than initially expected.

Besieux advocates for a more robust approach to experimentation. He encourages organizations to:

- **Embrace Experimentation:** By adopting a mindset of curiosity and openness to learning, organizations can test various interventions in a controlled environment. The goal should not be to validate preconceived notions but to discover what works and what doesn't in the specific context of the organization. Even interventions that fail to produce the expected results can yield valuable insights, leading to more effective iterations of the intervention and learnings for the organization.
- **Promote Intelligent Failure:** Fostering a culture of intelligent failure, as opposed to punishing all types of failure, can encourage more experimentation and learning. An *intelligent failure* is one where the organization learns something valuable despite the outcome not meeting initial expectations. This approach recognizes that not all experiments will succeed, but each one brings us closer to a more effective solution.

Thus, even with evidence-based interventions, it's necessary to adopt an experimental mindset, rigorously testing and iterating on the intervention to ensure its effectiveness in your unique organizational context.

This best practice of rigorous experimentation with EBCIs brings along an additional challenge: maintaining a grasp on the bigger picture and overarching goals of your changing organization while implementing and evaluating interventions. Balancing this attention to detail with a clear understanding of the broader organizational change objectives can be challenging. Each intervention, while valuable in its own right, is a piece of a larger puzzle and must be placed in the bigger picture of the organizational transformation.

The Emergence of a Shared Underlying Framework

When we interviewed a wide range of organizational leaders, they told us about the change management frameworks and models they use in their organization, including established ones such as ProSci/ADKAR,[4] McKinsey's 7S model,[5] and often with references to Kotter's 8-Step model.[6]

One thing that stood out in these conversations was that none of these leaders regard any single model as a definitive solution, a holy grail of sorts. Instead, they assess which frameworks or models best fit the specific organizational change they are dealing with, customizing them accordingly. Their pragmatic approach reminded us that while models provide a valuable starting point, they require thoughtful application, always remaining mindful of the unique needs of the context at hand. In the words of Natasja van Rens, HR director at Dura Vermeer, "Why do you reach for external support who's going to make your organization fit some model as opposed to experimenting with changing yourselves?" Similarly, Kati Terza, global transformation and change manager at Royal HaskoningDHV, invites other change managers to think about what makes their organization unique. "Science and theory are important, but you always have to start with the current state of your organization. Once you know your unique culture, it enables you to more effectively leverage the science and theory to drive real and lasting change."

Furthermore, in these conversations, we found that many of these models, while useful and often validated, were conceived and tested in the context of the 20th century. As such, they might not fully account for the radically different and complex realities of the 21st century—a business landscape often characterized by complexity and uncertainty. Blindly following these models without taking this shift into account could limit their effectiveness.

It was fascinating to find that, often unbeknownst to these leaders, there was a recurring theme in their approaches to managing change, especially the behavioral dimension. Similar to how top sales/marketing managers, product designers, and policymakers often intuitively apply principles from behavioral science without necessarily knowing the underlying mechanisms of action, we saw a pattern. Over and over, leaders alluded to an underlying approach to change, distinguishable from the usual suspects we mentioned before, that centered on three core components:

- **Prioritizing Change:** Recognizing the most important actions that need to be undertaken for the change and prioritizing them
- **Embedding Behavior:** Translating these priorities into tangible behaviors and, if possible, helping stakeholders form habits around them
- **Tweaking the System:** Ensuring that organizational systems, processes, and policies align with and reinforce these changes in habits and behavior

This underlying approach isn't an alternative change model or methodology. Instead, it functions as an invariant framework that provides a structure that complements their existing approach. It aids leaders in designing and selecting interventions and ensuring there's alignment and coherence among them. This way it can fit within any change management approach, helping change managers more effectively navigate the complexities of behavioral change within their organizations.

We have seen this approach manifest in various ways across organizations. One such example is Johnson & Johnson, the world's largest and most diversified healthcare products company. While working on elevating their change leadership maturity to the next level, we noticed they utilize a variation of this framework, meticulously planning for change by setting clear goals and priorities, then driving this change by translating these goals into tangible behaviors. The change is finally reinforced by ensuring the alignment of their organizational systems with these new behaviors. All three elements are parallel processes instead of sequential phases. They are related to one another and the goal is to find and keep balance between them at any stage of the project.

Another example of this approach can be found in Aegon, a multinational life insurance, pensions, and asset management company. We spoke to Clim Parren, former chief people officer at Aegon, who shared a similar approach. Instead of resorting to a detailed change plan, they adopt a framework that highlights their priority of "helping people live their best lives." This priority is translated into three key behaviors—tuning in (understanding the evolving needs of their customers, fostering empathy and proactive action), stepping up (taking initiative and leading the way in supporting customers through their life journeys), and acting as a force for good (striving to make a positive impact every working day, focusing on trust, inclusivity, and sustainable practices). Aegon ensures the alignment of their organizational systems and processes to reinforce these behaviors. To help deliver the change and to reinforce the behaviors, Parren noted that Aegon uses the ProSci's ADKAR model and McKinsey's influence model because it has proven its compatibility.

Dutch behavioral scientist and author Ben Tiggelaar describes a similar version of this underlying framework, which he calls "The Ladder."[7] It comprises three steps and can serve as an invariant framework for change:

- The top rung is about setting clear goals and prioritizing them. Tiggelaar identifies this as the ultimate goal or result one aspires to achieve.
- The middle rung is behavior. This level is about the specific, well-defined behaviors required to inch closer to the goal.
- Tiggelaar refers to the bottom rung as "support." This is the supportive infrastructure crucial to achieving the behavioral goals. He insists that support systems aren't just nice additions, but non-negotiable prerequisites for change.

It now becomes clear that this simple and invariant approach to change can be adapted to wildly different contexts, whether a multinational conglomerate like Johnson & Johnson, an insurance giant like

Aegon, or the distinct challenges faced by individual professionals. Let's dive deeper into the components of this framework and see how they manifest in the context of organizational change.

The Necessity of Prioritizing Change

Organizational change often encompasses a vast range of potential actions that can be taken at all times. Change managers and organizational leaders must not only identify the critical actions necessary to achieve their desired outcome but also assign them a level of priority. This is not a one-off exercise done at the outset of the change initiative, but a continuous process that should be undertaken throughout the entire change journey.

Take, for instance, "Organization X," which has identified a trend of favoring extroverted employees in promotions, thereby skewing the balance in leadership positions. The leadership team of Organization X could identify a key action, such as "ensuring a fair and unbiased promotion process for all employees." This chosen action provides clear guidance for the change and helps leaders steer their teams accordingly.

However, simply identifying key actions isn't sufficient. It is essential to continually assess the landscape of change and adjust the order of priority of these key actions as necessary. This is not just something that takes place during the planning phase, but is a dynamic process that happens throughout the change journey. These actions must be specific, measurable, and bound by time, enabling an organization to track progress and make course corrections as needed. Failure to identify clear, actionable, and prioritized key actions can result in ambiguity and misalignment. This could lead to teams working at cross-purposes, hindering the change process and causing resources to be squandered and opportunities missed.

Embedding Priorities into Behavior and Habit Formation

For sustained behavioral change to occur, the priorities established must be broken down into precise, observable behaviors. This offers clear guidance for individuals within the organization to act upon, and provides the opportunity for habits to form, making new behaviors easier to recall and execute. Rather than a box to be ticked off, this too is a dynamic process where behavioral science really comes into play.

Continuing with the example of Organization X, the leaders identified that equitable promotion opportunities were truly a priority. Now they need to identify and cultivate behaviors that align with this goal. One way they could train talent managers is to routinely encourage all employees to apply for promotions, making this encouragement a standard part of performance discussions. By doing so, they aim to create a habit where talent managers regularly enable all team members, irrespective of their personality traits, to visualize and strive for growth opportunities.

However, transitioning behaviors into habits is rarely a straightforward process. The repeated, consistent performance of these behaviors, supported by positive reinforcement, is critical for their transition into automatic habits. When such new behaviors become ingrained habits, they can shift organizational culture, driving the desired change. It's important to note, though, that not all behaviors can or should become habits. The key is to foster a balanced blend of conscious, reflective behaviors and intuitive, automatic habits that together support the prioritized organizational goals.

Here, the COM-B model (Capability, Opportunity, Motivation-Behavior) is a particularly useful tool, introduced in Chapter 2. It offers a simple yet effective framework for understanding why a specific behavior is not occurring or not becoming a habit. To utilize the COM-B model, change managers can ask themselves three straightforward questions:

- **Capability:** Do the stakeholders involved have the necessary skills, knowledge, and abilities to perform the desired behavior?
    - Do they understand what the behavior involves and why it is necessary?
    - Is there no additional need for training or information?
- **Opportunity:** Does the physical and social environment enable and support the behavior?
    - Are there enough resources available (time, tools, equipment)?
    - Is there social support for the behavior, or is there peer pressure against it?

- **Motivation:** Are the stakeholders involved sufficiently motivated to perform the behavior?
  - o Are they aware of the "what's in it for them" (WIIFT)?
  - o Are there no existing habits that conflict with the new behavior?

If the answer to any of these questions is no, it may indicate areas that need further interventions to align them with the desired behavioral change.

Without carefully cultivating behaviors and habits that embody the set priorities, the change process can become haphazard and ineffective. It is equally important to identify and replace old habits that conflict with new priorities. Unhelpful habits or behaviors can act as obstacles to change, even when the goals themselves are well defined and supported.

Reinforcing the Change by Tweaking Systems

The final component lies in organizational systems. This refers to the processes, policies, and structures within an organization that can either support or hinder the desired behavior change. In Chapter 2, we discussed the importance of context in shaping and changing behavior. In managing change, you want to create a context that supports new behaviors and sustains changes, instead of impeding them. You can do this by tweaking the systems in your organization. This might sound like a big undertaking, but often comes down to small changes you apply to existing systems instead of complete overhauls.

For Organization X, systems would need to be optimized to support the new habit of encouraging all employees to apply for promotions. HR evaluation systems could be adjusted to automatically qualify employees for promotion once they meet a predetermined qualification threshold. This systemic change would remove potential bias and ensure the new habit becomes the norm. However, if systems and processes do not align with the goals and the desired behavioral changes, they can serve as significant roadblocks. For example, if HR systems still favor extroverted employees in their promotion criteria, the new habits and behaviors will struggle to take root, hampering the goal of equitable promotion opportunities.

Conclusion

As you can see, this framework is not a new or unique construct, but an invariant approach, articulated differently across various companies and settings but fundamentally addressing the same aspects. The bottom line is that prioritizing change, embedding those priorities into behaviors, and tweaking organizational systems to reinforce them is an excellent approach to changing organizational behavior, and therefore organizational culture.

However, an invariant framework that can be applied so broadly can be hard to put into practice, especially under the pressure that continuous change brings to those tasked to manage it. That is why, instead of slapping yet another name on this framework and leaving it at that, we have utilized it as a bedrock for the evidence-based change interventions in the coming chapters. These interventions provide a practical step-by-step approach that helps you prioritize changes, embed them in behavior, and tweak organization systems to reinforce these changes. We refer to them as *behavioral breaks* and you find three of them in each of the following chapters.

Congratulations on finishing the first part of this book! We've discussed the fundamentals of organizational change management and behavioral science. You've seen how these fields merge into behaviorally informed change management and have had a glimpse at the underlying framework for all evidence-based change interventions. Now it's time to explore the six change areas as well as their behavioral insights and evidence-based interventions. In the next chapter, you learn to apply behavioral science to the planning and risk management aspects of organizational change management.

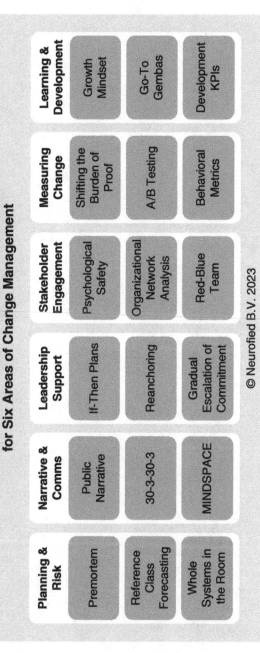

Figure 4.1 Eighteen evidence-based interventions in six areas of change management.

PART

II

Eighteen Interventions for Six Change Areas

5

Planning and Risk Management

JUST SOUTH OF the German capital Berlin in the state of Brandenburg lies the Berlin Brandenburg Airport. Between its conception in the early 1990s, its scheduled opening in 2010, and its actual opening in 2020, Brandenburg Airport became one of the most notorious examples of human error in planning and risk management. The story entails multiple delays, scandals, bribes, and multiple billions in cost overruns.[1]

As construction finally began in 2007, the airport's opening date was set for October 2011 with an initial estimated budget of approximately 2.8 billion euros. However, due to delays in the technical building systems, the need to install additional security screening lines, and one of its contractors going bankrupt, the opening date was pushed back to 2012. This is when things started going farther south.

After years of continuous delays and leadership changes, the airport's opening was denied just weeks before it was set to open. Inspectors identified approximately 120,000 defects, including fire safety concerns, malfunctioning automatic doors, and sagging roofs. They also discovered that about 170,000 kilometers of cable, located both inside and outside the airport, were improperly wired and posed a danger. With the efforts of multiple high-paid airport company managers over the course of more than nine years, the airport finally opened its gates in 2020. Just in time for the COVID-19 pandemic.

Bad luck and inevitable disasters aside, the planning and construction of the Brandenburg Airport seems to have been riddled with human error and cognitive biases. It's not an isolated case either. Thousands of academic papers and case studies describe how, time after time, managers make the same predictable mistakes when it comes to planning and managing risk. For example, 45% of IT change projects[2] and 86% of infrastructure projects[3] run over their original budget. It's highly likely that you, in both personal and professional contexts, have fallen victim to the planning fallacy and other biases yourself. We know we have.

While exploring these biases, it's worth remembering that their existence in our cognition doesn't reflect on our intelligence or ability—it's simply part of human nature. Every one of us, regardless of our intelligence or experience, is susceptible to biases because they are innate to how our brain works in navigating a complex world efficiently. Yet, acknowledging all this leads to an interesting question: Despite being ingrained, can we take steps to deal with the impact of these biases? Let's find out.

In this chapter, we examine the current approach to planning and risk management in organizational change initiatives, which often relies on roadmapping, linear planning, and an overall rational view and approach to managing risk. You discover how this approach, while theoretically sound, can lead to a number of problems and pitfalls, such as planning fallacies and biases, risk aversion, volatile and disappointing returns, and not accounting for black swans.

Planning and Risk Interventions

This chapter introduces behavioral insights that can help improve your planning and risk management process by taking the human factor into account. We cover three evidence-based interventions that help you with more realistic planning, better risk governance and mitigation, and improved ownership and accountability by mitigating bias:

- **Premortem:** This intervention encourages you to envision a future scenario where your change project has failed or succeeded in an extreme way, and retrospectively identify the reasons for this failure. This forward-thinking method enables more effective risk mitigation planning.
- **Reference-Class Forecasting:** This approach helps you use data from similar past projects to forecast the potential outcomes and risks of your current or upcoming change project. This evidence-based intervention assists in crafting a more realistic and objective project budget.
- **Whole Systems in the Room:** This collaborative intervention encourages all key stakeholders to participate in co-creating the change process. By integrating diverse perspectives and fostering a sense of shared ownership, this method significantly enhances the change initiative's resilience.

By the end of this chapter, you will have a deeper understanding of how to use behaviorally informed strategies to plan and manage risks in a way that increases the likelihood of success for your change initiatives.

As Ben Franklin said, "If you fail to plan, you plan to fail." Complex projects like strategy deployment, digital transformations, or mergers require meticulous planning and risk management. Tools such as roadmapping and project dashboarding come in handy to sketch a clear picture of the journey ahead, while keeping track of potential challenges. Engaging in qualitative risk analysis and curating a risk register are standard practices in this context. These steps help track recognized risks, their likelihood of occurrence, and the potential impact, allowing managers to prioritize risks. From there they can build a risk management plan that addresses the most significant risks as a priority.

On Biases in Planning and Risk Management

As you learned earlier in this chapter, the rational approach to planning and risk management, even with all its useful tools and technologies, still leaves room for human error. And quite a lot of it. To understand this better, it's worth taking a closer look at some of the cognitive biases associated with planning and risk. This list also includes some biases that you can see in multiple change areas:

- **Planning Fallacy** is a bias that leads individuals and organizations to underestimate the time, resources, and difficulty required to complete a project. This results in unrealistic timelines, inadequate resource allocation, and a lack of contingency planning. As a result, managers may fail to anticipate and plan for potential roadblocks and delays, which can lead to project failure or significant cost overruns.

- **Optimism Bias** is another bias that can contribute to poor planning and risk management. This refers to our tendency to overestimate the likelihood of positive outcomes and underestimate the likelihood of negative outcomes. This can lead managers to neglect potential risks and to underinvest in risk mitigation strategies.

- **Groupthink** can also lead to poor decision-making and inadequate risk management. In groupthink, individuals conform to the opinions of the group rather than considering alternative perspectives. This can lead to a false sense of unanimity, resulting in poor decision-making. To prevent these biases from impacting their planning and risk management processes, managers need to be aware of these biases and to actively seek out diverse perspectives and information.

- **Hindsight Bias,** also known as the "knew-it-all-along" effect, causes us to believe, after an event has occurred, that we predicted or could have predicted the outcome. It can prevent us from learning from our mistakes and adjusting our future plans and predictions accordingly.

- **Availability Heuristic** is a mental shortcut, or heuristic, that makes us rely on immediate examples when evaluating a specific topic, concept, or decision. In the context of organizational change, this could mean that managers might make decisions based on what information is readily at hand or easily recalled, which could lead to a skewed understanding of risks and planning.

We don't expect you to suddenly be aware of all of these at once, but this list should provide you with some patterns to look out for. And that brings us to the question of how to mitigate them. This is, of course, easier said than done, but the past decade of behavioral science in management (a subfield referred to as *behavioral strategy*) provided useful evidence-based interventions for planning and managing risk. These interventions aim to filter some of these biases out of the process, so let's explore three of them.

Mitigating Unseen Risks with a Premortem

Before we dive into the first evidence-based intervention for planning and risk management, let's explore a related strategy mentioned by Gerard Penning, the former CHRO at ABN AMRO who is currently a board member at Alliander, a Dutch energy network company. We talked about how he balances short-term and long-term change in his role as board member: "Scenario planning is one useful tool to bridge short- and long-term change. You create three scenarios and research how well prepared the organization is for each scenario. When we're talking about the energy transition, for example, are we prepared for a future in which hydrogen is the standard? The less predictable the future, the more important the learning agility of an organization becomes. Scenario planning is a tool that helps learning agility by making the future more predictable. It starts with curiosity and tickles the imagination." This is a beautiful example of, as we see it, an intervention in the wild. Many of you will know scenario planning, but a less well known yet just as useful intervention in the same category is called the premortem.

The premortem technique is a valuable tool in this regard. Invented by Gary Klein, research psychologist and fellow of the American Psychological Association and a leading expert on intuitive decision-making, the premortem is a method for identifying flaws in a plan that may otherwise go unnoticed.[4] If you have heard of a postmortem—an analysis conducted after a project has concluded to uncover what went well and could have gone better—you'll find this especially interesting. The premise of the premortem is simple: before a decision is made or a project has started, the team collectively imagines a future in which the project has failed and conducts an analysis to determine the reasons for this failure.

The meeting organizer states something like, "We are X months/ years ahead, and this project has been an unmitigated disaster. Why did it turn out to be so catastrophic?" Team members then write down their potential reasons for the failure in detail and share them with the group. It is important to note that broad participation from all team members is needed in order to ensure a thorough examination of potential risks and challenges. The participants of a premortem are typically those directly involved in planning and implementing the project or decision. They include:

- **Project Managers:** As the person who oversees the project from start to finish, the project manager should definitely be included in a premortem. They are aware of the project's overall goals and would be best placed to predict potential areas of failure.
- **Team Members:** This includes anyone who will be working on the project. Each team member brings a unique perspective and understanding of their specific role in the project. Their hands-on experience can be invaluable for identifying potential pitfalls.
- **Stakeholders:** These are individuals or groups who have a vested interest in the project. Stakeholders could include executives, clients, or other departments who are reliant on the project's success. They might have unique insights into potential risks that those directly involved in the project may overlook.
- **Subject Matter Experts (SMEs):** If the project involves specialized knowledge or expertise, SMEs should be involved in the premortem. They can identify risks related to their area of expertise that others might not anticipate.
- **Support Staff:** This could include members from HR, legal, or IT departments who can offer their perspective on potential challenges that may arise in their respective areas.

In essence, the goal is to have a comprehensive and diverse range of perspectives to fully explore potential challenges and risks. The greater the diversity of the group, the more potential risks you can identify and mitigate. That said, conducting a premortem with a smaller, less diverse group is always better than no premortem at all.

Where some teams love the idea of visiting the worst-case scenario and doubling down on all possible disastrous outcomes, this approach might be a bit discouraging (if not downright terrifying) for teams dealing with change fatigue or a recent setback. This is where we like to complement the premortem approach with a so-called *pre-parade*. Described by Roelaf Botha, venture capitalist and partner at Sequoia Capital, the pre-parade is a variation of the premortem that helps stakeholders capitalize on future opportunities by envisioning the best-case scenario and working backward from there. We found that this approach works especially well in sensitive changes for uncovering unseen risks and opportunities without decreasing morale. You can simply split the stakeholders in two groups (premortem versus pre-parade) and have them exchange risks/opportunities. You'll often find that there is a kind of metaphorical mirror in between them. Flip the best-case-scenario factors and you'll find ideas for factors that can cause the worst-case scenario and vice versa (a technique many professionals might know from flipping their weaknesses into strengths, for example, on their CVs).

The premortem technique differs from traditional risk assessment methods in two key ways:

- Most importantly, it takes advantage of the tendency for individuals to better explain past events than imagine future events, or **hindsight bias**. By imagining a future failure, the premortem allows for prospective hindsight.
- Secondly, the act of writing down potential reasons for failure and mandating participation from all team members helps to overcome the tendency for dissenting opinions to go unvoiced, the **groupthink** we discussed earlier.

The premortem technique is a valuable tool for identifying potential risks and challenges in organizational change initiatives. It can increase the success of your change initiative by anticipating and addressing potential obstacles before they occur.

The *behavioral breaks* you find here and in later chapters provide a practical step-by-step approach that helps you prioritize changes, embed them in behavior, and tweak organizational systems to reinforce your changes.

Behavioral Break: Premortem Intervention

1. **Plan and schedule:** Schedule a meeting with your team before finalizing your organizational change initiative. The number of participants is usually between 6 and 20. It's advisable to have your core team fully present and include at least one stakeholder from the participants described earlier in this section.

2. **Communicate the objective:** Clearly explain the purpose of the meeting, ideally ahead of time. The objective of the premortem is identifying potential risks and challenges before implementing the plan.

3. **Set the hypothetical scenario:** Begin the meeting by stating a hypothetical scenario in which the project has failed, for example: "We are six months ahead, and this project has been an unmitigated disaster. Why did it turn out to be so catastrophic?" You can also split the group in two here and assign a pre-parade to one of the groups. For long-term projects, you can adapt the timeline to three to five years.

4. **Include individual reflection:** Ask each team member to individually write down their potential reasons for the failure (or success, in case of the pre-parade) and keep them anonymous. Give them at least 5–10 minutes to think about this.

5. **Share perspectives:** Once all team members have finished writing, ask them to share their reasons with the group. Go around the room, one reason at the time, and, if possible, start with the most junior person. This will prevent senior leaders' perspectives from biasing the group (authority bias).

6. **Encourage open discussion:** Encourage debate among the team members to further analyze and understand the potential reasons for failure. This is where the premortem and pre-parade group can potentially debate each other as well.

7. **Identify common failures:** Take note of any recurring or common reasons for failure that were identified by the team members.

8. **Address potential risks:** Use these reasons to identify and address potential risks and challenges before implementing the plan. These risks can be logged in a risk register, a commonly used tool in change management.

9. **Assign risk mitigation tasks:** Appoint specific team members to tasks that will aim to prevent, minimize, or mitigate these identified risks and challenges.

10. **Monitor and review:** Monitor the progress of these tasks and review the premortem analysis regularly—for example, at a monthly meeting—to ensure that all potential risks and challenges have been addressed before implementing the plan.

You can use a premortem anytime at any scale when you want to de-risk a planning, process, or decision. If you're implementing one for the first time, we recommend you plan 60–90 minutes with your team, prepare the premortem well, and make sure you implement it step by step, using this behavioral break. The great thing about not just the premortem but all behavioral interventions is that the more you do them, the easier and more habitual they will get. In the long run, this simple intervention can have a major impact on a change initiative's ROI by diminishing unexpected cost overruns and shortfalls.

Reducing Cost Overruns with Reference-Class Forecasting

Although the premortem serves as a great tool to uncover a variety of risks associated with a project or decisions, some risks require more specific behavioral interventions, especially when it comes to financial risks such as in the Brandenburg Airport story. We have learned that cost overruns seem inevitable in projects that bring large-scale change, but missing the mark by multiple billions, or tripling your estimated budget, seems extreme. However, when we look at the literature, we see cost overruns in capital projects occur time and time again, in the most prestigious firms and contractors, featuring top-level fiscal analysts and financial planners. When smart people with great resources keep making the same predictable errors in their decision-making, there must be bias lurking around.

This pattern can be understood by considering how various cognitive biases work together. When we plan, we tend to be overly optimistic, underestimating the time and resources required—the planning fallacy we discussed. We also know already that optimism bias is causing us to anticipate positive outcomes more than negative ones.

Remember the **anchoring bias,** where we tend to rely too heavily on the first piece of information we encounter when making decisions? In this context, it means we might base our project timelines or budgets on initial estimates, even if they turn out to be unrealistic later. When these biases occur, they create what's known as an *inside view*: a skewed perspective that results in overly optimistic forecasts and a resistance to adjusting initial budget estimates, even after inaccuracies are spotted.

For example, when making an estimate for a project, a manager trapped in an inside view might focus on the specific details of the project at hand and ignore the fact that similar projects have taken longer and cost more in the past. This can lead to an underestimation of the resources required to complete the project. To mitigate this, behaviorally informed managers carefully consider the historical data and experiences of similar projects and use them as a benchmark to make a more accurate estimate and update continuously. This, unsurprisingly, is called creating an *outside view*.

The solution seems simple: teach managers responsible for project budgeting how to develop this outside view and remind them to use it whenever they are making important decisions. Unfortunately, this doesn't work at scale and over a long period of time. Since the inside view is caused by a cluster of unconscious biases, you will usually not be aware that you are stuck in an inside view while planning. Even more so, the larger the scale of a capital project, the more likely you are to see it as unique, and seemingly impossible to benchmark from an outside view.

Luckily, behavioral science has developed and refined an intervention to deal with this. Reference-class forecasting[5] (RCF) helps managers cultivate an outside view by gathering information from previous, similar projects, regardless of their success. By using the realized outcomes of real-life past projects rather than manipulated estimates of the current project, RCF enables managers to make more accurate and reliable top-down estimates of a project's true costs, schedule, and benefits.

First published in 2003 by Dan Lovallo (professor of strategy at the University of Sydney) and Daniel Kahneman (emeritus professor of psychology at the University of Princeton), this intervention is particularly useful because it helps managers avoid the common pitfall of focusing on easily recalled, similar projects that have succeeded and are close in time and space to the decision at hand. In other words, it combats the availability heuristic we discussed before. Instead, RCF allows managers to consider a broader range of historical data, which provides a more accurate picture of the resources and time required to complete a task.

RCF is a prime example of how behavioral interventions made it into policy. Since 2003, it's mandatory to perform RCF in the UK government for infrastructure projects over 40 million pounds, reducing cost overruns on capital projects from 38% to 5%.[6] Today, RCF is also a requirement for capital projects in countries like Denmark, Germany, Norway, Sweden, Switzerland, the Netherlands, and the United States.

In the coming sections, we explore a simplified step-by-step intervention plan for applying reference-class forecasting. As you go through this process, it's important to keep in mind that this version is simplified to make it more accessible. In its full implementation, RCF involves statistical computing that provides a more nuanced understanding of your project's potential outcomes using large datasets. While we won't be going through these more complex steps here, when it comes to implementing RCF we strongly encourage collaborating with data scientists in your organization, if possible. Provided they have the knowledge, skills, and access to statistical software to carry out these calculations, they can bring a level of accuracy and precision to your estimates that simply cannot be achieved without such data-driven insights. Think of this simplified RCF plan as an introduction to a new way of thinking about project planning and estimation, one that's informed by systematically reviewing data from similar past projects rather than relying solely on intuition and experience.

Behavioral Break: Reference-Class Forecasting Intervention

1. **Choose your reference class:** Start by identifying past change projects similar to the one you are planning. Consider key aspects, such as the nature of the project, its scale, its complexity, and the sector it falls under. Your aim is to find projects that share essential characteristics with your current project, providing a comparable reference class. You need to ensure the reference class is large enough to capture a range of outcomes (best practice is 20-plus projects, but even starting with 3–5 can help you improve your estimate and start building a reference class that improves over time), but remember that it doesn't require sophisticated statistical analysis. You just need a reasonable number of similar projects.

2. **Analyze the outcomes:** Next, review the outcomes of the projects in your reference class. Focus on final costs, completion times, and any other outcome measures that

are important for your current project. Look for patterns—are most projects going over budget? Do certain types of projects always take longer? Are there extreme cases where the project was a big success or failure? This step is all about understanding the landscape of past projects and noting down observations that might inform your current project.

3. **Make an informed estimate:** With your reference class chosen and your outcomes analyzed, it's time to make an estimate for your current project. Use the patterns you noticed in the second step as a guide. If most projects go over budget, for example, it would be smart to increase your initial cost estimate accordingly. The aim here is not to pinpoint an exact cost or completion date, but to create a more realistic range for these important project outcomes.

These steps should provide a good foundation for making more accurate forecasts without requiring statistical computations. However, if you have access to data analysts in your organization, they can help to strengthen the analysis by applying statistical methods to your data, allowing for even greater accuracy and confidence in your estimates. For example, when RCF is used for budget estimation in the public sector, their data scientists often have access to hundreds of past projects that fit the reference class. But even without their help, this simplified process can go a long way in improving the quality of your project estimates because it helps counter "this time it's different" thinking.

As you progress with RCF, you might notice that it can significantly enhance your planning and decision-making process. For instance, let's use some hindsight to reflect on how the Brandenburg Airport case could be improved. If we were to use a reference class of similar construction projects, we might find that the average cost of these types of projects is between 3 billion and 3.5 billion euros, as opposed to the initial estimate of 2.8 billion euros. This method, even without the detailed statistical computations, would yield a far more realistic estimate, significantly reducing the chances of a budget overrun.

Behavioral science is one of those rare examples where, in some cases, the public sector is a couple of steps ahead of the private sector. The interventions above, however, are just as applicable in commercial organizations. Putting together a reference class and correcting for intuitive budgeting errors requires some extra work, but judging from the numbers above, this is time well spent. Additionally, the more often you conduct RCF, the bigger your pool of useful reference classes will become and thus the easier and more reliable the RCF process will get over time. This is an opportunity for change teams to build long-term value for the organization by essentially building up a database of predictions and learnings. This is also an excellent opportunity to experiment with how other interventions might affect the project (more on this in Chapter 9 on measuring change).

So why not give it a go? You can start by putting together a reference class of around three to five projects the next time you're estimating a budget, and testing how this style of budgeting impacts cost overruns. If you notice success, present your results and the RFC method to the executive team and discuss how you can make it part of formal processes. There are plenty of RCF success stories to build a solid business case on.

Calibrating the Desired Degree of Risk

Planning fallacies and subsequent cost overruns clearly are types of risk that should be reduced as effectively as possible. However, on the far end of this spectrum we might find organizations that focus on relentlessly reducing all types of risk, which can lead to a different problem: excessive *risk aversion*. Especially in today's climate of continuous change and uncertainty, excessive risk aversion can sometimes pose an even bigger problem than risk-seeking because it reduces innovation, experimentation, and agility. A hybrid example is that of an organization where the C-suite decision-making (think acquisitions and capital expenditure) is bold, high-risk, and sometimes even impulsive, while downstream managers are bound to highly formalized decision-making processes that leave them little to no room to explore and experiment.

Risk-seeking decision-makers tend to be more prone to earlier discussed biases like **optimism, overconfidence,** and the **inside view.** On the other hand, risk-averse decision-makers are more likely to fall prey to biases like **loss aversion,** the tendency to avoid loss over pursuing gains, and **status quo bias,** the tendency to maintain the current state of affairs (even when that state is counterproductive). Thus, the key objective in managing risk is not reducing risk (or increasing it for that matter), but in calibrating the right *degree of risk* for the right circumstances. That said, now that we have discussed de-risking interventions like premortem and RCF, let's look at an intervention that helps cultivate a healthy degree of risk-taking in risk-averse scenarios.

When managing large-scale changes, attempting to plan and control risk without the involvement of a broad array of stakeholders is a recipe for failure. Instead, change managers should strive for integration and co-creation from the start, where the changes, their potential impacts, and acceptable levels of risk are discussed comprehensively with all stakeholders involved. Reflecting on experiences from industry professionals, the importance of this inclusive approach becomes even more evident. The vice president of HR at the multinational retail company we met earlier highlighted the success of a system-based approach when merging various brands into one unified HR system. The integration involved governance from the headquarters, sponsorships from brands, and a roll-out team comprising stakeholders from all the brands. This level of collaboration in planning and implementation fostered a shared sense of responsibility and streamlined the transformative process.

We spoke with the organizational capability director of a leading global healthcare company. She emphasized the role of co-creation in change initiatives and argued that merely informing employees about impending changes is insufficient. Instead, employees should be involved in the planning process, which fosters a sense of investment and commitment to the change. These insights underscore the value of a strategy that encourages broad participation and ownership which, in turn, aids in effectively calibrating and mitigating risk.

Using "Whole System in the Room" for Strategic Risk Management in Change

To approach risk management in a behaviorally informed way, change managers can adopt another evidence-based intervention: Whole System in the Room (WSR).[7] Derived from Marvin Weisbord's work in the field of organizational development, WSR asserts the importance of inclusive decision-making in change initiatives. In the context of organizational change, you can view it as an intervention in which representatives of each stakeholder group involved (referred to as "the system") discuss possible risks and co-create strategies to act on them. While similar to a premortem, WSR differentiates by involving a broader group of stakeholders, seeking to establish an acceptable level of risk for all parties involved, which, in certain cases, may mean agreeing to take on greater risks.

By creating a shared understanding of the necessity for change and the acceptable levels of risk, it reduces resistance and encourages collective action. We spoke with Wieke Scholten, Behavioral Risk Lead Partner at &samhoud, a consultancy that advises corporations on mitigating behavioral risk, about the application of this method. She describes that they conduct dynamic "system in the room" workshops. These sessions aim to create a shared comprehension of managing potential risks from the standpoint of every participant, and the collective understanding allows the team to develop more effective solutions.

> Whole System in the Room (WSR) lends itself well to the planning phase of change, where the risks and benefits of the proposed transformation are weighed and strategic decisions are made.

This intervention was deployed, for example, at ING,[8] a multinational financial services firm that, following a behavioral risk assessment, recognized a gap in cross-functional collaboration and ownership—key behavioral risk drivers. Using a design-thinking-inspired approach, the firm moved from problem identification to solution generation, leading not only to addressing the issue at hand but also fostering a significant transformation in the organization's risk culture.

As Scholten elaborates, the WSR sessions involve gathering all stakeholders involved in a certain risk management process, such as anti-money laundering processes in a bank. These stakeholders range from executives and global process owners to tech experts and frontline staff. This inclusive setting fosters a sense of shared responsibility and accentuates how each individual's actions contribute to the collective outcome. A significant outcome of this approach was the establishment of brief, weekly system-update meetings between risk managers and top leaders. Integrated into the regular meeting schedule, these meetings served as an early warning system, pinpointing potential behavioral risks at the outset of the change process.

The working mechanism underpinning WSR is its potential to mitigate biases like confirmation bias, groupthink, and anchoring bias, which can be particularly pronounced during periods of change. **Confirmation bias** tends to manifest when leaders or teams cherry-pick information that supports their preexisting beliefs or hypotheses. By involving a wide range of voices, WSR ensures that varying perspectives and potentially contradictory information are brought to everyone's attention. This acts as a natural check against the inclination to favor only confirming information. The WSR setting furthermore encourages robust debate and discussion, fostering a culture where dissenting opinions can be freely voiced, thus helping to avoid **groupthink**.

The WSR strategy is also designed to counteract **anchoring**, discussed earlier in this chapter. By facilitating the continuous introduction of new information and diverse perspectives from different stakeholders, it keeps the decision-making environment dynamic. As a result, the chances of getting stuck on initial anchors are reduced, promoting a more flexible and adaptive approach to planning change and managing risk.

Consider an organization undergoing a considerable transformation in its operational structure. Facing rough market competition, the company decides to transition from their traditional hierarchical model to a flatter and more collaborative structure. However, the transformation comes with a significant risk of disrupting the existing workflow and productivity. To manage this change, the company implements the WSR strategy, bringing together all stakeholders—from executives to frontline employees—in a series of workshops.

The focus isn't solely on flagging potential issues or risks but also on drumming up solutions together. This gives everyone a clear picture of the risks involved, sidesteps any finger-pointing, and underlines how every individual action can affect the whole group.

By using this strategy, the company gets a full understanding of the risks involved with the changes. This allows the company to decide how much risk it's willing to take on to achieve its goals. Rather than avoiding risks, leadership plans for them, making sure everyone knows their roles and responsibilities in the new structure. As mentioned, WSR lends itself well to the planning phase of change, where the risks and benefits of the proposed transformation are weighed and strategic decisions made.

This perspective on risk in change management resonates with the insights shared by Floor Huizer, transformation director at ABN AMRO. She pointed out how tightly regulated industries, such as banking, may tend to view risk as something to avoid, triggered by strict regulatory frameworks and scarred by past crises. However, she emphasizes, "Taking risks is at the core of our business. One should always play to win, and not play not to lose." In other words, the key lies not in avoiding risks but in recognizing, managing, and even embracing them as a fundamental aspect of business operations. Incorporating this mindset can be instrumental in the successful implementation and management of organizational change. Now, let's delve into the practical implementation of WSR.

Behavioral Break: Whole System in the Room Intervention

1. **Assemble your system:** Start by mapping out all the individuals and groups who have a stake in the planned change. These stakeholders represent your "system." Remember, the system is not just your C-suite or management team; it spans across all levels of your organization and may even include external stakeholders. A system map is different from a spreadsheet with stakeholder groups and names; it provides a more dynamic view on stakeholder

relationships. You can use open-source or in-house systems mapping software for this (including organizational network analysis, a technique we discuss in Chapter 8), but drawing it out on a whiteboard can go a long way too.

2. **Plan your session:** Once your system is assembled, plan a WSR session of ideally about half a day. The session needs to be scheduled at a time when maximum participation can be ensured, with the specific purpose of the meeting being communicated in advance. Make it clear that this session is aimed at gathering diverse perspectives about the upcoming change and fostering shared understanding to plan effectively. Make sure each stakeholder group is represented by the participants.

3. **Encourage diverse input:** At the start of the session, make sure to emphasize that all perspectives are not just welcomed, but vital. As the facilitator, your role is to create a safe environment for open discussion. Allow for disagreement but make sure to steer the conversation toward constructive outcomes. Use prompts such as:

   • "What are your initial thoughts on the proposed change?"

   • "What unique insights can you provide based on your role?"

4. **Identify and evaluate risks:** As you facilitate this conversation, you're looking to collaboratively identify potential risks (and opportunities) that the change could bring. This is where the strength of WSR shines. With a diverse range of stakeholders in the room, you're likely to get insights that wouldn't surface in a boardroom discussion. Encourage note-taking for these insights. Try using questions like:

   • "What potential risks do you expect with this change?"

(continued)

(continued)

- "How significant do you think they are in achieving our change objectives?"

5. **Harness collective intelligence:** Once all risks and opportunities are on the table, it's time to harness the collective intelligence of the room to find solutions. Steer the conversation toward deciding which risks are acceptable and which ones need mitigation strategies. Ask:

   - "Which of these risks can we accept as part of our change process?"

   - "Which risks do we need to devise mitigation strategies for?"

6. **Synthesize and plan:** Having a host of potential strategies is great, but the goal is to converge on a viable action plan. Encourage the stakeholders to reach a consensus on the way forward. This process ensures that the change plan is not top-down but shaped by the collective intelligence of the organization.

7. **Ongoing engagement:** The WSR approach isn't a one-off exercise. Keep the system engaged throughout the change process. Regular check-ins, updating stakeholders about progress, gathering feedback, and recalibrating the action plan based on real-time insights—all of these are integral to leveraging the full power of WSR.

When you apply Whole System in the Room, the approach will vary based on several factors, like the type and size of the change you're implementing, the structure and hierarchy of your organization, and the diversity of stakeholders involved. The prompts and questions offered in the above breakdown are not meant to be mindlessly copied and pasted but should be adapted to fit the unique context of your organization and change initiative. You can use the steps outlined here as flexible structure to be adjusted as necessary. WSR sessions can go from light and engaging to intense and from time to time even uncomfortable. However, done right, they can serve as a cornerstone for even the most complex of changes.

Conclusion

In this chapter, we explored a behaviorally informed approach to planning and risk management in the context of organizational change. The evidence-based interventions (premortem, reference-class forecasting, and Whole System in the Room) can complement and enhance your organization's existing risk and planning strategies.

Recalling the shared underlying framework from Chapter 4, these interventions help you identify and prioritize potential risks and opportunities in planning organizational change. They serve as practical tools to cultivate more effective behaviors and habits, such as envisioning future failure or success (premortem), collecting reference classes for budget estimations (reference-class forecasting), and fostering dialogue, debate, and active participation from all stakeholders (Whole System in the Room). Each intervention also provides a step-by-step process that can be adapted to your unique context, supporting the application of these interventions at scale. By reinforcing the desired behaviors and aligning them with set priorities, these tools can have a tangible impact on the efficacy of your planning and risk management efforts.

As we advance to the next chapter, we explore another area where applying behavioral science makes a big difference: narrative and communication.

6

Narrative and Communication

CLOSE YOUR EYES for a moment and envision yourself amidst a vast sea of people on a hot summer day in 1963. The Lincoln Memorial in Washington, D.C., was humming with anticipation. The energy was palpable as over 250,000 pairs of eyes turned to one man, Martin Luther King Jr. His voice began to narrate a history—not of a nation, not of an event, but of himself. He spoke of the Emancipation Proclamation, a turning point in his life and for every African American. It was personal, intimate, his own life intertwined with history.

As his speech progressed, King wove a tale that transcended his individual narrative, bringing together the struggles, aspirations, and experiences of those before him and those surrounding him. He spoke of a collective journey for equality, drawing in every person listening, making it our shared history. And then he shifted once more, his voice rallying for action, for now, echoing the urgency of making the promises of democracy a reality.

A few decades later, in Grant Park, Chicago, a similar narrative unfolded. Barack Obama, a name that was soon to be etched in the annals of history, shared his unique journey—a narrative of a mixed-race heritage, of an upbringing by a single mother and his grandparents.

It was his story, individual yet resonant. Yet his words reached beyond just his life. He told a narrative of shared hopes and dreams, a collective journey of the American people. And then, as if following an unseen compass, he steered the speech toward pressing issues like economic inequality and healthcare reform, underlining the urgency of the moment. A clarion call to act, to make a difference, to create a change—now.

Fast-forward to March 2022, weeks after the Russian invasion of Ukraine started, when Arnold Schwarzenegger took center stage. His narrative began with a tale from his youth, witnessing Yuri Petrovich Vlasov, a Russian, winning the World Weightlifting Championship. This awe-inspiring encounter and subsequent experiences with Russia shaped his deep-seated respect and affection for its people. His narrative wove personal memories with historical events, bringing his father's haunting experiences in the Second World War into focus.

As the narrative progressed, Schwarzenegger shared his personal story with the current predicament of Russian soldiers in Ukraine, offering perspective on the horrors of war. With increasing urgency, he appealed for immediate action to end the hostilities. He concluded his narrative with a stirring call for peace, directed squarely at Russian leadership, carrying the weight of his past experiences and the collective yearning of the world for peace. His concluding remarks acknowledged the bravery of Russians protesting the war, symbolizing a beacon of hope amidst dark times.

Three different eras, three different personalities, three different contexts, but one common thread—a narrative structure that moved from personal experiences to shared realities, finally culminating in a call for immediate action. You might be wondering, how do these historical narratives relate to the organizational change you are attempting to navigate? As we explore this chapter, we uncover how these narrative structures that were so effectively used by King, Obama, and Schwarzenegger can be adapted to unify and motivate your colleagues at work.

Narrative and Communication Interventions

In this chapter, we cover how you can optimize narrative and communication in organizational change initiatives with insights from behavioral psychology. We explore how the way that stories are told and the channels through which they are communicated can have a profound impact on the outcome of change efforts. Effective narrative and communication strategies can help generate buy-in, engagement, and alignment among stakeholders, while suboptimal strategies can lead to confusion, resistance, and disengagement.

Communication was one of the most commonly mentioned recurring challenges in OCM. Raymond van Hattem, HR director at Pro-Rail, a Dutch government organization responsible for the national railway network infrastructure, asked a question that kept resurfacing throughout interviews. "How do you reach everyone in the organization just as effectively? In my previous role at Rabobank I saw how effectively reaching 40,000 people is not doable. When I came to Pro-Rail, I thought it would be different with 5,000 people but it's still very hard to reach and engage people at scale." Kristel Buitink, VP of HR at CEVA Logistics, a global logistics and supply chain company, asked the same question and explained how it's not just about communicating to them but also about knowing the people so you can more effectively tailor communication: "CEVA uses flex workers a lot. These people come through a staffing agency and drive from other European countries here to work for X weeks/months and then return. It's very hard to find out what the experience of these people is and how to improve it."

We examine the current approach to narrative and communication in change initiatives, which often relies on a one-size-fits-all approach, relying on formal communication channels such as memos, reports, and presentations. However, this approach can lead to a number of problems, such as a lack of resonance with stakeholders, missed opportunities for engagement and feedback, and ineffective transfer of knowledge and learnings.

You learn about the importance of taking a personalized approach to narrative and communication in change initiatives, with behavioral interventions like these:

- **Public Narrative:** This intervention revolves around crafting a powerful, persuasive story that motivates and inspires action toward the change initiative. It provides a framework that helps you craft compelling narratives that connect on a personal level, build a sense of collective identity, and incite action.

- **30-3-30-3:** This intervention helps you use different communication channels effectively, such as social media, town hall meetings, and workshops, to reach diverse stakeholders and to ensure effective transfer of knowledge and learning.
- **MINDSPACE:** This framework can be used to enhance the content and delivery of your communication. It helps make sure your messaging is resonant and persuasive through nine behavioral science principles.

By the end of this chapter, you will have a deeper understanding of how to use behavioral insights in narrative and communication to drive successful change initiatives, and how to create messages that resonate with stakeholders and build momentum for change. Effective narrative and communication are the key to overcoming resistance and building a culture of continuous improvement and learning, where stakeholders are engaged, informed, and invested in the change process.

The Importance of a Strong Narrative and Open Communication

Humans are social creatures, and our brains are hardwired to make sense of the world around us by crafting and telling stories that connect the dots and address uncertainties. Particularly when change is happening, a strong narrative that clearly communicates the why, what, and how of the change initiative can help employees understand the purpose and direction of the change.

According to McKinsey & Company, a strong narrative can make a tangible difference in transformation success by mobilizing stakeholders and achieving business objectives with a shared understanding of what is changing and why. In fact, transformations where senior leaders align on a concrete change narrative and communicate openly and honestly about progress are six times more likely to succeed.[1]

Recall from Chapter 3 the discussion about PLUS retail, a supermarket chain that is in the process of merging with COOP, together becoming the third largest supermarket chain in the Netherlands. According to Judith Peters, HR director at PLUS retail, early communication of the change and a practical approach to implementation play a crucial role during such major transformations. This early communication of operational changes—such as transforming the store layout from COOP to PLUS, altering work clothes, products, and operational systems, but at the same time keeping some of the previous systems and procedures (i.e., HR systems in the stores)—was key to eliminating uncertainties among the employees about the upcoming changes. Moreover, a series of events with directors of both companies on stage signified unity, a common direction, and set an example of desired behavior. As Peters put it, "If the kids see that Mom and Dad are okay, they will also be okay."

> It's worth noting that the focus should not be on persuading people but rather on "understanding before being understood."

However, despite the best intentions, leaders and employees can be affected by cognitive biases that cloud clear communication. Leaders may fall into the trap of the **information bias**, where they delay communication while waiting for more comprehensive information. This behavior can breed confusion and distrust among employees. Nadine Beister, group director of HR at Achmea, one of the largest suppliers of financial services in the Netherlands, counters this pitfall, stressing the necessity of involving people early in the process: "People often think they need all the answers before they start communicating, but the earlier you communicate, the better."

Engage the team early, value co-creation, communicate openly—about what you do not yet know as well as what you cannot yet share—manage expectations, and avoid surprises. These approaches can all help mitigate such biases, fostering a shared sense of purpose, increasing trust and thereby easing anxieties.

Building on the idea of how narratives can shape organizational change, Michiel van Meer, the chief people officer at Aon Nederland & ASC EMEA, provides an illustrative example of the impact of language on effective communication. In 2019, Aon, an American professional services company, acquired a Dutch local group from Aegon, resulting in an addition of 2,300 people to their team. During their initial communications about the workings of the new company and the integration plans, they realized the use of numerous abbreviations made it difficult for the newly joined group to follow along. Recognizing this, they reduced unnecessary abbreviations and clarified their shared language, underscoring the idea that the use of complex language or insider terminology can undermine both the change narrative and strategy.

The lessons from this example are clear: do not assume your audience possesses the same knowledge you do. This phenomenon, known as the **curse of knowledge**, refers to a cognitive bias where individuals with extensive knowledge (in this context, organizational leaders) find it hard to understand and relate to those who lack the same information—for example, frontline workers. By actively encouraging all stakeholders involved to voice their concerns and provide feedback regarding the change, you can adjust your narrative and delivery method accordingly.

A narrative that clearly communicates the reasons, plans, and methods of change can guide employees through the process, providing a sense of purpose and direction. However, the way this narrative is delivered is equally important. Ensuring that the language used is clear and comprehensible for everyone involved is essential for maintaining engagement and avoiding confusion. Furthermore, creating a safe environment that allows for feedback, clarification, and dialogue can further enhance communication.

Current Approaches to Narrative and Communication

Evidence from both academia and business highlight that transparent and consistent communication plays a crucial role in shaping the understanding of the change among stakeholders, and plays a large role in determining the success or failure of the initiative. However, despite their importance, the current approach to shaping narrative and communicating them in change initiatives is often far from flawless.

Current approaches to change narrative and communication within organizations often involve a top-down strategy where key information and decisions about the change initiative are developed by senior leadership and then disseminated to the rest of the organization. This is typically accomplished through company-wide announcements, written memos, presentations, and workshops. The change narrative is often crafted by a select few, typically those at the top of the organizational hierarchy. In some cases, the language used is jargon-filled corporate speak, which may lead to confusion and misinterpretation, especially among those on the frontline, far away from headquarters. Additionally, communication is often one-way with limited opportunities for dialogue or feedback.

One of the main issues with this approach to narrative and communication in change initiatives is that it often relies on a one-size-fits-all approach. Change managers tend to use a generic narrative that does not take into account the unique context and needs of each stakeholder group. This results in a lack of resonance and engagement, and can lead to opposition. Moreover, the use of a single, all-encompassing narrative can also result in information overload, as stakeholders are bombarded with too much information, making it difficult for them to understand the change and how it impacts them.

Many interviewees also mentioned that not every change has an inherent "what's in it for me" (WIIFM) for everyone in the audience. Without a clear WIIFM, urgency and engagement are likely to dwindle. Barbara Lammers, CHRO at DPD, the second-largest parcel delivery network across Europe, explained, "In the end, it's all about how a change impacts us. And it should be. We have our own survival mechanism and work is near the bottom of the Maslow pyramid."

Another psychological principle that comes into play here is **framing.** This refers to the idea that the manner in which information is presented, or framed, affects how it is received and interpreted. For example, if you're told that a surgical procedure has a 90% success rate, you might feel more confident about going ahead with it than if you were told it has a 10% failure rate. Even though the statistical likelihood is the same in both scenarios, the way it's framed makes a difference in your decision-making. In the context of change management, understanding and applying framing can help managers tailor their communication to the unique needs and perspectives of different stakeholders. This can, in turn, aid in crafting a more compelling change narrative, mitigating resistance, and fostering buy-in and commitment among all involved parties. Therefore, as a change communicator, it's not just *what* you say, it's *how* you say it.

This resonates with Maarten van Beek, global HR director at ING Retail, a leading Dutch bank with a global presence. His insight takes it even a step further, extending it to the very language we use to describe change: "Change is a bit of a weird word. We are constantly moving and therefore changing. People generally respond better to 'movement,' perhaps because it doesn't trigger the idea of change aversion."

> By consciously choosing your words, you can guide the narrative in a way that feels intuitive and less aversive. The exact wording that you use, whether change, movement, or something else, depends on the context and culture of your organization.

Another issue with common approaches to communication in change initiatives is that they tend to be overly optimistic and positive, neglecting the potential downsides and challenges of the change. This can lead to unrealistic expectations and a lack of trust among stakeholders, who may feel that leaders are not being transparent and honest about the potential risks and challenges of the change. Furthermore, an overly optimistic narrative can also result in a lack of contingency planning, as leaders may underestimate the difficulties and risks involved in the change initiative. The pendulum can also swing the other way, although one rarely sees that in practice nowadays. If leaders are too transparent about the uncertainty and risk that a change brings, it might cause fear and confusion as well as a reduced trust in the capabilities of the leaders to successfully navigate the organization to the future state. This balancing act is at the core of the art of narrative and communication.

Constructing and communicating narratives on change initiatives also tends to suffer from a lack of diversity and inclusion. One common pitfall is not to involve different stakeholder groups and perspectives early in the communication process, which can lead to a lack of ownership and engagement among these groups. And as discussed, there can be significant group differences. Sales, tech, and finance departments, for example, have different cultures, priorities, and ways of working.

A behaviorally informed approach to communicating in these areas leverages group difference insights to tailor the narrative and/or communications to ensure everyone is aligned while acknowledging uniqueness. Recall that the focus should not be on persuading people but rather on "understanding before being understood." If you plan to communicate that the organization has a new purpose, you better be able to tell Thea the bookkeeper how her job is actually changing. Moreover, this lack of diversity can also result in **groupthink** because change managers may conform to the opinions and perspectives of the dominant stakeholder groups, neglecting alternative perspectives and information.

In short, conventional approaches to communicating change initiatives are sometimes inadequate, leading to resistance, unrealistic expectations, and suboptimal decision-making. To overcome these issues, change managers need to adopt a more context-specific and inclusive approach to communicating change. By doing so, they can increase the likelihood of success for their change initiatives and ensure that the narrative and communication process supports, rather than hinders, the change.

On Biases in Narrative and Communication

As with every other change area, it is useful to be aware of a few cognitive biases in the context of crafting narratives and communicating in organizational change management. This list is not exhaustive and remembering the names is not as important as understanding the patterns themselves:

- **The Framing Effect:** Framing can cause a tendency to react differently to information, depending on how it's presented. For example, in communicating change, leaders can present a new strategy in terms of potential benefits (gain frame) or avoiding pitfalls (loss frame). The frame used can significantly impact how the message is received and the attitudes toward the proposed change.
- **Information Bias:** This bias is the tendency for people to seek out more information before making decisions, even when it

doesn't add value to the decision. In change communication, this can lead to leaders delaying important communications because they feel they need more information first. This delay can create uncertainty and anxiety within the organization.

■ **The Curse of Knowledge:** This occurs when individuals, especially experts or leaders, assume others have the same level of knowledge or understanding. In the context of communicating change, this can lead to messages that are too complex or filled with jargon, making them difficult for employees to understand, which may result in confusion or misunderstanding about the change.

■ **The False Consensus Effect:** This is the tendency to overestimate how much others agree with us. In change communication, this can lead to leaders assuming that everyone is on board with the change, underestimating potential resistance or lack of alignment within the organization. This can hinder effective dialogue and engagement around the change initiative.

Engaging Storytelling with the Public Narrative

Reflecting back on the narratives presented at the start of the chapter, you might already have noticed the underlying structure that enabled them to resonate so powerfully with their audience. This shared structure, often referred to as a *public narrative*, is a method for communicating and catalyzing collective action that is rooted in personal story and shared values. (See Figure 6.1.) Developed as a framework for instilling social change by Harvard professor Marshall Ganz,[2] public narrative has found applicability far beyond social movements, and can serve as a transformative tool within your behaviorally informed change management toolkit.

Public narratives, as defined by Ganz, involve the weaving of three integral story strands: the narrative of self, us, and now. To understand how this works, consider how Arnold Schwarzenegger started his appeal to the Russian soldiers by sharing a personal story that resonated with the audience, revealing his deep admiration for the Russian people. This "story of self" connected him to his listeners on an emotional level, making his appeal more impactful. Similarly, Martin

Figure 6.1   Public narrative Venn diagram. Original idea by Marshall Ganz.

Luther King Jr. and Barack Obama, in their respective historic speeches, connected their personal journeys to the collective experience of their audiences. King, through shared dreams of emancipation, and Obama, by discussing common hopes and dreams of the American people, sketched out a "story of us," a tale of unity, shared values, and common grounds.

Finally, these leaders transitioned into the "story of now"—a rallying cry for immediate action. King, with his "Now is the time" refrain; Obama, with his urgent call for reform; and Schwarzenegger, with his plea for truth and peace, made an urgent case for action, compelling their listeners to act immediately in response to shared challenges.

This approach can be remarkably beneficial when applied to the context of organizational change as well. It provides a unique structure to communicate change initiatives, leveraging the power of storytelling to make abstract concepts like values and vision tangible and relatable through powerful framing. There are three main benefits of using public narrative in change communication:

- **Overcoming Resistance:** Change might trigger resistance in organizations. With public narrative, leaders can reduce this by fostering an emotional connection to the change, translating it into a story that resonates with the organizational values and goals, thereby inspiring employees and creating a sense of urgency for the proposed changes. Effectively mitigating resistance to change exceeds the scope of communication (covered in further depth in Chapter 8).
- **Building Trust and Shared Purpose:** Trust and shared purpose are crucial in any change initiative. Public narrative facilitates this by conveying personal and relatable story elements that articulate common experiences and motivations, fostering a sense of unity. This nurtures a sense of ownership and investment in the change initiative.
- **Clarifying Vision and Values:** A common challenge in communicating change is translating abstract ideas such as vision and values to concrete objectives that resonate with employees. Public narrative enables leaders to craft a compelling story that brings the change initiative's goals and potential merit to life. This helps employees understand and connect with their roles in the broader context of the proposed change.

Creating an impactful narrative is not an innate skill. It requires practice and refinement, making the public narrative technique hard to fully master, but some of its best practices are surprisingly easy to apply. For those willing to go above and beyond, there even exists a three-and-a-half-month course on public narrative at Harvard taught by Ganz himself.[3] Although we can't cover the full depth of this methodology in this book, you'll find a step-by-step guide to developing a public narrative for organizational change in the following behavioral break. As this intervention takes the shape of a framework, first focus on the building blocks of creating your narrative, and subsequently look into practicalities like who to involve and what to include.

Behavioral Break: Public Narrative Intervention

1. **Engage with your organization:** Before you begin crafting your narrative, it's crucial to engage with various stakeholders across the organization. This might include team members, managers, employees, and even customers. The goal of these engagements is to understand their perspectives and expectations regarding the proposed change. Gather as much information as possible about the context and nuances of the situation. This initial step serves as the foundation for your narrative, ensuring that it is grounded in the real experiences and needs of your organization.

2. **Identify your personal story (story of self):** Start by reflecting on your personal experiences, motivations, and values that align with the change. Make a list of these personal elements and how they relate to the proposed change. Remember, authenticity is key, so select a true story that communicates your commitment to the change.

3. **Understand and develop the collective story (story of us):** Interact with team members, stakeholders, and employees to understand their experiences, values, and aspirations. Recognize common themes and shared experiences. Use these insights to develop a collective narrative that communicates shared values and goals, fostering a sense of belonging and unity within the organization.

4. **Define the urgency of the change (story of now):** Present the current organizational challenges and the necessity of the proposed change. Develop a compelling narrative that underlines the urgency of these challenges and how the change initiative addresses them. Make sure the Story of Now ignites a sense of urgency and momentum toward the proposed change.

5. **Integrate the three stories:** Combine your Story of Self, Story of Us, and Story of Now into a unified and compelling public narrative. Although many narratives traditionally begin with the Story of Self, the structure can be adjusted to best fit your context. Depending on the situation, it might be more effective to start with the Story of Now, highlighting the urgency of change, or the Story of Us, emphasizing unity and shared values. Regardless of the starting point, make sure that your narrative clearly portrays your personal commitment, the collective identity, and the pressing need for the proposed change.

6. **Share and gather feedback:** Begin sharing your public narrative within your organization in appropriate settings. Encourage feedback and open discussion about the narrative. Listen to the stories and responses from others to understand how your narrative is being received.

7. **Refine your narrative:** Based on the feedback, refine and adjust your narrative as needed. Revisit each of the three stories and make sure they still resonate with the audience, align with the change, and evoke the necessary emotions and sense of urgency. Repeat this process as necessary, keeping the narrative alive and relevant throughout the change process (more on this in a moment).

By following these steps and using the public narrative method, you can create powerful stories that help inspire and mobilize employees and stakeholders toward a common goal. Whether you are leading a small change initiative within your team, or a large-scale organizational transformation, this technique can be an effective tool for engaging employees and building support for your change initiative. We also found this to be a highly energizing activity for most people, especially during off-site retreats when people have the time and mental capacity to zoom out and see the big picture. Make sure people have fun!

Although public narrative is a powerful tool and framework for communicating change, it's only as effective as the content it covers. That's why another common challenge is curating the information to use in your narrative and tailoring it to the different audiences you approach with it. The following section helps you collect information for your narrative, tailor it to different audiences, and gather useful feedback.

Collecting Information and Feedback on Your Narrative

A public narrative that truly resonates with stakeholders and communicates the rationale for change cannot be crafted solely within the confines of the boardroom or C-suite. It is important that the narrative is informed by diverse perspectives, stories, and data from throughout the organization. This requires managers to be open to feedback, actively seek out differing opinions, and consider multiple viewpoints when crafting the narrative.

> By engaging with employees, customers, and other stakeholders, leaders can gain valuable insights into how the change is perceived by and will impact various groups that can be used to identify potential roadblocks.

A collaborative approach not only results in a more robust and inclusive narrative, but also helps to build trust and buy-in from those who will be most affected by the change. Ultimately, a public narrative that is co-created with input from all stakeholders is more likely to be embraced and successfully implemented.

Julia Wittlin, change program manager at Microsoft Western Europe, a European branch of the American multinational technology company, provides valuable insight into how to implement this approach. She emphasizes the crucial role of the previously discussed WIIFM factor in change initiatives. According to Wittlin, in today's dynamic corporate environment, where changes are ongoing and often layered, a clearly articulated WIIFM for each stakeholder group helps prevent potential resistance and fatigue. "With so many different changes happening at the same time, it's important to create a change narrative that englobes most, if not all, of them. There is a need to create a story that makes sense to everyone and brings the vision and strategy together." The challenge is in how granular you want to go and how to prioritize this in a busy day-to-day agenda. Departments are a mix of various teams with different views and if not given careful attention, there is bound to be a WIIFM missing for specific teams (more on this in Chapter 8).

This approach doesn't merely involve broadcasting the WIIFM; it calls for an interactive engagement with different stakeholder groups to discover and clarify the unique WIIFMs pertinent to each group. By doing so, leaders can ensure that the benefits of the change are understood and resonate with the individuals in those groups. This not only strengthens the narrative's appeal but also builds trust and buy-in from the very people who are pivotal for the successful implementation of the change.

While involving different stakeholder perspectives in the narrative can bring valuable perspectives and insights, too many voices can lead to conflicting information, and an overabundance of opinions can hinder decision-making. It's important to strike a balance between including diverse viewpoints and maintaining a sense of focus and direction. One way to achieve this balance is by setting clear criteria and goals for the narrative and establishing a process for incorporating feedback and input from various stakeholders.

Jeroen van der Brugge, at the time of writing, organizational development director at Facilicom Group, has a lot of experience with crafting change narratives while leveraging the insights from a broad variety of stakeholders throughout the organization. Here are some of his practical guidelines in navigating this tradeoff in narrative and communication:

- Before you start writing a change narrative, make sure to *listen* to as many diverse stakeholders as possible. Instead of asking them what they think the narrative should include, ask them how they would feel about potential changes and how they expect to be impacted.
- Once you feel like you have gathered sufficient input, start crafting the narrative within your change or transition team. Avoid

having too many stakeholders in the initial writing process. The faster you can draft a working version, the sooner you can start honing it with stakeholder feedback.

- Asking for broad feedback throughout the organization is key, but the trick lies in *how* you ask for it. At this stage, avoid asking questions like "What should be changed about this narrative?" "What would you like to add?" or "What is missing?" because they will slow down the process and result in endless iterations over details. Instead, ask questions such as "What does this narrative do to you?" and "How does this narrative make you feel?" Questions like these help stakeholders detach from the superficial and tap into what they really value and need in the upcoming change.

Tailoring and Communicating Your Narrative with the 30-3-30-3

Communicating change is always a demanding task given its sensitivity and potential impact on all stakeholders involved. The dynamic nature of town hall meetings, workshops, ask-me-anything sessions, or show and tells each require a specific communication approach to ensure your message is properly absorbed. Falling into the extremes of over- or under-communication can hamper the effectiveness of the process. Over-communication (for example, a daily email loaded with operational details) can overwhelm your audience and often quickly leads to disengagement. Under-communication, either in the case of low frequency or content with limited information or relevance, can leave employees feeling neglected, confused, and unsure of their role in the change process or even the organization. Striking a balance between these extremes is hard but important. One tool in the BeSci realm has proved very useful for the change managers we've worked with: the 30-3-30-3 intervention.

The 30-3-30-3 offers an intuitive guideline to craft the change narrative in four distinct versions, each aimed at catering to diverse needs and attention spans of your audience: a 30-minute, a 3-minute, a 30-second, and a 3-second version. This last addition, which is often left out, is designed to serve as an easy-to-recall motto or mantra that encapsulates the essence of the change.

We often get questions regarding which order to craft these versions in. The truth is that it doesn't matter too much. Some find it easier to start with the core idea (3s) and build a story around it (30m), while others want to see the big-picture (30m) before distilling the essence (3s). When we facilitate 30-3-30-3 sessions, we usually work in the order used in the following behavioral break.

Behavioral Break: The 30-3-30-3 Intervention

The **30-minute version** is comprehensive and detailed, perfect for town hall meetings where an in-depth discourse on the change, its context, reasoning, and expected results is feasible and necessary. It's an opportunity for change leaders to clarify details and address queries, providing transparency about the change process.

The **3-minute version** is a condensed summary of the change narrative, ideal for presentations to the executive leadership or external stakeholders. This version emphasizes the key messages, the strategic importance, and the anticipated organizational impacts of the change, without delving into granular details. This 3-minute version can also be used as a short update for other teams at the start or end of their meetings without overwhelming the audience.

The **30-second version** is akin to an elevator pitch, best suited for quick informal discussions or brief encounters with colleagues. It provides a swift overview of the change's purpose and its broader implications, expressed in clear and simple language, free from technical jargon.

The final, and perhaps most impactful, is the **3-second version**. This distilled motto or mantra, encapsulating the essence of the change initiative, serves as an anchor for your narrative, giving your change a recognizable name and form that sticks. This ultra-short narrative might seem trivial, but it can significantly enhance the memorability and internalization of the change message, making it more accessible and personal.

One of the most common pitfalls in implementing the 30-3-30-3 rule is cramming too much information into each format. Given how much there often is to communicate, it can be tempting to make a 3-minute version that has about half the content of the 30-minute format and requires an auctioneer's speaking speed to keep up. Resist this temptation! As discussed, our brain has limited memory and to find meaning in words, we need time to ponder. It's no coincidence that the leaders we discussed in the introduction of this chapter speak slowly. Albeit a very different context, in the Navy Seals they have a saying for this that we found useful to internalize: "Slow is smooth and smooth is fast." Regardless of whether we're talking about a tactical mission or crafting and delivering a change narrative, rushing often leads to its own set of challenges.

We spent considerable time chasing the source of this intervention but could not find it. The closest we got was a mention that someone learned it through the lean methodology. Forgive us for not including a source this time; however, we've seen the value in action plenty of times to share it publicly. By leveraging the 30-3-30-3 rule in conjunction with the public narrative framework, change managers can construct a multifaceted yet consistent change narrative. The public narrative approach helps create a motivating and authentic story that spurs action, while the 30-3-30-3 rule provides a strategy to tailor that story to specific audiences and communication channels. This integrated approach can help ensure that the narrative of change is not just heard but understood, remembered, and acted upon.

Strategic Focus in Change Communication

Next to the crafting of a compelling public narrative and tailoring it with the 30-3-30-3 rule, another important step for change managers is to pinpoint the best application of their communication efforts for maximum influence. It's important to note that the response to change varies across stakeholder groups. Including those with the highest potential for engagement at the start of a change initiative can go a long way. One insightful strategy is proposed by Kiki van den Berg, global director of HR (CHRO) at Rabobank, a Dutch multinational banking and financial services company. She counsels change managers to primarily target the "people in the middle." This group, which typically represents around 60% of the stakeholders, neither resists the change nor advocates for it passionately. By channeling your efforts toward engaging this group, you can generate momentum that can gradually tilt the balance toward the understanding, acceptance, and eventual embrace of the proposed change.

While focusing on these groups can facilitate the change process, make sure to avoid creating an echo chamber of consensus. As a change manager, surrounding yourself solely with "yay-sayers" can stifle critical thinking and blindside you to potential pitfalls. Actively seeking criticism and dissent from a broad range of stakeholders can provide invaluable insights, even though it might be challenging. Ideally, include not only early adopters but also those in the late majority and laggards part of the distribution. These last two groups might be the most important in terms of identifying risks and issues. We discuss concrete interventions for engaging diverse perspectives and managing dissent in Chapter 8, but first let's explore another evidence-based intervention.

MINDSPACE: An Evidence-Based Tool for Communicating Change

You might have noted that most of the interventions discussed in this chapter are primarily focused on structure, rather than content. This is because when it comes to narrative and communication in change initiatives, there is no one-size-fits-all solution for the content of the message. Every change effort is unique, with its own set of challenges, stakeholders, and objectives. As such, it is much more useful to have a framework (like public narrative) and structures (such as the 30-3-30-3 rule) to guide the development of communicating organizational change, rather than a rigid set of content guidelines.

However, constructing a strong narrative is challenging, and adjusting and tailoring it to different stakeholder groups adds another layer of complexity. This is where another evidence-based intervention might prove to be valuable. A tool that helps shape both the content and the delivery of the message with behavioral science principles can boost the persuasiveness and effectiveness of change communication. The MINDSPACE framework we discussed in Chapter 2, developed by the Behavioural Insights Team (BIT)[4] can help you here.

MINDSPACE represents nine of the most robust influences on our behavior, as described by behavioral science: messenger, incentives, norms, defaults, salience, priming, affect, commitment, and ego. Each of these components provides a lens through which we can assess and refine our communication strategy. Each component in this framework is backed by a wealth of research—enough to fill an entire book of its own. However, it's not necessary to go through the full depth of this research to effectively apply the MINDSPACE framework to communication. In fact, the beauty of this framework is that it has been designed to be readily applied by practitioners, especially those without a research background. To keep it simple, here is a brief description of each component in the context of change management:

- **Messenger:** This aspect highlights the importance of the communicator's credibility and trustworthiness in change management.
- **Incentives:** Here, the focus is on how the benefits of change are communicated, and how these motivate employees to adapt to new practices or behaviors.
- **Norms:** This refers to the power of collective behavior in influencing individual actions.
- **Defaults:** This component emphasizes the importance of making new behaviors the "new normal," and making it easier for people to adopt them.
- **Salience:** This emphasizes making the change message stand out and be remembered by linking it to the roles or tasks of individual stakeholders.
- **Priming:** This relates to using subtle cues in communication that encourage desirable behavior and promote action.
- **Affect:** This component focuses on the emotional responses that the change process can evoke.
- **Commitment:** This involves fostering a sense of responsibility and reciprocity among stakeholders.

- **Ego:** This considers framing the change in a way that aligns with employees' personal or professional identities to increase motivation and participation.

Much like policymaking (for which the framework was originally developed), the communication of organizational change aims to (re-) shape behavior. Instead of compelling action through strict regulations or incentives alone, successful change communication often requires a subtler, more behaviorally informed method that can bring about significant changes in behavior at low cost and high effectiveness. Keeping with this, MINDSPACE provides a robust framework to guide the development of change communication strategies and captivating narratives.

Translating this into the context of change communication, the MINDSPACE framework can be used to ensure that your communication strategy is as effective as possible. It will help you make sure you don't miss anything important in your narrative. In the following behavioral break, you find an overview of each component of MINDSPACE, with prompts to enhance your communication.

Behavioral Break: MINDSPACE Framework Intervention

Component	Question	Action Prompt
Messenger	Is your message being delivered by a trusted and influential source in the organization?	Identify credible individuals (e.g., change champions) who can act as the messengers of change. Organizational network analysis (discussed in Chapter 8) can help you here.

Component	Question	Action Prompt
Incentives	Does your communication clearly highlight the personal and professional gains from the change? Are potential losses acknowledged and addressed?	Craft your message to highlight the "what's in it for them," and ensure employees that potential drawbacks are addressed up front.
Norms	Are you leveraging social norms and pointing out how others are successfully engaging with the change?	Use examples of successful engagements with the change in your communications and role-model the desired behavior. (Chapter 7 goes deeper into tools to facilitate role-modeling.)
Defaults	Have you made the new behaviors as easy as possible to adopt, setting them as the "new normal"?	Make it easy for people to engage in new behaviors by removing hurdles and making them the standard procedure.
Salience	Is your message capturing attention, using novel, relevant, and concrete information?	Avoid jargon. Use normal language and real-life examples to make your message memorable. Find a way to help your audience visualize the change's outcomes.
Priming	Are there subtle cues that can make people more receptive to the change message?	Incorporate positive, action-oriented language or information that aligns with people's existing beliefs and values.

(continued)

(continued)

Component	Question	Action Prompt
Affect	Are you considering the emotional impact of your message and aiming to evoke positive emotions toward the change?	Frame your message to spark positive emotions and directly acknowledge and address potential negative emotions.
Commitment	Are you providing opportunities for public commitments to the change?	Create opportunities for leaders to make public commitment and lead by example. In written communication, make it easy and appealing for employees to sign up for training sessions/workshops that are part of the change initiatives.
Ego	Does your message allow individuals to feel good about themselves when they engage in the desired change behaviors?	Align your message with individuals' personal values and goals, and highlight their role in the success of the organization. Strive to frame any changes, even those that might have negative impacts, in a way that respects individuals' dignity and doesn't come across as a personal attack, helping them save face where possible.

As you develop your change communication strategy, you can continuously refer back to this framework. Involve your communication team, managers, and change leaders in this process, making sure everyone is aware of and understands the MINDSPACE components. Establish a routine check-in, perhaps at the end of every week, to review your communication materials with this tool and make any necessary adjustments.

Conclusion

This chapter emphasized the role of crafting a compelling change narrative and communicating it effectively. It discussed the obstacles often faced in this context, including cognitive biases like the framing effect and the curse of knowledge, and the challenge of one-size-fits-all communication strategies.

In summary, while each change initiative is unique, the need for a captivating narrative and effective communication is universal. The tools and insights provided in this chapter can help you build powerful narratives and design effective communication strategies that are sensitive to your organizational context and resonate with all stakeholders.

As we move on to the next chapter, which focuses on leadership support, remember that these interventions are not stand-alone solutions but tools to enrich existing practices. By sharing them with organizational leaders, project managers, and internal communications teams, you can tailor them to your organization and make them your own through experimentation.

7

Leadership Support

THERE'S AN AGE-OLD riddle that goes something like this: "If a change initiative launches in an organization but no leader is there to drive it, does it make an impact?" Alright, we might have stolen that from our colleagues in philosophy, but it does highlight a painful truth that's all too familiar for change managers. Even when you do everything right, change initiatives can still seem to fail due to a thousand reasons, it seems. This makes it near impossible to identify what exactly went wrong. However, during the 40 interviews we conducted for this book, there was one element that never remained unspoken: the role of leadership in driving change.

Imagine you are leading a project to implement a new customer relationship management (CRM) system in a large organization. You have done all the necessary research, engaged stakeholders at every level, carefully crafted a plan to ensure a smooth rollout, and have been working tirelessly to execute it. However, despite your best efforts, the initiative fails to gain traction because one or more senior leaders do not provide the support this project needs. This is usually reflected in other change areas such as stakeholder engagement, planning and risk, or narrative and communication. It could be that they do not fully understand the benefits of the new system, or they feel like they're *too busy* to role-model the change themselves and try to delegate it. Without their support and involvement, your carefully laid plans fall apart, and the change effort grinds to a halt.

Leadership Support Interventions

Every leader is a change leader refers to the fact that all (and especially) senior leaders have an important responsibility to proactively support change initiatives. But it's also the role of change managers to gain the support of senior leadership and keep them engaged throughout the change effort. This chapter explores both sides of the coin. Change managers learn insights and practical, evidence-based interventions that help ensure leaders buy into the changes, stay engaged, and provide sufficient sponsorship and guidance. For change leaders, there are insights and interventions that help you take a proactive, important role in driving the change by communicating, role-modeling, engaging stakeholders, and supporting the change management team.

Through real-world examples and practical advice, this chapter dives into the importance of leadership support and how to secure it. We cover common pitfalls like a lack of understanding of the change initiative and problems with resource allocation. The chapter also provides three evidence-based interventions:

- **If-Then Planning:** This technique simplifies the process of remembering and executing new habits, especially in stressful times. Particularly helpful for leaders aspiring to be role models, If-then planning connects specific situations with desired actions.
- **Re-Anchoring:** This technique helps leaders consciously assess and adjust their initial assumptions. It aids in resource allocation based on the specific needs of the current change initiative, rather than being influenced by past experiences or historical data.
- **Gradual Escalation of Commitment:** This intervention encourages a venture capitalist-like approach to risk and support calibration during bottom-up change initiatives. By making incremental commitments, leaders avoid large gambles and allow for an innovative and lean approach to proving the efficacy of the initiative.

After this chapter, you will have a better understanding of how to secure leadership support to create a more successful change effort. You will be able to identify and avoid the pitfalls that can lead to failure and implement practical strategies to gain the support of senior leadership.

Current Approaches to Leadership Support

Most seasoned change managers are well aware that the success of any organizational change initiative depends heavily on leadership support. However, in many organizations, this support is often viewed as a small formality crammed into the calendar of their busy leaders, with little consideration given to how they genuinely contribute to the change effort. As a result, change managers face a variety of challenges when it comes to securing adequate leadership support, especially during long-term change initiatives.

A common problem in securing and maintaining leadership support is a general lack of understanding regarding the change and its purpose in senior leadership. This can happen when change managers fail to clearly communicate the need for the change, the goals, and how it will benefit the organization and their department or team.

> When senior leaders (as with other stakeholders) don't understand the purpose of the change, they're less likely to get behind it, leading to a lack of sponsorship, engagement, and role-modeling.

One of the most common barriers to securing leadership support is the lack of communication between change managers and the leadership team. Change managers may focus too much on the day-to-day tasks of the change effort, leaving little time for regular communication with senior leaders. As a result, leaders may not have a clear understanding of how the change effort is progressing, what the challenges are, and how they can help. Difficult sponsors—we've all encountered them at some point—can pose an even bigger problem. Change managers may have to deal with sponsors who are not fully committed to the change, have competing priorities, or, in rare cases, are (sub)consciously sabotaging a change initiative.

Lack of role-modeling is another common problem, especially when it comes down to *maintaining* leadership support and *reinforcing* the change. People look to their leaders for subtle cues on what behavior is and is not appropriate. And most of us tend to focus more on what you do than what you say. If senior leaders fail to model the behaviors they expect from their teams, the change effort is likely to fail because they are actually signaling it is not a top priority. Leaders must be willing to take the first steps in implementing the change and demonstrate its importance through their actions, not just their words. This can mean attending key meetings, actively participating, and being involved in communications. But it also shows why it's so important that when a company is, let's say, implementing a new performance management system, senior leaders are the first to embrace it and use it to evaluate their own performance. Without this kind of role-modeling, employees are likely to resist the change, leading to a lack of engagement.

This problem was discussed with Roger van Lier, the P&O director a.i. at the Municipality of Amsterdam as well, who emphasized the role of leadership in driving change. He observed that several reorganizations might have been avoided if management could have put more effort in organically instigating change through role-modeling and inspiring colleagues. He pointed out that the absence of such proactive leadership often results in reactive changes.

Martin Sitalsing, the head of Police Central Netherlands, covered this issue from his experience in the public sector. Sitalsing asserts that for large changes, especially within a traditionally conservative organization such as the police, action-driven cultures often pose a large barrier. In a "24/7" profession with high turnover, you can't easily take personnel out of the front line to sit down and reflect because it's not a priority over their service to the public.

Furthermore, Sitalsing stresses the importance of credible leadership. He subscribes to the "skin in the game" philosophy, which calls for leaders to exemplify the change they want to bring about in their teams and build credibility by personally having a stake in the risk of the change succeeding. This makes role-modeling integral to the change management process. By this, he underlines the necessity for leaders to act as catalysts for change, rather than just endorsing it.

In essence, Sitalsing makes the point that credible leadership demands active role-modeling of engagement, consistency between words and actions, and personal accountability in driving change.

In line with these views, Marjon Kaper, director of People & Community at ANWB, a Dutch travelers association, also put her emphasis on empowering leaders in change initiatives. She advised, "Empower them, give them autonomy, and hold them accountable. Leaders should focus on solving issues. This involves about 50% explaining where we go and 50% on how to get there." The objective here is to empower leaders to effectively support the change—helping them solve issues and clearly communicating the role of bottom-up change initiatives in driving the desired change.

On Biases in Leadership Support

As we discuss the process of securing and fostering leadership support, it's important to be mindful that cognitive biases and heuristics can often pose significant barriers by influencing how leaders perceive and react to change initiatives. While a broad range of biases and other factors can affect leadership support, let's discuss some of the most common and relevant ones:

- **Status Quo Bias:** We tend to prefer the familiarity and comfort of the existing situation over any change. It's similar to an "If it ain't broke, don't fix it" mindset. For example, a chief marketing officer might be reluctant to move toward a data-driven marketing approach because the traditional methods they have used so far seem to work just fine.
- **Availability Heuristic:** Technically a heuristic, or mental shortcut, rather than a cognitive bias, this tendency involves basing decisions on information that is readily available or easily recalled. In a change management context, leaders might disproportionately remember unsuccessful change initiatives, leading to pessimism toward new proposals. For instance, if a previous attempt at organizational restructuring led to employee unrest and resistance, leaders might be overly cautious about supporting a new restructuring initiative.

- **Sunk Cost Fallacy:** This is the tendency to continue investing in a decision, primarily because of the resources already committed, regardless of potential future returns. For example, a leader may continue to invest in a failing project because they've already committed significant resources, not because they believe the project will succeed. While often referred to as a cognitive bias, the sunk cost fallacy is technically a logical fallacy. The difference is subtle but important.

> **Cognitive biases** are unconscious, systematic thinking patterns that can cause predictable errors in our decision-making and judgments. On the other hand, **logical fallacies,** like the sunk cost fallacy, are errors in reasoning, often arising from incorrect logical arguments. Both can significantly influence decision-making processes, albeit in slightly different ways. In this book, we collectively refer to these psychological principles as biases.

While this list is not exhaustive, it covers common cognitive biases and heuristics that can influence leadership behavior in organizational change that are worth keeping in mind. The evidence-based interventions explored in this chapter are designed to mitigate these potential barriers. They aim to encourage desired behaviors and help shape the ideal environment for robust leadership support.

Real-World Challenges in Leadership Support

Leadership is an area with loads of variety across different sectors and industries. This became apparent during our interviews, where we discussed the challenges of leadership support in organizational change.

Kiki van den Berg, global director of human resources at Rabobank, provides valuable advice on the importance of appointing the right leaders to the right changes in larger organizations. She emphasizes that each change initiative has a unique profile that should be matched to the style and profile of the leader or sponsor assigned to it. By doing so, HR and the board can set up a change effort for success or failure. Selecting the right leader is key for maintaining productive leadership support because it ensures that the person overseeing the initiative possesses the necessary skills, expertise, and commitment to drive the change effectively. A well-matched leader can inspire and motivate their team, navigate challenges, and make informed decisions.

To exemplify this, think about an organization undertaking a cultural shift toward sustainability. This change profile would need a leader passionate about sustainability; able to integrate it into business operations, strategy, and brand identity; and foster an inclusive culture. HR and the board would map the requirements of the change initiative and match them with potential leaders' profiles. For instance, a suitable leader could be one who has led sustainability projects, is trained in sustainable business practices, and recognized for their commitment to corporate responsibility.

Van den Berg also highlights the need for formal systems that allow employees to provide feedback to sponsors or leaders. Especially in hierarchical organizations, providing honest feedback to senior leaders can be challenging. HR can play a lead role by ensuring that such feedback loops are embedded into performance management systems used to evaluate high-level leaders and sponsors. This open line of communication can help leaders make better-informed decisions and address any issues that may arise during the change process. Furthermore, it fosters a culture of transparency and trust, where employees feel heard and valued.

Kati Terza, global transformation and change manager at Royal HaskoningDHV, shares her experiences in addressing the challenges that busy leaders face in effectively sponsoring and leading changes and their people through change. She points out that leaders may not always have the ability (e.g., time, skills) to properly fulfil their sponsor roles, which can negatively impact leadership support in a given change. To address this issue, Royal HaskoningDHV provides sponsorship sessions to senior leaders, creating awareness of their role and equipping them with the formal and soft skills needed to lead and sponsor change effectively. Sponsorship sessions could entail clarifying leaders' unique roles and responsibilities, developing strong communication and stakeholder engagement abilities, and teaching them how to address resistance and monitor progress. Through workshops, group discussions, and hands-on exercises, leaders learn about change management principles and leading by example.

Jeroen van der Brugge, who was organizational development director at Facilicom Group at the time of writing, brings attention to the fact that making a rational business case for change is sometimes not enough to secure sustainable sponsorship. Change managers must also engage leaders emotionally. In cases where C-suite leaders are not engaged enough with a change that could be critical for the company's future, van der Brugge suggests framing the conversation to make leaders think about the footprint they want to leave at the company or how they want to be remembered as a senior leader. These tactics tap into a leader's sense of purpose and courage, and can be a powerful motivator for engagement and sponsorship. However, van der Brugge cautions that these kinds of tactics should be used wisely and with care, as they can be tricky to navigate, depending on the personality of the leader/sponsor and your relationship with them.

Now that we have gained some insight into real-world leadership support challenges and how they are tackled by industry leaders, let's see how these strategies can be further enhanced by applying evidence-based interventions.

Facilitate Role-Modeling (or Anything Else) with If-Then Plans

While crafting persuasive change narratives and using transparent communication (as discussed in the previous chapter) are key responsibilities for leaders, it's equally vital to embody the desired attitudes, values, and behaviors they want their teams to adopt. This is where a popular yet often misunderstood technique takes center stage: role-modeling.

At first glance, role-modeling appears straightforward. However, putting it into practice and executing it effectively is more challenging than it seems. In the context of organizational change, role-modeling refers to the practice of leaders exemplifying the desired attitudes, values, and behaviors associated with the change initiative, thereby setting a positive example for employees to follow. By doing this successfully and consistently, leaders can inspire and motivate their teams to adopt new ways of thinking and working.

While leaders often recognize the significance of role-modeling, actually transforming their behaviors to set an inspiring example for their teams can be an uphill battle. This struggle stems from the fact that the behaviors essential for role-modeling are often deeply ingrained habits, which are notoriously difficult to change, especially when faced with stress, uncertainty, and time pressure.

To support leaders in overcoming these challenges and becoming effective role models, change managers can leverage evidence-based interventions, such as "if-then planning." Conceived by psychologist Peter Gollwitzer,[1] this technique is rooted in habit science and empowers individuals to create specific plans for modifying their behavior by connecting a particular situation (the "if") with a desired action (the "then"). This approach can be particularly advantageous for leaders striving to role-model change, as it simplifies the process of remembering and executing new behaviors, even under stress.

If-then planning, also known as implementation intentions, is a behavior change technique rooted in behavioral science and neuroscience. The underlying mechanisms that make if-then plans effective in changing habits are as follows:

- **Enhanced Cognitive Accessibility:** If-then plans help individuals more easily recognize the situational cues related to their desired behavior. By explicitly linking a specific situation with a desired action, if-then plans make it more likely for individuals to notice and act on these cues when they arise.
- **Automaticity:** The creation of if-then plans forges strong mental associations between a situation and the desired behavior. In neuroscience terms, this association happens in the basal ganglia, an area of the brain vital for habit formation. With time, the planned behavior becomes automatic when the situation occurs, reducing the need for conscious thought and utilizing less of the prefrontal cortex (planning and risk), which is responsible for higher cognitive processes and uses a lot of energy.
- **Goal-Directed Behavior:** If-then plans help to keep individuals focused on their goals by providing clear and specific instructions on how to achieve them. This clarity reduces the cognitive load associated with decision-making and problem-solving,

allowing individuals to devote more mental resources to enacting the desired behavior.

■ **Habit Disruption and Replacement:** If-then plans disrupt old habits and foster new ones by associating a novel, alternative behavior with a specific cue. Regularly practicing this new behavior in the context of the cue weakens the neural pathways of the old habit, while strengthening the new one and eventually substituting the old habit with the desired behavior.

The benefits of if-then planning are manifold. It helps leaders pinpoint critical situations where role-modeling is essential, devise concrete plans for implementing the desired behaviors, and ultimately facilitate the adoption of these new behaviors throughout the organization.

Implementing if-then plans sounds straightforward, but following through can be surprisingly hard. Let's break it down into a step-by-step intervention plan in the following behavioral break.

Behavioral Break: If-Then Plans Intervention

1. **Pinpoint desired behaviors and situations:** Engage with change leaders to highlight the specific behaviors essential for successful organizational change. Weigh the business goals and potential impact of these behaviors on the transformation process. Additionally, identify situations where these behaviors are most effective.

2. **Establish triggers (if):** Working closely with change leaders, outline the triggers or cues that will initiate the desired behaviors. Detail the situations that call for the new behaviors to be executed. Be as specific as possible here. Collaboration implies a shared effort, with change managers providing guidance and leaders bringing their personal insights and expertise.

3. **Develop the if-then plans:** Assist change leaders in generating their if-then plans, connecting the triggers

from Step 2 with the desired behaviors. Every plan should open with the trigger (if) and depict the specific behavior to be performed (then). Propose that change leaders keep their plans straightforward and feasible.

4. **Rehearse and internalize the if-then plans:** Support change leaders in rehearsing their if-then plans, facilitating the absorption of the new behaviors. This could involve role-playing exercises, or practicing in real-life scenarios. Repeated practice helps solidify the mental links between triggers and desired behaviors, making new behaviors instinctive over time.

5. **Track progress and adapt if necessary:** Regularly check in with change leaders to gauge their progress in enacting their if-then plans. Discuss any hurdles they encounter and explore potential if-then plan adjustments if necessary.

6. **Promote sharing the if-then plans:** Encourage change leaders to disclose their if-then plans with their teams and inspire team members to develop their own if-then plans. This could facilitate widespread adoption of new behaviors throughout the organization.

7. **Implementation guidelines:** For effective execution, change managers, potentially with the support of a behavioral science expert either within the organization or an external consultant, should facilitate a dedicated session to assist leaders in creating their if-then plans. This session could span one or two hours, depending on the scope and complexity of the behaviors to be developed. Follow-up sessions should be scheduled every two to four weeks, providing an opportunity to monitor progress, discuss challenges, and make necessary adjustments to the plans. This collaborative process enables leaders to take an active role in their behavioral changes, under the guidance and support of the change managers and behavioral science professionals.

If-Then Plans in the Wild

Here's how if-then plans can be put into practice with a real-world case. Imagine an organizational change aimed at enhancing employee engagement in a large tech company. Recognizing the significance of active listening as a critical leadership behavior, the change manager, with the assistance of a behavioral science expert, collaborates with a department head in a dedicated session. The objective of this session, which lasts approximately one and a half hours, is to identify and outline if-then plans to address key situations where active listening can enhance engagement, such as during team meetings, one-on-one conversations, and performance reviews.

In this session, they pinpoint specific triggers or cues for the department head to actively listen. For example, when a team member starts sharing their perspective during a meeting, that's a cue for the department head to engage in active listening. Accordingly, they create an if-then plan stating, "If a team member shares their perspective during a meeting, then I will make eye contact, nod in agreement, and paraphrase their points to demonstrate understanding."

To reinforce this new behavior, the change manager and the behavioral expert facilitate practical exercises for the department head, including role-plays and application of the plan in real-life cases. As the department head repeatedly practices this plan, the link between the trigger and the desired behavior of active listening strengthens, gradually becoming more automatic.

Following the initial session, the change manager schedules regular follow-ups every three weeks with the department head to track progress, address challenges, and make necessary adjustments to the plan for improved outcomes. The department head is also encouraged to share their if-then plan with the team and motivate team members to craft their own if-then plans for active listening. This step promotes a culture of continuous improvement and aids in the adoption of active listening behavior across the organization, initiating with the leader as the role model.

Guiding change leaders through the process of creating and implementing if-then plans can help change managers effectively support them in role-modeling new behaviors during organizational change. This can have a ripple effect throughout the organization, promoting the successful adoption of change at all levels. After all, if an organization's leadership isn't changing their behavior, then why on earth would their employees?

Interventions for Senior Leaders

So far, we have focused on how change managers can ensure that organizational leaders remain engaged during important changes. We have explored how change managers can support leaders in providing effective sponsorship, guidance, and role-modeling throughout the change process. Now it's time to switch perspectives. As a senior leader, you play a critical role in facilitating, sponsoring, and leading change within your organization. What's key to remember here is that leadership starts (and sometimes ends) with your behavior. Your actions and decisions have a significant impact on the success of any change initiative.

Interviews with organizational leaders we conducted allowed us to see the breadth and depth of change leadership. Inca van Uuden, HR director at Essent, highlights that change management necessitates a unique blend of transactional and transformational leadership, emphasizing vitality, resilience, and a balance of courage and care in leadership. Michiel van Meer, chief people officer at Aon Nederland & ASC EMEA, built on this by explaining how leadership should develop mental resilience akin to a professional athlete. This resilience equips leaders to navigate constraints in resources, budget, and time to uncover the optimal route forward.

Critical to this mental resilience is the ability to acknowledge errors in your thinking (which, believe it or not, becomes even harder at the leadership level), and having the tools at your disposal to make more objective decisions. Such unbiased decision-making is pivotal to the success rate of a change initiative, particularly in resource allocation.

Re-Anchoring for Fact-Based Allocation of Resources

One critical success (or failure) factor underpinning successful change is the correct allocation of resources at the leadership level. Distributing adequate resources to the right sections of an organization ensures that change initiatives receive the necessary support and investment, setting them up for success. However, especially in the case of budgeting, leaders almost always fall victim to a particular cognitive bias, anchoring. This can become problematic when you're facing large-scale unprecedented changes that require significant resources.

Imagine a company called GreenTech that specializes in renewable energy solutions. They have recently developed a cutting-edge solar panel technology that could revolutionize the industry. The leadership team decides to undergo a major organizational change to shift focus from their existing product lines to this new technology.

During the planning process, the leadership team must allocate resources for the upcoming change initiative across business units involved in the change. Leaders have historically allocated a specific budget for change projects each year, which has been sufficient for their previous, possibly less ambitious endeavors. As they discuss the budget for this new initiative, the team members unknowingly find themselves anchored to their past budgets, believing that a similar division of budget across their business units will be sufficient for each team to play their part in this transformative change.

However, as the project unfolds, it becomes evident that the new solar panel technology requires a much larger investment in research and development, manufacturing, and marketing. Because the leadership team is anchored to their past budget allocations, they fail to recognize the increased resource needs for these particular business units in this change initiative. As a result, the project remains underfunded, struggles to gain traction, causes friction between units, and ultimately fails to achieve its full potential.

This example highlights the danger of **anchoring bias** in resource allocation across business units during organizational change. In the case of GreenTech, the leadership team was unconsciously anchored to how resources were allocated to similar previous change initiatives, for example, an expansion of their existing product portfolio. This intuitive anchoring led the leadership team to assume that the current change initiative would require a similar allocation of resources. However, if they had objectively assessed the situation and carefully considered the unique requirements of the new solar panel technology, they would have realized that this change initiative demanded a completely different allocation of resources. Since anchoring, like all unconscious biases, influences our thinking without our awareness, this is easier said than done.

One evidence-based way to address the challenge of anchoring bias in resource allocation is a technique called "re-anchoring." This method, described by Dan Lovallo and Olivier Sibony,[2] helps leaders consciously assess and adjust their initial assumptions. By doing so, they can allocate resources based on the specific needs of the current change initiative rather than being influenced by past experiences or historical data. The following behavioral break explains how it works.

Behavioral Break: Re-Anchoring Intervention (for Resource Allocation)

1. **Become aware of anchoring bias:** Before making resource allocation decisions, leaders should recognize the potential influence of anchoring bias on their judgment. This awareness allows them to question their initial assumptions and seek diverse perspectives. Simply bringing anchoring bias and its potential harm under the attention of the leadership team can be a start.

2. **Gather relevant information:** Collect comprehensive information on the specific requirements of the current change initiative, including research and development, manufacturing, marketing, and any other aspects that may need resources. This information helps leaders make informed and objective decisions. Let your business analysts shine here, if you can!

3. **Create a second anchor:** Develop a second anchor, solely based on the relevant information gathered, that represents a more accurate resource allocation for the current change initiative. This second anchor should be completely independent of their historical data or past experiences. Leaders can decide to undertake this step

(*continued*)

(*continued*)

themselves, but it might be even better to leave this to your business analysts. They are less likely to be anchored, since they did not make last year's budgeting decisions.

4. **Compare and evaluate both anchors:** Compare your initial anchor (based on historical data or past experiences) with the newly created second anchor (based on current change initiative requirements). Analyzing the differences between the two anchors helps leaders realize how much their initial estimate was off.

5. **Foster open discussions:** Include a segment in your regular leadership meetings dedicated to reviewing and discussing resource allocation decisions. In this segment, leaders can share their assumptions, offer different perspectives, and collectively reevaluate initial decisions based on the second, data-driven anchor. This approach not only helps reduce the anchoring bias but also promotes objective decision-making.

6. **Adjust resource allocation decisions:** Based on the comparison of both anchors, as well as the open discussions, leaders should revise their initial resource allocation plans to better match the specific needs of the current change initiative.

Re-Anchoring in the GreenTech Scenario

Let's apply this behavioral break by imagining you are one of the leaders sponsoring the change at GreenTech.

Your first move is to raise the awareness of anchoring bias among the leadership team. In a meeting, you open a dialogue about the potential pitfalls of anchoring bias and how it can skew resource allocation decisions. This discussion encourages the team to question their initial assumptions, setting the stage for a more objective evaluation of the unique resource requirements of the new solar panel technology project.

Following this step, you assign your business analysts to gather comprehensive data on the specific resource needs for the new project. This task covers a detailed investigation of areas like research and development, manufacturing, and marketing. By involving business analysts, you leverage their objectivity to set a fresh anchor. In case business analysts are not available, leaders can undertake this task, while striving for as much objectivity as possible.

After the data is gathered, you work with the team to generate a new, data-driven anchor, which is rooted in the specific needs of the current change initiative. This second anchor incorporates the unique resource demands of the project, creating a more accurate picture of the allocation needs.

Now you encourage the team to compare the initial anchor, which was influenced by past experiences, with the newly formed data-driven anchor. This comparison and evaluation stage is key to revealing any disparities and helping the team realize the extent of anchoring bias in their initial estimates. You include a segment in existing leadership meetings dedicated to reviewing and discussing resource allocation decisions where the leadership team can share their assumptions, and challenge their initial resource allocation decisions in light of the second, fact-based anchor. This environment of open dialogue fosters objective decision-making.

Finally, informed by the second anchor, open discussions, and comparison insights, the leadership team revises the initial resource allocation plan to better align with the specific needs of the new solar panel technology project. As a result of your efforts, your team is now better equipped to make informed resource allocation decisions, avoiding the underfunding of critical aspects of the change.

Notably, the re-anchoring technique can not only be applied to allocate financial resources effectively but also to manage and allocate another key currency: time. It can assist leaders in obtaining a more objective view of time as a resource, and help allocate and safeguard it more effectively. As the senior organizational change manager we interviewed at a global healthcare company points out, time itself is a critical resource, requiring conscientious allocation to drive effective organizational change. Leaders must proactively increase capacity for change, safeguarding time for their teams to process, reflect, and manage the mental load associated with change. She underscores this, highlighting capacity management as a primary objective in her work with change, where time is considered the "ultimate currency." She points out that leaders often grapple with the balance of workload and mental load versus the needed time to process and reflect on changes. "I don't have the time" might not be just a simple statement, but could represent a form of bias where leaders fail to safeguard their own time and space, and that of their employees, to drive change.

The re-anchoring technique is a good example of an evidence-based change intervention that utilizes bias (creating a second anchor based on facts) to counteract bias (the initial anchor influenced by past resource allocation). You might have recognized the similarity between re-anchoring and reference-class forecasting (discussed in Chapter 5). While both interventions aim to reduce bias, they differ slightly in focus and approach.

> **Reference-class forecasting** is most effective when decision-makers possess a deep understanding of a specific change project and need to estimate the necessary resources. By constructing a reference class using a wide array of external historical data, overconfidence and overoptimism in planning can be mitigated. Conversely, **re-anchoring** is best applied when decision-makers lack detailed operational knowledge of a particular change or must decide on resource allocation across multiple change initiatives. In such cases, historical data, which is useful in reference-class forecasting, might only further skew the decision-makers' perception and bias them toward previous budget allocations.

Gradual Escalation of Commitment

While allocating resources for change accurately from the beginning and setting the organization up for success using interventions like re-anchoring are both essential, leadership support and sponsorship do not end there. Leaders must continually monitor and reassess whether support and resources are being allocated correctly, especially in the context of bottom-up change. Bottom-up organizational changes, such as grassroots innovation, employee-driven process improvements, and cross-functional collaboration initiatives, hold immense potential for creating value.

This point was also beautifully illustrated by Pieter Versteeg, CHRO at Sodexo, a French food services and facilities management company that operates in approximately 55 countries, has more than 400,000 employees, and serves 100 million customers daily. COVID-19 significantly impacted their business and triggered an urgent need for change. Pieter shared how Sodexo Netherlands made a strategy change aimed at performance improvement, integrating services, launching new brands to deal with the future of work, incorporating sustainability elements, and improving the employee experience—the area in which he is most active as CHRO. This new strategy, if it were to be successful, had to be accompanied by a cultural change. All this effort paid off in 2022 with a better performance.

However, what stood out in this process was not a conventional top-down imposition of change, but a co-creative initiative. They turned to their development program for high-potentials and asked them, "We want a cultural change but not top-down. We'd like five leaders among you to lead this project. This is the number one priority next year. Who dares to take on this challenge and comes up with a plan of how to go about this? You can be sure of one thing and that is that we will support you." Like everything in life, it goes with "falling and getting up," but these employees truly played a pivotal role in leading the change process, fostering the new key competencies such as entrepreneurship, responsibility, positive energy, and flexibility.

This case underscores the potential of bottom-up change when supported by adept leadership, clearly showing the importance of continuously assessing and adjusting resource allocation. However, these initiatives require careful calibration of risk and support from leadership. Leaders must carefully balance their support for bottom-up innovation and change, ensuring sufficient resources for promising initiatives, while at the same time avoiding continued investment in projects that don't yield anticipated returns—a scenario often referred to as "sunk costs" (the same one that the sunk cost fallacy is named after!).

To address these challenges, leaders can employ an intervention called gradual escalation of commitment. As Olivier Sibony describes in his book *You're About to Make a Terrible Mistake*,[3] this approach involves making incremental commitments instead of taking big gambles, much like venture capitalists who increase their financial commitment at each stage based on a company's past achievements and future plans. Aside from bypassing lengthy approval processes and big risks, gradual commitment also incentivizes employees working on change to take an innovative and lean approach to proving their initiative, without taking on large gambles that could negatively impact their careers. Leaders responsible for sponsoring change through resources allocation could use gradual escalation of commitment, as illustrated in the following behavioral break.

Implementing a gradual escalation of commitment process within an organization requires overcoming several obstacles related to processes and culture. Companies could, for example, engineer exceptions to the annual budget process or create a dedicated unit to manage these projects like an internal venture capitalist. Moreover, leaders need to allocate time for progress reviews at each stage, even if these discussions seem small-scale compared to larger investments.

Behavioral Break: Gradual Escalation of Commitment

1. **Identify and assess bottom-up change initiatives**: Encourage employees to propose change ideas and evaluate them based on potential impact, feasibility, and alignment with the organization's strategic goals. For instance, consider an employee who proposes the adoption of a new internal communication platform to enhance collaboration and streamline information flow. You would then evaluate this proposal, weighing its prospective benefits, implementation costs, and fit with the company's overall strategic direction.

2. **Allocate initial resources and set intermediary objectives:** Provide sufficient resources for promising initiatives and define measurable, time-bound objectives. For instance, allocate a small budget and a six-month time frame for the initial pilot phase of the new communication platform, with the objective of increasing employee engagement by 5%.

3. **Implement a sunset clause with specific criteria:** In advance, determine the conditions under which an initiative will be discontinued. Establish clear criteria, such as a target outcome and deadline (in this case: achieving a 5% improvement in employee engagement within six months). If the project fails to meet these criteria by the specified deadline, the initiative will be terminated by default to minimize sunk costs and improve resource efficiency. Make sure these criteria are modest, not moonshots.

4. **Monitor progress and adjust resource allocation:** Regularly review progress against intermediary objectives and adjust resources based on performance and potential for long-term success. If the pilot phase shows promising results, consider increasing the budget and expanding the platform's adoption across incrementally bigger parts of the organization.

The most significant challenge, however, lies in shifting the risk- and loss-averse culture that tends to get in the way of bottom-up experimentation and innovation in many large enterprises. Project proponents must accept that their initiatives will be continually scrutinized and challenged, similar to start-up founders seeking their next round of financing. Generally, however, employees do not have the same tolerance for risk and financial expectations as entrepreneurs, which could potentially impact their willingness to propose or back risky yet potentially beneficial initiatives. Additionally, senior executives must learn to "pull the plug" on a project if it hasn't reached its objectives at a particular stage of development. This can be difficult due to the sunk cost fallacy discussed earlier, even with a gradual escalation of commitment process in place.

Nevertheless, by granting employees the necessary safety and resources to pursue bottom-up change initiatives, organizations can unlock a wealth of benefits. By encouraging innovation, enhancing employee engagement, and bolstering overall organizational resilience, companies can effectively harness the creative and problem-solving skills of their workforce. Moreover, fostering an environment where employees feel empowered to drive change cultivates a sense of ownership, which often translates to increased job satisfaction and employee retention. We further discuss these topics when we turn to cultivating psychological safety in the next chapter.

Conclusion

This chapter dissected the challenges of leadership support in organizational change. We discussed obstacles such as communication gaps, lack of role-modeling, and the struggle in allocating resources objectively. To navigate these hurdles, you as a change manager or leader now have three evidence-based interventions to experiment with.

We introduced if-then planning, re-anchoring, and gradual escalation of commitment. Linking these insights back to the underlying framework from Chapter 4, we see that gradual escalation of commitment mainly focuses on prioritizing the change by making sure the most promising initiatives get adequately supported. If-then planning helps embed the behavior by cultivating supportive habits at scale, whereas re-anchoring tweaks the system to reinforce the change by debiasing the resource allocation process. They provide a structured approach for objective and informed decision-making, mitigating biases, and enhancing effectiveness.

This chapter offers a meaningful starting point to applying BeSci in leadership support, equipping you with the behavioral insights and evidence-based tools to start experimenting. Now let's turn our attention to an equally important challenge: engaging the stakeholders in your organization.

8

Stakeholder Engagement

CONSIDER A FICTITIOUS multinational fashion corporation embarking on an enterprise-wide digital transformation initiative. The new strategy, meticulously crafted by top management and external consultants, promised quite the package: streamlined operations, enhanced productivity, and a culture primed for innovation.

The execution of this strategy began with a top-down rollout. Armed with beautifully designed slides, timelines, and objectives, senior management set out to transmit their vision to the organization. Town hall meetings were organized, newsletters were dispatched, and training sessions were scheduled. The goal was simple: equip everyone with the knowledge and tools needed to navigate the digital transformation. Yet the flow of information was from the top to the bottom, with little opportunity for feedback or dialogue.

Despite the clear advantages presented by the transformation, the transition from planning to implementation revealed some unexpected complications. The workforce—comprising a wide array of stakeholders from fashion designers and project managers to administrative staff and even top-level executives—found themselves grappling with the changes. Their involvement had been limited to receiving information about the impending transformation, with little say in the planning process. This lack of engagement began to breed distrust. As the people at the heart of the change, the employees felt overlooked and disconnected from the company's new direction. The unfamiliarity with the proposed changes and the uncertainty about its implications triggered fear, leading to resistance on multiple fronts: reluctance to adopt new digital tools, concerns about job security, and a decline in morale.

Unfortunately, the resistance wasn't met with understanding or patience. Instead, it created a vicious cycle, as management's doubling-down response further eroded the sense of psychological safety among the employees. Psychological safety, a cornerstone of successful change initiatives, is what allows stakeholders to experiment, make mistakes, and learn, without fear of reprisal. In its absence, the transformation project began to falter and was ultimately halted in its tracks.

Stakeholder Engagement in Change Management

This scenario underscores the essential role of stakeholder engagement in organizational change. It highlights the importance of trust, inclusivity, and psychological safety, and serves as a stark reminder that even the most carefully planned change initiatives can run into difficulties if not all stakeholders impacted are feeling included and engaged in a change initiative.

The experience in this scenario is far from unique. In fact, you might recognize this narrative because it is quite common in many organizations undergoing significant change. In this chapter, we aim to explore the topic of stakeholder engagement and shed light on the complexities, challenges, and opportunities that it presents from a behavioral perspective.

Stakeholder engagement is an area that requires change managers and facilitators to be at the top of their game. It involves dealing with multiple stakeholder groups, each with its own interests, concerns, and perspectives. It's about creating a conducive environment where stakeholders feel safe to experiment, make mistakes, and learn from them. It also involves many other people-centered activities, such as recognizing (silent) resistance and acknowledging early signs of change saturation or fatigue, and addressing them proactively.

Yet engaging stakeholders isn't simply about preventing resistance or managing dissent. Done right, it becomes a process that enables organizations to harness the collective intelligence, creativity, and commitment of their people. This includes ensuring diversity and inclusion, promoting transparency and open communication, and co-creating solutions that are embraced by all (or at least, by most).

This process is not easy and should never be confined to the upper echelons of the organization. Change champions, ambassadors, or agents—those stakeholders throughout the organization who dedicate a portion of their time to facilitating change—play a leading role in this process. They act as a bridge between different levels of the organization, helping to foster understanding, facilitate communication, and drive alignment with the change objectives.

Stakeholder Engagement Interventions

Throughout this chapter, we explore three evidence-based interventions designed to improve stakeholder engagement during organizational change:

- **Psychological Safety:** First, we explore strategies to promote psychological safety within your team. By fostering an environment where stakeholders feel secure in expressing their ideas and concerns, you'll be able to cultivate an environment for open dialogue and creative problem-solving, encouraging deeper stakeholder engagement.
- **Organizational Network Analysis (ONA):** ONA, an innovative analytical tool, allows you to understand the informal hierarchies and networks of influence that are at play within your organization. Recognizing these interconnections can help you identify key influencers and potential change champions, ensuring a comprehensive engagement of all relevant stakeholders.
- **Red-Blue Team:** A method designed to stimulate constructive conflict. This approach not only urges teams to critically examine their plans and assumptions, uncovering potential weak

spots in your strategy, but also creates a platform for active stakeholder participation, offers room to discuss resistance, and promotes a culture of speaking up.

By the end of this chapter, you will be equipped with new tools to effectively engage stakeholders, ensuring your change initiatives are robust, inclusive, and strategically sound. You will be better positioned to leverage the power of diverse perspectives, challenge groupthink, and navigate the complexities of your organization's informal networks of influence.

Stakeholder engagement is one of those change areas that, at times, feels more like an art than a science. As change managers, you have already been making significant strides in this area. You've been managing resistance to change, alleviating change fatigue, and addressing uncertainties in your communication plan. Nonetheless, the inherent toughness of this task means that there's always room for improvement and growth.

First and foremost, effectively engaging stakeholders requires recognition and respect for the diversity inherent in the individuals and groups impacted by any given change. As Tessa Peetoom, global director of DEI at ALD|LeasePlan, underscores, this diversity necessitates a flexible strategy that can adjust to the unique needs and preferences of different stakeholder groups. Some stakeholders may respond best to a more directive approach that provides clear guidelines and structure. Conversely, others may thrive under a more collaborative style, where they can feel genuinely listened to and appreciated. The aim is not to elevate one approach over the other, but to act on the need for a wider spectrum of engagement strategies.

Adding to this, the organizational capability director at the global healthcare company shares her organization's strategy of a distributed change management structure. This approach allocates key roles in driving change to every leader within the organization, with the scope of the audience for the change being determined by the extent of the project—whether that is at a national, regional, or departmental level. This distributed method enables widespread engagement and responsibility across the organization.

On Biases in Stakeholder Engagement

Engaging stakeholders in organizational change effectively requires an understanding of the mentality that underlies their attitudes and behaviors toward change. It is here that many traditional stakeholder management approaches tend to fall short. A reason for this might be that engagement strategies are often based on the assumption that employees will react to change in a fully rational way. However, the principle of bounded rationality discussed in Chapter 2 teaches us that human behavior is not always rational. Understanding the underlying cognitive biases to these behaviors can help change managers empathize and engage with stakeholders in a more meaningful way.

Three common biases that interfere with successful stakeholder engagement during change are reactance, status quo bias, and loss aversion:

- **Reactance:** Reactance stems from our desire for autonomy. When we sense an attempt to limit our choices, our instinct is often to resist. Think of it like dealing with a pushy salesperson, or a memory from kindergarten when you were made to sit in a corner. In the workplace, reactance can cause employees to resist change if they see it as a threat to their independence, even if the change is beneficial. It often signifies a lack of early involvement, co-creation, or communication.
- **Status Quo Bias:** This bias reflects our preference for what's familiar and stems from our need for control and energy conservation. It can trigger resistance to any disruption of existing routines, thereby hindering the adoption of change.
- **Loss Aversion:** People tend to prefer avoiding losses to acquiring equivalent gains. If stakeholders perceive the change as a potential loss—whether that's job security, professional routines, or their sense of identity—they are more likely to resist it. This aversion to perceived loss can further amplify resistance to change.

These biases, which can subtly infiltrate the change process and interact with many other behavioral drivers, make it difficult to pinpoint the exact sources of resistance. Therefore, conventional stakeholder engagement strategies, which risk overlooking these nuances, often fail to achieve and sustain the desired level of engagement.

The shortcomings of conventional engagement strategies highlight the need for a behaviorally informed approach, one that not only understands these biases but also employs evidence-based interventions to mitigate them effectively. Such an approach prioritizes creating an environment that fosters psychological safety, allowing stakeholders to openly express their thoughts and concerns. It facilitates constructive dialogue, builds trust, and promotes a culture of continuous learning—the prerequisites for successful stakeholder engagement.

The Importance of Psychological Safety

Harvard Professor Amy Edmondson, a leading authority on psychological safety, describes the concept as a shared belief within a team that it's safe to express ideas, admit mistakes, or raise concerns without fear of punishment or blame.[1] The word "shared" deserves close attention here. Leadership can't simply claim their organizational environment is psychologically safe. Each employee has to actually believe it and experience a safe environment that fosters open communication, enabling them to contribute their unique perspectives and insights.

> Remember that **psychological safety**, a cornerstone of successful change initiatives, is what allows stakeholders to experiment, make mistakes, and learn, without fear of reprisal.

Establishing such an environment is not an overnight event but a progressive journey that requires unwavering dedication, particularly in existing work climates marked by intimidation or conflict. To make this more practical, let's consider a situation where an employee, having fought tooth and nail for the sponsorship of a specific project, must confront the harsh reality of disappointing returns.

In the absence of psychological safety, the employee might fear a backlash or even public shaming for the project's failure. But in a psychologically safe setting, the manager's response takes an alternate path, asking, "What have we learned from this?" This response pivots the focus away from pointing fingers to a quest for knowledge, fostering a culture where taking risks, voicing diverse viewpoints, and embodying one's authentic self is not just permitted, but encouraged.

This idea is mirrored in the real-world practices of ABN AMRO, as shared by Wies Wagenaar, global head, Center of Expertise for Behaviour, Ethics, and Learning. Her team deploys an intervention known as "Reflection Dialogues," with goals that are multifold: to cultivate a culture of psychological safety and shared goals among all stakeholders, to identify the root causes hindering change, and to co-create solutions for improvement. All dialogues are oriented toward fulfilling ABN AMRO's purpose, "Banking for better, for generations to come," and are reinforced through structured manuals, "train-the-trainers" programs, and hands-on facilitation. Interestingly, Wagenaar's team leverages the "Whole System in the Room" approach (as described in Chapter 5) to achieve these ends.

The advantages of cultivating psychological safety are manifold, from increased team engagement and better decision-making to an organizational culture of continuous improvement and learning. Remember, psychological safety is not an individual attribute but a collective attribute, influencing group behavior and, by extension, overall organizational performance. In teams, departments, or entire organizations reflecting high psychological safety, it is important to note that these are usually not places where everyone always agrees or is overly nice to each other. Instead, it is characterized by constructive conflict, healthy tension, sharpness of ideas, and intelligent failure. These aspects are only possible due to the trust and safety provided in the organization. In a psychologically safe environment, disagreements are welcomed as opportunities for growth and innovation. It encourages individuals to challenge assumptions, engage in robust discussions, and explore different perspectives.

Cultivating Psychological Safety

The process of instilling psychological safety, particularly important when managing stakeholders in an organizational change scenario, is, according to Edmondson, anchored in three key stages: setting the stage, inviting engagement, and responding productively.[2] Setting the stage involves laying out the complexities of the task ahead and highlighting the essential role of each team member in the change process. In doing so, you're emphasizing the importance of their input and reinforcing their value to the team.

The next stage, inviting engagement, is about proactively soliciting feedback and providing opportunities for stakeholders to express their thoughts. This involves creating spaces where all voices are heard and different perspectives are valued. The final stage, responding productively, requires welcoming all types of feedback and treating missteps not as faults deserving of blame, but as opportunities for learning and development. This framework sounds simple (as practical frameworks should), but can be surprisingly hard to embed in an organizational behavior and processes.

This is partly attributable to psychological safety being a broad and nuanced concept. Thus, interventions are better framed as flexible guidelines rather than rigid instructions. We'll go over two practical interventions inspired by Amy Edmondson's framework: a diagnostic questionnaire and several strategies for cultivating a psychologically safe environment.

The first intervention is a seven-item questionnaire developed by Edmondson to help leaders diagnose the level of psychological safety within their teams. The responses to these questions provide valuable insights into whether team members feel safe to take risks, make mistakes, or voice their opinions. You can find a tool that helps you run this survey in your team on Edmondson's website.[3]

Behavioral Break: Psychological Safety Questionnaire

1. **Preparation:** Prepare the seven-item questionnaire that includes the following questions:
   - If you make a mistake on this team, is it not held against you?
   - Are members of this team able to bring up problems and tough issues?

- Do people on this team sometimes accept others for being different?
- Is it safe to take a risk on this team?
- Is it not difficult to ask other members of this team for help?
- Would no one on this team deliberately act in a way that undermines my efforts?
- Working with members of this team, are my unique skills and talents valued and utilized?

2. **Distribution:** Distribute the questionnaire among the team members. Ensure anonymity to encourage honesty and openness in responses.

3. **Evaluation:** Upon analyzing the questionnaire responses, look for patterns and their implications. The questionnaire is constructed such that yes answers are indicative of a psychologically safe environment. Therefore, an abundance of no responses, especially uniform across the team, could indicate an issue with psychological safety. Look out for any questions that consistently score low—these might point to specific areas of concern that require immediate attention.

4. **Action:** Use the evaluation results to develop an action plan for improving psychological safety within your team. This might involve addressing specific issues identified in the questionnaire or implementing general strategies or interventions to promote psychological safety.

This brief psychological safety questionnaire is designed to be utilized more frequently and independently of standard annual climate or employee engagement surveys. Offering a rapid and quantifiable snapshot of the team's current psychological safety provides a baseline for identifying areas for improvement. Additionally, its repetitive use can effectively gauge the success of interventions, demonstrating whether they've had a positive impact on the team's psychological safety.

The second intervention involves the application of several strategies inspired by Edmondson's work to nurture a psychologically safe environment.

Behavioral Break: Strategies for Cultivating Psychological Safety

1. **Focus on performance:** Start by making the business case for psychological safety. Emphasize and communicate that open dialogue matters for improving results, particularly in knowledge-intensive work. Understand that senior executives value psychological safety when they grasp its role in resolving complex issues. There is a wealth of concrete data available you can use to make your case, like Edmondson's work on psychological safety and learning behavior in teams.[4]

2. **Admit your own mistakes:** Develop a culture of transparency by acknowledging your own mistakes and sharing what you've learned from them. This action underscores the acceptability of errors as a part of the learning process and should be habitualized by all organizational leaders and managers.

3. **Encourage input and direct communication:** Actively invite your team members to share their thoughts and ideas. Foster a culture of open dialogue by asking open-ended questions that allow team members to express their perspectives. David Hulsenbek, CHRO at Salta Group, for example, encourages colleagues to directly approach others whose behavior they seek to understand and simply ask them about it. This approach may lead to uncomfortable situations initially, but in the long run it enhances mutual understanding and strengthens the team's psychological safety.

4. Provide constructive responses to feedback: Make it a practice to respond to feedback in a way that values the contribution and encourages further dialogue. This could involve expressing appreciation for the feedback and asking clarifying questions to fully understand the perspectives being shared. If-then plans (discussed in Chapter 7) can be a great tool to form habits around these behaviors.

Remember, these strategies are not about maintaining constant comfort or always being "nice." Instead, they aim to create an environment where team members feel safe to take risks, make mistakes, and express their ideas without fear of negative consequences.

One organization where psychological safety plays an essential role is Van Oord, a leading marine contractor with over 155 years of experience. The Dutch company operates in the global market, focusing on areas of climate adaptation and offshore energy. When we interviewed their chief people officer, Meike Salvadó-de Reede, she explained why psychological safety is so important when creating a safety culture: "Our construction workers deal with very large equipment in potentially high-risk situations, and we want to make sure no one gets hurt. To ensure physical safety, an environment of psychological safety is essential. It's important that anyone who sees unsafe behavior feels like they can speak up, regardless of role and seniority. We measure the number of incidents and the data clearly shows that the focus on psychological safety is having a positive effect."

To foster a culture of psychological safety, Van Oord developed several strategies that are in line with the research described in this chapter. They use safety observation cards that allow anyone to log unsafe practices as soon as they are spotted. This straightforward tool keeps safety in everyone's mind, especially while operating or working with heavy machinery. They also adopted an ambassador approach where employees from different levels of the company, including top executives like Salvadó-de Reede, act as safety leaders and role models. They lead by example, encouraging their colleagues to speak up about potentially unsafe situations, to be transparent about making mistakes, and to provide constructive feedback continuously, turning every incident into a learning opportunity. This also aligns with the role-modeling discussed in the previous chapter and the importance of sponsorship from the top.

As Salvadó-de Reede emphasizes, their safety culture isn't about being nice; it's about being kind. This means sometimes making the hard calls, ensuring that everyone takes responsibility for their safety and the safety of others. By setting clear priorities, role-modeling behaviors, and providing the necessary resources and support systems, van Oord has fostered an environment where safety is a shared responsibility. This strategy is another real-world example of the underlying framework for behavioral change (discussed in Chapter 4), where priorities, behaviors, and systems are aligned to drive sustained change.

While cultivating psychological safety helps individuals feel secure in voicing their ideas and concerns, it's equally important to recognize the channels through which these ideas and concerns travel. In every organization, beyond formal hierarchies, there exist informal networks of communication and influence. These networks often remain unseen but play a pivotal role in how information is exchanged and change propagates. Understanding these networks, which are not always apparent in an org chart, can greatly enhance the effectiveness of stakeholder engagement.

Understanding Your Stakeholders Beyond the Org Chart

Imagine a well-established company with a deeply entrenched hierarchy, departments defined cleanly, and a clear org chart representing this. This company is about to implement a major strategic change, impacting pretty much every department and every role. Senior leadership believes that they can effectively manage this change by cascading it down through the established lines of command—a classic top-down approach.

Yet as the change process rolls out, unexpected issues begin to crop up. Information is getting lost, resistance is growing, and the initiative seems to stall. Leaders become frustrated; the change process, on paper, should be running smoothly given their design based on formal hierarchies. However, the reality of the situation is far from it. They soon realize they've overlooked something critical: the hidden, informal networks that power the flow of communication and influence within their organization.

In this company (as in many others), there are key individuals, not necessarily high-ranking, who hold significant influence. They are the ones colleagues turn to for advice or information, the ones who bridge gaps between departments, and the ones who can encourage or impede change without a formal mandate to do so. The story of this company underscores the significant value of understanding and factoring in organizational networks in change management. It highlights the disconnect that almost always exists between the formal hierarchical structure and the actual informal networks that exist within an organization.

Organizational Network Analysis

By overlooking these networks, even the most well-planned change initiatives can encounter unforeseen resistance and obstacles. Hence, this section covers the concept of a tool called organizational network analysis (ONA), explores its application in the context of stakeholder engagement, and explains how understanding and leveraging these hidden networks can help to enhance employee engagement and drive change to both formal and informal networks.[5]

ONA is an analytical tool based on social network analysis that examines the informal structure of an organization by assessing and mapping the relationships and interactions between individuals (see Figure 8.1).[6] The dots indicate employees within a team or department, and the lines between them show connections to their colleagues. Bigger dots with more connections indicate that these stakeholders might hold a position of influence within their team or department. The relevance with regard to change management lies in its ability to uncover informal hierarchies, providing an insightful perspective into who truly influences the flow of information, decision-making, and ultimately, the overall organizational culture. This knowledge is invaluable when planning and implementing change initiatives because it helps identify key influencers and channels through which change can be effectively communicated and embedded.

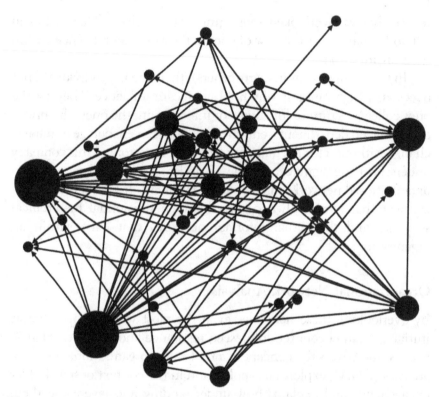

Figure 8.1   Organizational network analysis (ONA) visual.

As is probably clear by now, relying solely on org charts and formal vertical hierarchies can provide a skewed representation of an organization's true dynamics. These formal, static structures often fail to capture the organic exchange of information and influence within an organization, leading to gaps in stakeholder engagement during change management. To address this, understanding horizontal hierarchies and informal networks is vital. It enables change managers to identify key influencers, known as "central nodes" or "knowledge brokers" in ONA terms, who can champion change initiatives and cascade them effectively throughout the organization. Every change manager is aware of the importance of change champions; ONA will help you find out where they are hiding.

As we are writing this book, we are applying ONA in practice in an ongoing project within a large department of the Dutch government, aiming to enhance diversity and inclusion (D&I). To effectively promote cultural diversity and eliminate barriers to the promotion and retention of diverse talent, ONA has proven indispensable. It provided us with a dynamic and objective view of the employee landscape, in which it became instantly clear how diverse the informal networks are, and which groups are systematically excluded.

In practical terms, conducting an ONA involves several key steps. Initially, an ONA survey is conducted, capturing the various connections and interactions within an organization. This data is then transformed into a network map using specific software tools (we like to use RStudio, but there are many different options) that visually display *nodes* (people or groups within the organization) and *ties* (relationships or interactions between nodes).

Analysis of this map allows for the identification of central nodes and knowledge brokers, as well as disconnected or peripheral nodes. It's also important to pay attention to the strength of ties, which may indicate the frequency and quality of interactions. Ultimately, the goal is to create a more balanced network, where information and influence flow effectively and inclusively.

Behavioral Break: Organizational Network Analysis Intervention

1. **Identify the need:** Start by recognizing the situations where ONA could provide valuable insights. This could be a large-scale change initiative, a D&I project, or any situation where you need to better understand the communication patterns and informal networks in your organization.

2. **Assemble a team:** Given the data-intensive nature of ONA, it's advisable to collaborate with your data analysts or data scientists. You need not be an expert yourself, but partnering with those who are familiar with data can be beneficial and speed up the process by quite a bit.

(continued)

(continued)

3. **Define the scope:** Decide on the boundaries of the network you want to analyze. It could be a specific department, a team, or the entire organization. If you first start experimenting with ONA, it's advisable to start with a smaller team. However, you need at least 25 people to create a useful network map.

4. **Collect data:** Gather data on communication, collaborations, and relationships within the defined scope. The easiest way to do this is through an organizational network survey in the relevant team/department. These resources are freely available. Always ensure the collected data is anonymized and complies with regulations.

5. **Visualize the network:** This is where your data science team shines. Using appropriate software, they will visualize the network, with individuals as nodes and relationships or interactions as ties.

6. **Analyze the network:** Examine the network to identify key individuals—the central nodes, knowledge brokers, and peripherals. This is key to understanding the existing informal hierarchy and communication pathways. As ONA becomes standard procedure in change management, you'll find yourself getting better at analyzing these networks rapidly.

7. **Interpret the findings:** This step involves, quite literally, connecting the dots. Who are your central nodes? How can they aid in your change management efforts? Do you have potential change agents in the peripheral who should be better integrated? This step will often trigger valuable insights for your change strategy.

8. **Develop an action plan:** Based on your findings, build a strategic plan to engage the identified key stakeholders. Consider interventions that leverage their position in the network for effective communication and change adoption.

> **9. Monitor and iterate:** Remember, change is a process, not a one-time event. Monitor the effectiveness of your strategy, revisit the network analysis periodically, and adjust your approach based on the changing dynamics of your organization. Administering ONA before and after a change intervention or entire program can, for example, be a great and objective way to evaluate the effectiveness of your intervention on employee engagement of inclusivity.

Since ONA is quite a technical and analytical tool, the first time may seem a bit daunting. However, the more often you apply it, the more intuitive it will become. Remember, ONA is not an end in itself but a means to a greater end—a useful tool in your change management toolkit that empowers you to engage your stakeholders more effectively.

In our conversation with Clim Parren, former chief people officer at Aegon, he highlighted the potential benefits of ONA. He sees it as a great tool for managing complex stakeholder engagement in large organizations and providing a more objective understanding of organizational dynamics. Parren believes that ONA gains insight into informal leadership within the organization and leverages that to ensure changes reach all stakeholder groups.

Navigating Resistance

While cultivating psychological safety and understanding social networks within an organization are powerful strategies, they do not form a complete solution for stakeholder engagement during change initiatives. To get an even stronger grasp on stakeholder influence, change managers need to tailor their strategies to the different styles in which their stakeholders engage. Resistance is, for example, not merely an obstacle to change, but a complex form of stakeholder engagement in its own right (given that the resistance is active, not passive). Understanding and shaping engagement could therefore benefit strongly from a deeper understanding of different types of resistance and how to act on them.

In *The Science of Successful Organizational Change*, Paul Gibbons discusses four Ds of resistance—Destruction, Distancing, Delays, and Dissent.[7] Destruction involves acts like refusal to participate or corruption of information. Distancing can manifest in stakeholders being unavailable or showing lack of engagement. Delays come in the form of procrastination or, sometimes purposefully, not meeting deadlines. Dissent can be expressed both covertly and overtly, with covert (or silent) resistance posing a bigger problem. This 4D model should not be confused with the 4D model of appreciative inquiry (discussed in Chapter 3).

Contrary to popular belief, resistance is not inherently negative. In fact, it's an expression of engagement—though not the kind we usually want. It's a sign that stakeholders are involved enough to have an opinion, even if it's in opposition. Understanding the reasons for resistance allows change managers to address these concerns and turn resistance into support. We can learn from how the field of customer support handles this. Complaints are not good for business, but also present opportunities. Solving their problem in a quick and empathic way can often turn those customers from "complainers" to "ambassadors."

To manage resistance, a one-size-fits-all tactic rarely works. Julia Wittlin, change program manager at Microsoft, emphasized the significance of comprehending the root causes of resistance and eliminating the obstructions for better stakeholder engagement. For those ends, Gibbons offers a holistic model of resistance,[8] differentiating between various causes of resistance and outlining potential reasons behind them.

This model doesn't only offer a deepened understanding of resistance, but it can also significantly improve well-established change management tools like change impact analysis and stakeholder maps. By incorporating this model into your change impact analysis, you can better anticipate and understand the different types of resistance you might encounter during a change initiative. Meanwhile, when constructing stakeholder maps, the holistic model encourages a more nuanced view of stakeholders. Rather than viewing stakeholders simply as individuals who will either support or resist change, the model encourages you to consider their unique perspectives, fears, habits, and values.

Table 8.1   Gibbon's holistic model of resistance.

Cause	Reason
Rational	They possess insufficient or wrong facts, or disagree with reasoning based on those facts.
Habitual	They have a will to change, but habitual behaviors produce lack of adoption or relapse.
Emotional	They are angry at or afraid of a proposed change.
Pragmatic	They need to know how, as well as what and why, and they need the skills to do what is asked of them.
Identity	They see change as a threat to "who I am" or how they see themselves.
Fairness	They perceive a lack of justice or fairness in the process or outcome.
Ideology	The change is contrary to their values, philosophical stance, or morals.
Liberty	They expect self-determination, freedom, and the ability to self-actualize.
Social	There are social disruptions to important relationships or loyalty to others harmed by the change.
Cultural	Organizational norms, rituals, language, and values reinforce old patterns of thinking and behaving.
Political	They think and act in tribes and value political loyalty and status.

Engaging Resistance Through Constructive Conflict: Red-Blue Team

Despite acknowledging the importance of diverse perspectives and harnessing a tailored approach to ease resistance to change, an organization can often find itself stuck in a pattern of conformity due to hierarchical structure or conflict avoidance culture. This forms the basis of our next intervention, the **Red-Blue Team exercise**, which builds on the foundation of psychological safety to spark constructive conflict, debate, and dissent.

This Red-Blue Team intervention is rooted in military science, where it has been used for over a century to understand rivals' intentions and simulate strategies and tactics for potential weaknesses and threats.[9] In the context of organizational change, this intervention promotes idea generation, decision-making, and a culture of constructive conflict. It works beautifully for important decisions that can have a lasting impact on the trajectory of the organization, particularly where hierarchical structures and conflict avoidance culture are prevalent.

The Red-Blue Team intervention is structured to facilitate a space for discourse and debate, prompting team members to constructively challenge the perspectives put forward. A facilitator—who is usually the leader or manager but can also be external—ensures a safe environment where all viewpoints can be freely expressed and acknowledged. The team is divided into two, each assigned a specific role in a debate about a predefined statement that is crucial to the decision or innovation at hand. The Blue team argues in favor of the statement, while the Red team debates against it. Each team generates strong arguments that contribute to a fuller understanding of the matter at hand. The intervention is not about winning the debate. Rather, it aims to promote a deeper understanding of the topic through the exploration of diverse viewpoints.

From a behavioral perspective, the Red-Blue Team intervention addresses cognitive biases such as status quo bias, authority bias, and groupthink, which often hinder the decision-making process. These biases can reduce stakeholders' willingness to speak up, instigate constructive conflicts, and explore more effective options. Through Red-Blue teaming, these biases can be mitigated by leveraging the environment and processes rather than attempting to alter people's inherent thinking patterns.

This exercise can be a real lifeline when stakeholders are disengaged or even show animosity toward a change initiative but have not yet shared this openly. This could be due to uncertainty they experience, or not having sufficient information to fully engage with the change. The Red-Blue team exercise provides them with a safe space, as well as a direct incentive to engage in debate and explore different arguments for or against the proposed change. This will not only make their voices be heard, but also include them in creating possible solutions discussed in the exercise.

To understand its relevance to change management, consider a common change challenge: the integration of new technology into an organization's operations. This decision can profoundly impact the workflow, the employees' roles, and the customer experience. Equally suitable challenges could be a major shift in the company's strategic direction or the implementation of a new sustainability initiative. Each of these represents significant potential change that could elicit strong reactions and resistance from stakeholders.

In a real-world example, we facilitated a Red-Blue Team exercise with a leading Dutch online retailer's leadership team. One of the significant debates was on this contentious topic: "We should stop participating in Black Friday." This decision carried serious implications for their market positioning, customer expectations, and profitability. The Red-Blue Team intervention was instrumental in bringing to light the multifaceted aspects of this complex decision. To make sure the stakeholders fully committed themselves to their respective teams, we provided red and blue armbands. This twist that was meant as a fun add-on seemed to have a surprising effect on the vigor with which the leaders argued. However, the exact underlying cause of this heightened engagement remains somewhat of a mystery.

With that context, let's delve into the step-by-step behavioral breakdown of how you can conduct a Red-Blue Team intervention yourself. This exercise can be done rapidly in 30 minutes, but for the best outcomes, at least an hour and a half is advised to include discussing learnings and reflection, especially at the first try.

Behavioral Break: Red-Blue Team Intervention

1. **Identify the change challenge:** Define the change challenge that would benefit from constructive debate. This could range from implementing a new technology to deciding a shift in strategic direction or introducing a sustainability initiative. Create a guiding statement around this change, like "Implementing this new technology will significantly improve our efficiency."

(continued)

(*continued*)

2. **Form the teams:** The assigned facilitator creates two diverse teams—the Red and the Blue—ideally with members from various departments or levels within the organization to ensure different perspectives. The Blue team will defend the change initiative, while the Red team will critique it.

3. **Develop arguments:** Both teams independently develop their arguments. The Blue team outlines the benefits and potential advantages of the change, while the Red team identifies possible drawbacks and risks. The goal is to consider the change challenge from all possible angles. Depending on the magnitude of your challenge, this phase can take anywhere from 15 minutes up to weeks and, in some cases, even months!

4. **Present arguments:** The Blue team first presents their case, followed by the Red team presenting their counter-arguments. A facilitator ensures every viewpoint is heard, understood, and recorded for future reference.

5. **Facilitate open dialogue:** Teams engage in an open debate, challenging each other's arguments while searching for shared understanding and potential solutions. This is where constructive conflict unfolds, providing space for dissent and fostering a psychologically safe environment.

6. **Synthesis:** Once all perspectives have been aired and understood, the teams come together to find common ground. Shedding their Red-Blue identities, they integrate the insights from the exercise and work on a collaborative change strategy that addresses the benefits and potential drawbacks identified during the debate.

7. **Action planning:** Based on the synthesis, the unified team develops an action plan for the change initiative. This plan should incorporate the diverse viewpoints and solutions identified during the exercise, ensuring the resulting change is robust, inclusive, and well-rounded.

Underpinned by psychological safety, the Red-Blue Team intervention serves as an effective tool in the arsenal of any change leader, adeptly managing resistance, providing space for debate and dissent, and ultimately driving alignment toward change.

Conclusion

As stated at the beginning of this chapter, stakeholder engagement often feels more like an art than a science. However, the discussed behavioral insights and evidence-based interventions serve as useful tools to start experimenting with the science-side. Due to the sensitive nature of stakeholder engagement and the wide variations in how stakeholders perceive change and its impact on them, it's absolutely key to tailor these interventions to your people and context before implementing them at scale.

As we move to the next chapter about measuring change, remember that a more personalized approach not only makes these interventions more effective, but it also resonates more deeply with your stakeholders. A little extra personalization can go a long way.

9

Measuring Change

How DO YOU measure behavioral change across thousands of stake-holders? How do you find out how they feel about the change? What KPIs, OKRs, or other kinds of metrics are useful to collect and analyze? Who can benefit from reporting on the progress of change? If it can be such a cumbersome process, is it worth measuring the soft side of change in the first place? In this chapter, we answer these and other questions with scientific articles in one hand and interview notes in the other.

As with all other chapters, the aim is not to reinvent the wheel with entirely novel methods of measuring change that replace conventional ones. Instead, we present a deep-dive into some of the challenges change managers and leaders might encounter in this area, behavioral insights that are relevant for them, and three evidence-based interventions that can enhance or complement your measurement strategies.

Measuring the Impact of Change

Why measure change management in the first place? It's a good question with many answers, the first of which has its roots in economics. If you cannot prove the value of change management efforts for the organization's goals, it's hard for the board and sponsors to justify a growing investment. When you can provide transparent reporting on how change management contributes to project and organizational success, the case builds itself. This was one of the things that Bas Zwart, global leader of change management at Johnson & Johnson, emphasized when we asked him which advice helped him and his team get to where they are: "Don't celebrate the deliverable but the value to business. You almost want to think like an internal consultant and focus on communicating the value of change solutions for other teams and departments." And to connect the dots: a variety of interviewees mentioned that the main reason they work(ed) with large consulting firms such as McKinsey and Bain in change projects is that they have the data. Because of their global reach and experience, they can see which change strategies historically worked in which organizational contexts at a much more granular and practical level than most scientific or in-house studies. Proper measurement is an opportunity for change management teams to build these capabilities in-house, a valuable asset for any organization.

Another, probably even more important, benefit of measuring change management effectiveness is that it enables continuous improvement for your change management team and in turn, other stakeholders. When you select relevant metrics and measure progress and performance in them, you can take a more data-driven approach to improving the quality of your support services. As you saw in Chapter 1, developing the right internal change capabilities is a recurring challenge for change management teams, and without measuring change effectiveness, it's hard to know where to start. If, on the other hand, you can spot patterns in weaknesses and risks across change projects, you'll quickly find out where to focus your attention for maximum impact. Quality measurement functions as a compass for spotting opportunities of improvement.

On a project level, measuring change effectiveness helps you monitor how things are going, which often gives insight into any potential risks and opportunities you can then address. If stakeholder feedback suggests that many people are not aware of how the changes will affect them, you might want to increase the frequency and/or content of communications. If the data indicates that the group of employees who signed up for the new wellness program do not have a lower absence rate, you can change the program's structure or incentives to counteract the potential causes, such as lack of engagement or low perceived benefits. Obviously, it's not as simple as we describe here, given how hard it is to isolate cause and effect, but luckily this is exactly what science is for. Later in this chapter, we discuss some common measurement challenges and relevant behavioral insights.

When done properly, clarity on and active measurement of the success metrics for a change management project also help a variety of stakeholders involved. For people on the project team (i.e., change managers, change leaders, change agents, or project/program managers), it helps in identifying, prioritizing, and implementing the required change activities. Executives and project sponsors benefit from higher certainty that the project is likely to lead to the desired results as well the ability to see how things are evolving and provide proactive guidance based on other organizational factors that the project team might not be aware of. Although not always leveraged, there is also value for the people who are affected by the change and the organization at large. Communicating the progress, wins, and even challenges helps them understand how this change affects the organization as a whole and, in turn, their own role. They might even reach out to the project team with additional feedback or insights, which, as discussed previously, is key to embedding the change in and across the organization.

The importance of measuring change effectiveness to prove the value might also differ based on the company culture. When we spoke with the business manager of customer success at a multinational technology corporation, she explained, "Almost any decision is data-driven, even outside change management. Whenever you see an intervention, it's backed by data to explain the why and the how. Our culture also supports a strong vision, so the data helps explain that vision. When you can combine these two elements, you will see people rumbling behind the efforts." Given the prevalence of digital transformation efforts, more and more organizations are gaining access to a lot of data and are developing a data-driven mindset along with it. This means that the coming years are likely to bring a transition in how we measure the effectiveness of change management, resulting in new challenges. As the manager we spoke to puts it, "The challenge is not the data, but which data to use, in the sense that you get what you measure."

Measuring Change Interventions

This chapter covers three evidence-based interventions you can apply to measure the effectiveness of change initiatives:

- **Change Measurement Toolkit:** Uses specific tools like behavior change assessments, pulse surveys, and organizational climate surveys to measure the impact of change initiatives and the actual behavior change resulting from them.
- **Shifting the Burden of Proof:** This approach aims to foster realistic evaluation of change initiatives' progress by starting all project items with a "red status." This approach urges the project teams to actively provide evidence to justify a move toward "green status." This process reverses the typical approach of assuming success until failure is evident and ensures that every step taken toward the project's completion is evaluated properly.
- **A/B Testing Change:** Tests change initiatives by implementing changes in a subset of the organization (group B) while maintaining the status quo in a control group (group A). This experimental approach allows you to isolate change initiatives and measure them objectively. You can also use A/B testing to experiment with the evidence-based interventions in this book.

Measuring the Hard and Soft Sides of Change

Measuring change can refer to two things: measuring how the change initiative is progressing and measuring the effectiveness of change management efforts. Measuring how the change is progressing is often one of the easier aspects of a change initiative. It mainly involves measuring the hard side of change management, which is relatively straightforward and objective: there is a plan with clearly defined deliverables and milestones set on a collectively agreed upon timeline, so the question simply becomes "Are we on schedule?" There might be additional questions regarding the quality of deliverables and the timeliness of milestone achievements, but these questions can often be answered with a definitive yes or no. When the new tech support software replaces the old and all processes are adapted, some might consider the change to be finished. It might officially be, but did it lead to the desired results? It might be that the number of support tickets has grown significantly or that people, instead of adopting the new system, reach out directly to tech support employees. A full progress bar does not mean it's fully effective.

In the words of Floor Huizer, transformation director at ABN AMRO, "It is difficult to measure change holistically. Sure, we can track deliverables, but do we actually measure their effectiveness?" She advocates for the development of clear, relevant change metrics that are tied to specific deliverables, performance results, and behavioral changes to track progress, focus attention, and create ownership. Yet Huizer warns against potential biases that the usual suspects like engagement surveys might produce due to subjective judgment of the surveyor. And because it measures people's engagement, not the intended change.

Marjon Kaper, director of People & Community at ANWB, also mentioned that concrete indicators are instrumental to clarify for stakeholders how they can support the change initiative, especially as a way to empower people with an entrepreneurial mindset. This is also where perspective matters: if a leader simply wants the change done without much regard for how people feel about it, measuring can be as simple as focusing exclusively on the hard side. This approach, as you probably expect, has many challenges and is more likely to result in short-term failure and long-term fatigue. It is also not at all human-centric.

Measuring the effectiveness of change management efforts is much harder. It involves measuring both the hard and the soft side. The hard side combines the aforementioned elements and adds other "hard metrics" to the mix such as KPIs, OKRs, or other data points your organization might already collect. The soft side of change is ironically much harder to measure because of its intangible and subjective nature. Where you can lean on digital analytics and timelines on the hard side, you'd ideally quantify things like leadership support, psychological safety, and change fatigue on the soft side. Granted, developments in the intersection of behavioral and business analytics have enabled more quantitative data points, but it still takes significantly more time, energy, and know-how than tracking whether we're on schedule—a fact that can entice some people, at their own peril, to ignore it altogether.

As emphasized by Michiel van Meer, chief people officer at Aon Nederland and ASC EMEA, both hard and soft sides of change measurement can be enhanced by the application of behavioral science methods and principles. One such method is qualitative interviewing. This approach delves into individual experiences, interpretations, and sentiments about the change, painting a holistic picture of its impact, which can provide more nuanced insights than purely quantitative measures like surveys.

Furthermore, van Meer suggests a "feedback loop" approach, characterized by an "antenna network" that tests ideas and gathers raw feedback before the full implementation of change initiatives. These antennas, ranging from team leaders to frontline employees, gather unfiltered feedback from various levels and departments and provide leaders with a broader perspective toward proposed changes, and a mechanism to test ideas before full-scale implementation or scaling.

In essence, measuring the effectiveness of change management is a multifaceted process, involving an intersection of behavioral and business analytics. It requires a combination of well-defined metrics, behavioral science methods, and continuous feedback mechanisms not only to track the progress of change initiatives but also to gauge their impact on organizational behavior.

Good Metrics Follow the Use Case

You find many examples of change metrics in this chapter, but how do you know which ones are most relevant for your situation? The short answer is that it depends on your use case. Making your promotion process more inclusive requires you to measure success differently than when you're implementing a new IT system or revamping your approach to L&D. If it's a top-down change initiative, there might already be a set of KPIs or OKRs that you can use to point your arrows at. In many cases, however, change is bottom-up and creating a set of metrics is part of the process of getting leadership buy-in. So what are use cases that you can draw inspiration from when choosing metrics that measure change effectiveness for your unique context? Let's go through some common examples of use cases and metrics.

Two of the most common use cases in organizational change are forecasting how a change might affect the organization and how prepared the organization is for the change. That's why two of the most common tools in OCM are the **Change Impact Analysis** and the **Change Readiness Assessment**. The former maps the impact of the change on the organization and its people by measuring the number of units/stakeholders impacted, the severity of these impacts, and how different changes might impact different stakeholder groups. This information is collected through stakeholder engagement and is essential for areas ranging from planning and risk management to narrative and communication.

The next step is often to map stakeholders' readiness for the proposed change by measuring things such as their awareness and support of the change, current and future capabilities required, and their willingness and ability to learn what is needed. For maximum value, this process of measuring change readiness should not only occur at the start of a project but also as it progresses, since these are useful insights for, again, planning, narratives, and such.

Another, increasingly digital, element of every change is communications. One part of this is tracking the reach, engagement, and outcomes of emails. Did people open the emails? Did they click on links or forward the email? Did they perform the requested action(s)? With the rise of instant messaging platforms like Slack and Microsoft Teams came new opportunities to gauge the effectiveness of communications.

Tessa Peetoom, global director of DEI at ALD | LeasePlan, sets an example by stressing the significance of a data-driven approach in measuring their DEI efforts, with a particular emphasis on root cause analysis. Leveraging the HR tool Workday, LeasePlan measures several metrics, such as:

- The number of women in the organization and at the top level
- The number of nationalities within the organization and at the top level
- The success rate of their succession planning

These metrics, gathered from an HR tool, contribute to the broader governance, performance measurement, and peer review processes.

Additionally, they also conduct surveys to measure aspects that reflect the culture and inclusivity of the organization. Three key metrics that they focus on include:

- Employees' feeling of belonging
- Whether employees feel they can bring their whole self to work
- The perceived inclusivity behavior of managers and teams

These survey metrics provide a more qualitative measure of the cultural shift within the organization, thereby complementing the more quantitative metrics gathered from their HR tool. This balance of quantitative and qualitative measures forms a comprehensive view of the effectiveness of DEI initiatives, providing insights to refine strategies and promote a more inclusive workplace while keeping people at the center.

It's good to look out for potential challenges when dealing with qualitative and quantitative data. In many organizations, these types of data are often collected and analyzed in different departments. For example, HR might handle qualitative data collection through interviews, surveys, and focus groups, while IT departments may manage larger volumes of quantitative data. The challenge arises when these different types of data fail to be integrated, which could lead to an incomplete picture of the situation. An insightful perspective on integrating qualitative and quantitative data for a more accurate measurement of change comes from Diana Chiang, behavioral data scientist at the University of Warwick. She walks us through a hypothetical use case that illuminates the power of merging these two types of data.

Imagine an established company making a substantial internal process change, transitioning from SharePoint to a more advanced platform. Accustomed to SharePoint, the employees now need to adapt to this novel system. To facilitate a smoother transition, the change initiative is designed to be more of a bottom-up approach, where the employees themselves are key drivers of the change.

One method to assess the impact of this change would be to ask qualitative questions on a large scale, such as "How has this change been affecting you?" "What challenges have you faced during this transition, and how have you tried to overcome them?" and "In what ways has the new system improved or hindered your daily work routines?" The responses, logged and transcribed, would provide a wealth of qualitative data. Rather than leaving it in its raw, qualitative form, however, Chiang suggests employing quantitative analysis techniques.

Natural language processing, for example, could be used to sift through the responses, identifying recurring key phrases, words, and themes. This type of analysis could reveal the main issues employees face during the transition by weighing the valence of each theme and prioritizing them accordingly. Themes could range from relatively straightforward concerns such as a need for more guidance, to more complex problems like difficulties integrating the new system into their existing workflows on personal devices.

Even subtler issues could be uncovered with this approach. For instance, employees over a certain age might express less confidence in handling the change, or certain demographics might face unique challenges not immediately apparent from a quick review of the responses. By converting qualitative responses into quantifiable data, a more nuanced understanding of the change impact becomes possible. This allows the organization to gauge not just the prevalence of certain sentiments or issues (e.g., "How many employees expressed the need for more guidance?"), but also their relative severity and their specific contexts.

Although this comprehensive approach to blending qualitative and quantitative data is not yet widely exploited in change management—with exceptions like industry leaders such as Google—it holds vast potential. By embracing this method, organizations can gain a deeper understanding of their employees' (and customers'!) experiences, allowing for a more effective, people-centered approach to managing change.

On Biases in Measuring Change

So what cognitive biases should you be aware of when it comes to measuring change? Here, you can find an overview of these and other cognitive biases that commonly occur while measuring change that you can briefly visit at all times:

- **Black Swan Effect:** This cognitive bias can exacerbate issues over time, as stakeholders tend to dismiss low-probability yet high-impact events that may negatively impact change progress. In the realm of measuring change, such an unforeseen event can severely impact the progress of the change initiative.
- **Paradox of Choice:** This refers to how an abundance of choices can paradoxically lead to restricted freedom because of choice overload. When it comes to selecting metrics for measuring change, too many choices can lead to complexity and lack of focus. This can result in scattered attention and suboptimal results, as stakeholders try to optimize all metrics simultaneously.
- **Surrogation:** This cognitive bias refers to our tendency to lose sight of the strategic construct that a measure is intended to represent, leading to acting as if the measure is the construct of interest. For instance, an organization might focus solely on a metric like financial performance, thereby losing sight of broader strategic goals, such as sustainability.

A real-world example illustrating the harmful impact of bias in measuring change comes from Wies Wagenaar, global head of the Center of Expertise for Behaviour, Ethics, and Learning at ABN AMRO. She emphasizes the pitfall of surrogation, which causes us to focus too much on a number or metric, losing sight of what that number is actually intended to represent. Wagenaar points out how this leads measures to become decoupled from the strategic constructs they aim to capture. "We find that the systems and processes within banks that employees must use are extremely complicated, almost impossible to manage, and require a lot of manual work. What often gets measured, however, is only the time employees spend on the actual system," she notes. "As a result, it seems that employees have more than enough time and the blame lies with them. In reality, they are working extremely hard, and we see a high turnover rate because the workload is too intense and the procedures are too complex." This is why one of Wagenaar's priorities is to leverage behavioral insights to reduce needless complexity in systems and empower employees to work as efficiently and responsibly as possible.

Now that we've explored the change area of measuring change from a behavioral lens, it's time to get practical. In this next section, we walk you through four practical interventions based on behavioral science.

Beyond the Net Promoter Score

Change programs are frequently assessed through tools like the Net Promoter Score (NPS) and annual engagement surveys. The NPS can serve as a quick gauge of how well a change initiative is received among employees or stakeholders on a scale of 0–10. These are widely used tools that can indeed be helpful in assessing the value of change programs; however, these instruments may fall short in measuring what truly matters: sustained changes in behavior and their alignment with organizational goals. Regrettably, change initiatives often aren't evaluated adequately or, in some cases, at all.

On the other hand, the process of designing and implementing change programs and interventions often comes quite naturally to seasoned change professionals. The strategy formulation, identifying the need for change, and the roll-out of new initiatives—this is what change managers are trained in. Yet the crucial step of evaluating the effectiveness of these initiatives beyond the NPS often does not get the attention it deserves.

The NPS is not at all a bad metric but, as discussed, it's more reliable when combined with other metrics. One issue lies in the fact that what is *perceived* to be effective in terms of change (and thus earns a high NPS score) often does not correlate with what is effective in changing behavior. And behavioral change is what leads to new results. The heart of the issue is that there is often a disconnect between what people *say* they will do (or even what they believe they will do) and what they actually end up doing. This phenomenon, known as the **intention-action gap**, is well documented in behavioral science and can occur for a variety of reasons, including social desirability bias (where people respond in a way they believe is viewed favorably by others), forgetfulness, or changes in circumstances.

Furthermore, while the NPS captures a snapshot of impressions at a particular moment, it does not track behavioral changes over time. For instance, someone might give a high NPS score immediately after a positive customer service interaction, but this does not necessarily mean their behavior will change in the long run—they might still switch to a competitor, discontinue using the product, or fail to recommend the service as they initially indicated.

For these reasons, relying solely on the NPS to measure the success of change initiatives can be misleading. Instead, it's advisable to use the NPS in conjunction with more robust metrics that capture behavioral change directly. This also relates to our previous discussion regarding the surrogation bias. Only using the NPS is likely to lead you astray.

Measuring Behavioral Change

Measurement strategies that seek to provide more insight into the effectiveness of an organizational change initiative should be aimed at measuring actual changes in behavior. Here, metrics should provide an index or percentage that represents the proportion of employees who, as a result of a change initiative, have actively started to change their behavior in their daily work routines. In essence, these "behavioral metrics" should capture the real-world impact of a change initiative by measuring the shift in everyday practices.

For instance, consider a change program that your organization has launched to bolster digital transformation. The initiative focuses on enhancing digital literacy, fostering digital innovation, and promoting the adoption of the many advanced digital tools and workflows available. Instead of forcing these on employees, you seek to motivate them to adopt changes on their own volition. The anticipated behavioral changes could involve more frequent use of digital collaboration tools, increased participation in digital skills training, or more proactive involvement in digital innovation projects.

Strong behavioral metrics should evaluate these critical aspects: Did the program equip learners with the necessary tools and knowledge? Are they applying these learnings in the relevant contexts, such as team meetings or specific tasks? What obstacles are they encountering, and how can these be mitigated? Behavioral metrics do not simply rely on the subjective question of "Would you recommend it to. . .?" but rather focus on the *frequency of behaviors*, such as how many times in the last week an employee used a specific digital tool.

To understand why this is a more reliable indicator of actual behavioral change than the NPS, imagine asking employees this question: "How many times in the last week have you utilized the new digital collaboration tool for project discussions?" Responses could range from "not at all" to "multiple times per day." This frequency-based question gives you insights into how the new behavior (use of the digital collaboration tool) is becoming part of the employees' regular activities and might slowly turn into habits. Frequency-based questions are usually restricted to the last week because this time frame is close enough for accurate memory recall.

All responses indicating engagement in the new behavior, even once a week, can inform behavioral metrics. Suppose that, out of 1,000 employees, 700 reported using the new digital tool at least once in the past week. In this case, the behavior change would be 70 percent, which means a significant proportion of the workforce is adapting to the desired change. One of the key benefits of behavioral metrics is their ability to provide a comparison with other metrics such as NPS scores. While NPS scores are valuable in capturing how much participants appreciate the program, behavioral metrics provide a measure of how much actual change the program has brought about in terms of behavior.

So what would a toolkit for measuring change that includes behavioral metrics look like? There are thousands of useful and thoroughly validated measurement instruments that, depending on the use case, each have their pros and cons. However, we have found the following three measurement instruments to be exceptionally useful in gauging change effectiveness both stand-alone and in conjunction.

- **Behavior Change Assessments:** To assess changes in employee behavior, a behavior change assessment should be administered two to four weeks post-training. This self-report assessment measures the frequency with which employees engage in the newly introduced behaviors during their work routines. To mitigate biases associated with self-reporting, a complementary survey is sent to colleagues or direct reports to gain additional perspectives on the observed changes.
- **Pulse Surveys:** Pulse surveys are brief check-ins that look like short versions of behavior change assessments. They can be deployed at regular intervals, like 3, 6, 9, and 12 months post-training. These brief surveys can often be completed in less than two minutes and provide insight into how new behaviors are sustained over time, indicating whether the change initiative continues to yield value.
- **Organizational Climate Survey:**[1] This time-tested pre- and post-intervention survey gauges organizational attitudes regarding specific topics like psychological safety; diversity, equity, and inclusion; cultural change; or other themes relevant to the organization. It paints a picture of employee experience, indicating the change's broader impact on the organizational climate.

Although this list is far from exhaustive, these instruments highlight the importance of identifying and measuring which behaviors or habits are targeted for change—a crucial component of any change initiative's overarching framework. That being said, the real challenge lies in knowing when to apply which instruments to measure the successes of specific organizational changes you are working on. Although this is a highly context-dependent process, we have outlined some broad steps you can take in the following behavioral break.

Behavioral Break: Change Measurement Toolkit

1. **Identify the desired behavioral changes:** The first step to effectively measure a change initiative is to identify the desired behavioral changes. These changes should be behaviors or habits that align with the goals of your change program and the broader strategic objectives of your organization. For instance, if your organization is undergoing a cultural shift toward greater inclusivity and diversity, the desired behaviors may involve proactive engagement with diverse colleagues, active participation in diversity training programs, and demonstrating respect and acceptance of diverse ideas and perspectives. However, translating high-level organizational objectives like fostering inclusivity into specific, measurable behaviors can be a complex task. In this context, the expertise of behavioral scientists or HR professionals with formal training in psychology or behavioral science becomes invaluable. These specialists can help pinpoint specific behaviors that directly support your strategic goals. Their insights can guide the process, ensuring that the defined behaviors align with your strategic goals and are practical and achievable within your organization's context.

2. **Choose the right measurement instruments:** Given the behaviors you've identified, determine the most suitable measurement instruments. Depending on the nature of your initiative and the resources available, you could consider tools such as behavior change assessments, pulse surveys, the organizational climate survey, and of course NPS surveys. Where you can find scientifically validated organizational climate and NPS surveys online in abundance, behavioral change assessments and pulse surveys are very context specific and are usually tailor-made by

(continued)

(continued)

HR/behavioral science professionals to fit the specific behaviors you seek to change.

3. **Implement the chosen measurement instruments:** Deploy the measurement tools at the right time. Timing plays a critical role in capturing meaningful insights from your measurement tools. Generally, an NPS survey is conducted immediately after a training session ends. Behavior change assessments typically follow two to four weeks post-training. Pulse surveys can be scheduled at 3, 6, 9, and 12 months after the training completion. The organizational climate survey can be conducted before and after the change initiative. Remember, these time frames serve as guidelines but your organizational context or the nature of the change initiative might warrant altered timelines. Use these tools to enhance or complement your existing measurement instruments, ensuring a comprehensive view of your change program's impact.

4. **Analyze and act on the data:** After collecting the data, analyze it to identify trends, areas of success, and areas that need improvement. If the data reveals that some behavioral changes are not taking hold as expected, this is an opportunity to revisit the initiative and consider adjustments. Keep stakeholders informed about your findings and your plans for continuous improvement. Remember, the ultimate aim is to ensure your change initiative results in meaningful, sustained behavior change that aligns with your organizational goals.

Knowing *what* you intend to change provides the clarity needed to frame your assessment tools, determine the questions to be asked, and evaluate the change initiative's success effectively. Measurement is not an afterthought but an integral part of the entire change process, incorporated from the outset.

While the comprehensiveness of this particular measurement portfolio may not be feasible for every organization, a minimal approach is strongly recommended. Organizations should, at the very least, administer an NPS survey at the end of every training program and deploy behavior change assessment two to four weeks post-training, both for participants and their direct reports or colleagues. This minimum approach enables organizations to capture immediate reactions to the training and, subsequently, the early indications of behavior change.

Watermelon Project Dashboards

Now that we have focused on developing a high-level overview for assessing change initiatives, we can turn to other more real-time strategies to effectively evaluate and manage specific change projects in action.

Typically, from a project management viewpoint, change initiatives are evaluated through a reporting method known as the **traffic light system**. This system allows project stakeholders to report to the steering committee by indicating the status of the overall project and deliverables or phases using a set of universally understood colors. Green implies smooth progress, amber or yellow indicates caution or neutrality, and red signals a problem that needs immediate attention.

This traffic light system's appeal lies in its simplicity and intuitiveness. It provides a quick snapshot view of the project's health, highlighting areas that demand immediate attention and ensuring an efficient tracking mechanism. However, like most measurement tools, the traffic light reporting system is not immune to distortion and misuse.

One significant pitfall of the traffic light system is a deceptive trap known as the watermelon phenomenon. This term finds its roots in the characteristics of a watermelon, vibrant green on the outside, yet strikingly red on the inside. When applied to project management, this phenomenon describes a scenario where stakeholders (influenced by biases we'll discuss shortly) present an outwardly healthy green-only dashboard, masking internal complications and issues, much like a watermelon conceals its red interior under a green shell.

The perpetrators that are at least partially responsible for the distorted view are cognitive biases that cloud our judgment. For instance, **overoptimism bias** leads project stakeholders to underestimate potential problems and overestimate their ability to deliver on targets. Simultaneously, the **planning fallacy** makes them believe they can complete tasks more quickly and cheaply than realistically possible, often ignoring past experiences that suggest otherwise. In addition, the **black swan effect** exacerbates this issue over time, causing stakeholders to dismiss low-probability yet high-impact events that may negatively impact change progress.

This skewed representation can lead to missed early intervention opportunities, and these concealed problems can grow into critical issues that jeopardize the entire initiative's success by the time they're uncovered. To prevent this kind of reactive dynamic, it helps to recognize and address the watermelon phenomenon in its early stages to ensure an accurate reflection of the project's health and timely management of potential risks. To counter this watermelon effect, change managers can implement an evidence-based intervention known as "shifting the burden of proof." This concept, outlined by Olivier Sibony in his book *You're About to Make a Terrible Mistake*, encourages challenging the status quo as a default choice.[2]

Picture a project kickoff meeting where the dashboard is, by default, filled with red lights. The responsibility now shifts to the stakeholders who need to demonstrate, with convincing proof, why their project segments are on track and warrant a shift to amber or green. For example, a team responsible for implementing a new software solution might need to provide evidence of completed training sessions, successful dry runs, and positive feedback from a control group before their light can change from red to amber or green.

Not only does this approach counteract overoptimism, but it also pushes stakeholders to be more objective in their progress reporting. It can become a best practice, mandated by the steering committee, to foster a culture of rigorous and realistic progress assessment. Given the reversed dynamic (guilty until proven innocent), it's important to mention the role that culture and role-modeling play here. The initial red dashboard is not "bad" and it should not become a dynamic where presenters feel threatened by an overt need to prove themselves. That could lead to the same biases we aim to mitigate! But when there is psychological safety and a growth mindset in all those present, this collaborative way of progress mapping is likely to filter out many of the previously discussed biases.

Behavioral Break: Shift the Burden of Proof Intervention

1. **Start with red dashboards:** Begin by adjusting your traffic light system and start all project elements in the red status. This means that every component is considered off track or not yet ready until proven otherwise. While this might initially feel counterintuitive, remind everyone involved that this doesn't represent a failure, but it's an innovative way to counteract biases and encourage objective reporting.

2. **Define clear criteria for status shifts:** Set explicit and objective criteria for what constitutes a shift from red to amber and eventually to green. For instance, a shift to amber might require a detailed plan with key milestones, while a shift to green could require evidence of milestones achieved on time and within budget, or successful completion of pilot tests, ideally including soft metrics. Ensure the shifting criteria are clearly communicated and documented at the start!

3. **Communicate the new system:** When you consider piloting this system, explain it to the involved stakeholders in advance through a team meeting or written communiqué. Ensure everyone understands the reasoning behind this shift, the new criteria for status changes, and the overall goal of reducing bias and fostering more accurate reporting. Invite questions and feedback to ensure understanding and buy-in.

(continued)

(continued)

4. **Encourage honest reporting and open discussion:** When stakeholders present their reports, encourage them to provide evidence to justify their status shifts. This approach should stimulate more transparent dialogue about real challenges and progress, rather than a simple green light check-in. Facilitate a culture where discussing red and amber status components are welcomed as opportunities for improvement, not as signs of failure. Perhaps you can even celebrate shifts.

5. **Provide support:** To help your team adjust to this new system, offer your support. This might be in the form of additional resources to help meet criteria for status shifts, or simply being available for advice and guidance as they navigate this new approach. This is also an excellent opportunity to collect feedback.

6. **Review and adapt:** After a few reporting cycles, gather feedback on this new system. Are you seeing more accurate reporting? Are watermelon dashboards less prevalent? Adjust the approach as necessary, taking into account lessons learned and feedback received. If you see good results, try scaling up the pilot with other teams.

The benefits of adopting this "shifting the burden of proof" approach are multifold. Primarily, it serves as a debiasing mechanism, promoting objectivity and discouraging overoptimistic reporting. Furthermore, it catalyzes more productive and solution-oriented dialogue between the steering committee and change project teams during meetings, as discussions become focused on proving progress and addressing hurdles. It might take up a little more time than sprinting through all-green dashboards, but has the potential to transform status update meetings from simple reporting sessions to collaborative, problem-solving platforms.

Applying Scientific Rigor: A/B Testing Your Change Initiatives

Even with unlimited access to high-fidelity data, state-of-the-art analytical tools, and advanced measurement instruments, managing substantial change in an organization can still be challenging due to inevitable biases and other obscuring factors. While such biases may not be that big a deal for smaller change initiatives, it's wise to limit their impact as much as possible when dealing with significant, pilot-tested organizational change initiatives. Interestingly, we can borrow a helpful tool from the scientific method to mitigate these biases, called **A/B testing**.

> A/B testing enables you to compare different approaches side by side and choose the most effective one.

Science offers us various strategies to evaluate the effectiveness of interventions, each with their own strengths and limitations.[3] On one side of the spectrum, we have opinion surveys similar to the NPS, and on the other, we have randomized control trials (RCTs)—the gold standard of experimentation. Imagine RCTs as a balanced coin toss; participants are randomly assigned to an experiment group or a control group. The experimental group experiences the proposed changes, while the control group carries on with the status quo. All other variables are kept the same (as much as possible).

By observing the outcomes of both groups and comparing them, we can confidently tell whether the changes caused any noticeable differences. Why is this important? Well, this random assignment helps to eliminate any bias, ensuring you get untainted and reliable results. However, while RCTs are rigorous, they can be resource-intensive, requiring substantial time, knowledge, and resources to conduct correctly, making them a tough fit for rapidly changing organizations. Here's where the quasi-experimental design comes into play—it's a method that strikes a balance between feasibility and robustness, making it a solid choice for change managers.

Quasi-experimental studies involve observing the effects of an intervention on a group and comparing it to a similar group without the intervention. However, unlike RCTs, these studies do not involve randomization, making them more similar to the method of A/B testing, which has been adapted from scientific experimentation into fields such as conversion optimization and user experience design.

A/B testing is often used to compare two versions of a web page or a product feature. In the context of organizational change, this methodology proves highly beneficial as well. Let's take the example of a large company planning a significant shift in their working approach—say, transitioning from a traditional in-office setup to a remote-first culture. The organization could systematically A/B test this new way of working across different departments or divisions, thereby controlling for as many external factors as possible. This approach helps to isolate the effects of the proposed changes and provides the opportunity to optimize based on the gained insights before scaling it across a bigger part of or the entire organization.

However, we have to recognize that A/B testing, much like quasi-experimental design, has its limitations in a complex organizational context. Unlike a controlled lab environment, where scientists can isolate variables, real-world settings are full of uncontrollable factors that can influence the outcome, like a sudden viral cat video that takes over the office chat. Also, unlike RCTs, departmental divisions for A/B testing can't be randomized. But here's the silver lining: perfect scientific rigor isn't the goal here. Instead, your aim is to glean valuable insights about the impact of the proposed changes and understand their nuances across different departments and stakeholder groups.

As you A/B test your change initiatives, combining both hard and soft metrics can aid in assessing the intervention's effectiveness across different departments. Hard metrics could include quantifiable measures like productivity levels or customer satisfaction scores. In contrast, soft metrics could focus on aspects like employee feedback, team collaboration levels, or overall morale. A/B testing helps identify which metrics are most influenced by the change, providing valuable data to guide the broader rollout. The following behavioral break goes over this process step-by-step.

Behavioral Break: A/B Testing Change Intervention

1. **Identify the change initiative:** The first step is to clearly define the change you want to test. It could be a shift in work culture, introduction of new technology, or an overhaul of organizational processes. For example, a company might want to transition from a traditional office setting to a remote-first work culture.

2. **Form a hypothesis:** Before you start gathering data, formulate a clear hypothesis that outlines your expectations. For example: *We expect a remote-first culture to increase productivity.* This hypothesis forms the basis of your A/B test and helps you define clear success metrics.

3. **Determine the A/B groups:** Divide your organization into two groups. One will be your "A" group (control group) that continues with the status quo, and the other will be your "B" group (experimental group) that experiences the proposed changes. It's important to note that these groups should be as similar as possible in terms of size, function, and demographics.

4. **Define your metrics:** Identify both hard and soft metrics that will measure the effectiveness of the change. Hard metrics could be productivity levels, error rates, or customer satisfaction scores, while soft metrics could include employee feedback, team collaboration levels, or overall morale.

5. **Implement the change:** Apply the proposed changes to the "B" group while the "A" group continues with the existing ways of working. Ensure that the intervention is the only variable changing for the "B" group during the testing period.

6. **Collect data:** Gather data based on the predefined metrics over a set period. Remember, it's important to

(continued)

(continued)

collect data from both groups over the same time period to ensure comparability.

7. **Analyze results:** After the testing period, analyze the data. Look for significant differences between the two groups in terms of your defined metrics. Did productivity increase in the "B" group? Was there a boost in employee morale or customer satisfaction scores?

8. **Draw conclusions:** Based on the results, infer if the implemented change had a positive, negative, or neutral impact by comparing it to your initial hypothesis. Can your hypothesis be rejected or validated?

9. **Refine your change initiative:** If the change initiative was successful, consider refining it based on the feedback and data obtained and start planning for a wider rollout. If the initiative was not successful, use the insights gathered to understand why and make necessary adjustments.

The duration of A/B testing can range from a few weeks to several months, depending on the nature of the change, the metrics used, and organizational factors. Short-term changes and hard metrics might warrant shorter periods (two to four weeks), while long-term changes and soft metrics might require several months. The size and complexity of the organization can also affect the testing duration. Ensure that the period allows sufficient time to accurately assess the impact of the change initiative.

In a nutshell, using a simplified A/B testing approach for significant change initiatives offers a practical and systematic way to test, measure, and refine your strategies. Remember, perfect scientific rigor isn't the goal here. Instead, aim to gain high-quality insights about the impact of the proposed changes and understand their nuances across different departments and stakeholder groups, before going full scale.

Conclusion

This chapter tackled recurring complexities and challenges of measuring change, a practice that doesn't always get the attention it deserves due to the many other urgencies inherent in organizational change. However, if you fail to properly measure the impact of what you are changing, it becomes near impossible to drive lasting change. You've made new additions to your evidence-based toolkit, including a broad set of measurement instruments that help you assess the full impact of change initiatives, prioritizing actual behavioral change over other, more subjective measures. For example, by A/B testing change initiatives, you can gain a more nuanced understanding of what works and what doesn't.

With the capabilities to measure and evaluate the effectiveness of change initiatives in place, you can take the next step—converting these insights into learning experiences. In the upcoming chapter, we explore the role of learning and development in change management.

10

Learning and Development

LEARNING AND DEVELOPMENT (L&D) is one of those areas that different people view very, very differently. Some seize every opportunity to have their organization invest in their professional development and career. Others think of most training days or programs as mandatory sessions they have to attend in order to further the organization's goal. Still others are more concerned with the social and fun aspect of training than the developmental side. As you probably know, there is a lot that organizations can do to shape the L&D experience and learning culture one way or another, but both in our experience with clients and through the interviews, we keep seeing how this topic has a lot of complexity beneath the surface.

What Is L&D?

Learning and development (L&D) broadly refers to the strategic function in an organization focused on the continual growth and improvement of the skills, abilities, and knowledge of employees. It encompasses a range of activities, tools, and strategies used to promote learning, professional development, and skill enhancement among staff. L&D

programs can include on-the-job training, online courses, workshops, coaching, mentorship, and more. The aim of L&D is to align employee growth with the organization's goals, fostering a culture of continuous learning, enhancing performance, and ultimately driving business success. For change managers, understanding the principles of L&D can help shape effective change strategies. By designing L&D initiatives that align with the objectives of the change process, change managers can ensure that employees are prepared for and capable of adopting new ways of working.

At most large organizations, there are usually dozens or even hundreds of simultaneously active L&D programs that offer a variety of opportunities to develop skills and know-how. Some are relevant to many roles, while others are specialized to specific job functions, business units, levels of seniority, or even regions. There may also be leadership or talent development programs, technical skill training, compliance training, or soft skills development courses. More organizations are also offering some kind of continuous learning programs to their employees, where they can choose courses based on their own interests and career goals, often in the form of an online learning platform such as LinkedIn Learning.

As you can imagine, the number of active L&D programs can vary widely across organizations because they depend on the organization's size, industry, strategic objectives, complexity, and commitment to employee development. Still, quantity matters less than quality. It's more important to ensure that each program is relevant and aligned with individual and organizational goals than it is to offer a broad range of just-in-case training programs. It also pays off to learn more about the impact of your L&D programs. If there is a clear impact, you can double down on what works. If the impact is lower than expected, you get the opportunity to rethink how L&D can add more value. Either way, it clearly moves you forward.

Let's explore one challenge before deep-diving into a beautiful case from one of our interviews. As you know, we asked most interviewees how they would like to leverage behavioral science for their organization. After behavioral change, L&D was the most common answer.

Consider the words of Raymond van Hattem, HR director at Pro-Rail, a Dutch government organization responsible for the maintenance and extension of the national railway network infrastructure, the allocation of rail capacity, and controlling rail traffic: "How do people learn? How do they develop? What do they need to grow more? We implemented three big L&D programs where people can freely spend their L&D budget but we found lots of people don't spend it. Why?" Usually this was followed up or preceded by a conversation about employee engagement because the topics are deeply intertwined. So what can an organization do to keep their people engaged and what role can L&D play here? Let's consider the answers to those questions through a use case.

The L&D Journey of dsm-firmenich

The Dutch company DSM (now known as dsm-firmenich after a recent merger) is challenging conventional wisdom to solve this exact issue. We sat down with their VP of learning and development, Marco Mullers, who shared their insightful and fascinating behavioral business tale to revitalize their learning culture. Despite having a solid L&D strategy and a comprehensive catalog of learning resources, DSM wasn't making significant progress in terms of fostering a culture of continuous learning. In contrast to many organizations, they were actually measuring the effectiveness of their L&D efforts and found year after year that the actual impact of L&D efforts was alarmingly low. This called for a transformation in the way they approached learning, spearheaded by the newly brought-in Mullers.

Combining their research insights with a thorough SWOT (a strategic analysis tool that evaluates strengths, weaknesses, opportunities, and threats related to a project or organization) and impact analysis, Mullers's team identified three main problems: learner engagement was dismally low with their L&D content often going unused, the L&D team wasn't delivering what the business needed in a timely manner, and employees' (perceived) readiness for the future was lagging behind that of competitors. Put bluntly, they found that L&D was—as in many organizations—underutilized, too slow to react, and often irrelevant. One insight they gained from this was that the biggest challenge was not the quality of the L&D content but making sure people actually used it! This led them to thinking about how to make learning fun. Drawing an analogy with Apple's successful marketing tactics, Mullers commented, "If Apple launches a new iPhone, they don't just put it on the website and wait for people to come and get it." He saw clearly that the way L&D was branded within the company, its promotion strategy, and the incentives offered to the employees were all out of sync with the modern dynamics of learning. But in his view, learning could be both extremely valuable and fun!

So they resolved to take a different route and change their approach to L&D. The first step was to increase engagement, and Mullers recognized that learning should be something employees intrinsically want, not something pushed top-down. The focus was taken off promoting specific learning content that served the organization and was redirected to promoting the inherent fun in learning itself. A shift in language was made around L&D and they even hired a marketing company to rebrand L&D within the company. Their consciously warm and quirky catchphrases, such as "learning makes your heart happy and soul sing" and "learn to love to learn together," became a strategic element in sparking an interest in learning.

Complementary to their L&D offering on core business competencies, they subscribed to LinkedIn's learning platform, which introduced a large library of original and fun learning content ranging from professional development topics all the way to drumming, photography, and cooking. They still emailed people to encourage learning but they only promoted these fun courses intending to foster a love for learning.

When they looked into how people were using the learning library, the results were enlightening. Despite promoting fun, nonbusiness topics, 90% of what employees chose to learn was connected to DSM's core competencies! The strategy won them a LinkedIn award for talent, but much more importantly, their activation rate skyrocketed and, as people had fun with learning, their learning agility grew.

Mullers's new strategy also targeted the issues of slow responses and employees' future readiness. His team stopped building expensive, large-scale L&D programs and instead started to think of themselves more as facilitators of learning. They provide tools, platforms, and support to the business units, allowing them to take the lead in designing their own learning modules. Instead of conducting one lengthy *Learning Needs Analysis* once a year (common practice in L&D 101),

Mullers and his team started measuring learning needs briefly and constantly, tracking search keywords, identifying the roles hardest to fill, and assessing capability needs throughout the year.

An example of this strategy in action was when the CEOs of DSM and Firmenich announced the big reorganization. Within hours of the announcement, the L&D team had assembled two lean learning pages on SharePoint, one for leaders and one for employees, offering content on dealing with and leading this change. This strategy, which they refer to as **dynamic skill responding**, valued timely and relevant content over polished, lengthy courses. It served as a lifeline amid the stress and uncertainty brought by the reorganization, because it brought some control back to stakeholders. This type of just-in-time learning, although it wasn't nearly as time-intensive as creating an entire L&D program, proved to be among the most engaging learning opportunities for their employees. The point is that having it when people need it proved much more important than having it perfect at launch. And you can then continue to make it better over time.

Mullers's ongoing journey with DSM's L&D transformation is a powerful testament to the shift needed in modern learning and development strategies. His key takeaway: **As an L&D leader, you cannot afford to think that others learn like you do.** Adaptation to the evolving learning landscape is the key to fostering a vibrant, efficient, and impactful culture of learning in any organization—even if that means crafting 30-second, split-screen educational videos for TikTok to engage your Gen Z employees.

Learning and Development Interventions

Learning and development is a resurfacing theme in organizational change projects. To make the move from current to future state, chances are high that at least some stakeholder groups have to gain knowledge, develop skills, or adopt a new mindset. Given this psychological nature of L&D, you can leverage insights from behavioral science to design L&D programs that are more human-centric, targeted, and effective. In this chapter, we explore the role of L&D in driving organizational change, discuss the current approaches to L&D and their limitations, and delve into how behavioral science principles can be applied to enhance L&D initiatives. This chapter covers three evidence-based interventions:

- **Growth Mindset Language:** This intervention involves creating a language toolkit designed to evoke a growth mindset. The toolkit includes language patterns, phrases, and cues that highlight the potential for development and the value of effort. Instead of feedback emphasizing fixed traits, the toolkit encourages growth-oriented feedback. This not only helps employees see their potential but also reshapes organizational communication to promote continuous learning and improvement.
- **Go-to-Gemba:** This intervention promotes first-hand learning by encouraging stakeholders to visit *gemba*—the places in other teams/departments where actual work occurs. It provides insights into different roles, processes, and the impact of changes, fostering empathy, enhanced communication, and shared learning.
- **Developmental KPIs:** Incorporating developmental key performance indicators (KPIs) offers a balanced focus between performance and continuous learning. While traditional performance metrics remain important, incorporating developmental KPIs—such as the percentage of employees attending upskilling workshops or average time spent on personal development—challenges biases that place disproportionate emphasis on results. This shift encourages a culture that values the learning journey and fosters an environment of continuous personal and professional development.

The Importance of L&D in Change Management

L&D might not be the most upstream change area but it is still at the heart of successful organizational change management. When executed well, L&D programs empower employees to embrace new processes, technologies, and roles, ultimately enabling organizations to achieve their strategic objectives and drive long-term growth. Apart from this long-term value, it can also be an excellent tool for a variety of short-term benefits, ranging from speeding up adoption to facilitating two-way communication by providing a space for discussions about the change to clarify doubts and address concerns.

There is also a semblance of yin-yang in the relation between L&D and OCM. Organizational change is not a one-time event but a continuous process that requires a consistent commitment to improving L&D efforts. Change initiatives are also often the sprouts out of which L&D initiatives can bloom. L&D, in turn, is the catalyst that enables individuals and teams to acquire the knowledge, skills, and competencies necessary to navigate the complexities of change. By fostering a learning culture and investing in employee development, organizations can increase engagement, boost morale, and reduce the resistance that often accompanies change initiatives.

Michiel van Meer, chief people officer at Aon Nederland & ASC EMEA, underlines the necessity of integrating change management as a standard part of L&D programs, especially for leaders. Leaders are constantly juggling scarce resources, tight budgets, and stringent deadlines. This necessitates not just effective management, but also resilience in the face of setbacks, a curiosity to explore new solutions, and the courage to go beyond your comfort zone. Thus, for van Meer, change management and leadership development are inseparable, and L&D programs must ensure the development of these competencies.

Perhaps one of the best descriptions of why L&D is so important for any organization that aims to thrive in the long term came from someone who—we assume—has not spent much time thinking about L&D in organizations, Albert Einstein, who said, "Problems cannot be solved with the same mindset that created them." Whether problems are caused by suboptimal decisions from leaders, hardly observable destructive habits among groups of employees, or even the organizational structure and systems, those problems can only be solved by evolving our behaviors. **Root cause analysis** can help you identify which things (behaviors, decision-making processes, structures, or processes) deserve attention, which empowers you to choose the appropriate forms of learning for the right audience. It could be (a combination of) leadership development and talent development, or it might need more general or specific L&D programs that address the root cause.

Let's illustrate this in an area where it is clearly observable: diversity, equity, and inclusion (DEI). Most organizations, large and small, are still in the early stages of identifying their challenges, strategy, and suitable forms of learning. Once you know where to focus first (e.g., cultural, gender, or neurodiversity, with the latter emphasizing that conditions like autism, ADHD, and dyslexia are not disorders but rather different forms of cognitive functioning that have their own strengths and challenges), you would ideally experiment with some approaches to find the one (or few) that work best for your unique organizational culture. It's worth noting how one of our clients developed their L&D strategy for DEI. They invited a variety of organizations to develop a DEI training based on their unique expertise, ranging from art- and game-based to our evidence-based approach. Their employees could then choose which of the hosted trainings appealed most to them and subsequently provide their feedback to the L&D team. This then enabled them to make informed decisions about how to design their strategy while selecting suppliers that connect well with their people and culture.

L&D initiatives act as a bridge, helping employees move from familiar territory to new landscapes introduced by change. They equip employees with the necessary tools, techniques, and know-how to adapt to new processes, systems, and roles. Whether they are effective in doing so depends heavily on their relevance and applicability, which is why a strategic approach to L&D has to take into account the evolving dynamics of the workplace. Great L&D aligns current and future organizational needs with the learning goals and opportunities of its employees.

Let's look at it through the lens of the COM-B model you might be familiar with now. If the organization's interests heavily outweigh the employees' interests, motivation and engagement are likely to dwindle, reducing the effectiveness of any L&D program, even with easy access (Capability) and repeated requests (Opportunity). But when aligned with their own goals/purpose, people can be highly motivated to learn and develop mindsets, skills, and capabilities that help the organization and themselves thrive. Effective L&D programs stimulate intellectual curiosity, foster skill acquisition, and promote a sense of personal and professional growth. This usually leads to increased employee engagement, morale, and buy-in during the change process.

Employees who feel valued and invested in are more likely to embrace change, making the change process smoother and more effective.

Change is often met with apprehension and resistance, as it disrupts the familiar and propels us into the unknown, at least as far as our brains are concerned. By focusing on the development of key skills and mindsets, L&D can help foster resilience in the workforce. Resilient employees are better equipped to navigate the turbulent waters of change, remain productive amid uncertainty, and adapt to new realities. Thus, L&D initiatives that prioritize resilience not only enable individuals to thrive during periods of change, but also contribute to the long-term success and agility of the organization. We get into the how later.

Current Approaches to L&D

When you look at most L&D programs, they are underpinned by a mixture of traditional and modern methods. Traditional methods, such as classroom training, seminars, workshops, and on-the-job training, continue to hold their ground. These methods are proven, relatively cost-effective, and accessible to various learning styles. Viewing L&D through a behavioral science lens reveals several opportunities for improvement that allow organizations to reframe change as an opportunity for learning and skill development, instead of merely a challenge to navigate.

Currently, many organizations rely on one-off training programs. Though they often receive high satisfaction ratings or NPS (think back to the previous chapter), their effectiveness in ensuring long-term learning and skill development is not necessarily guaranteed. This raises questions about the metrics used to gauge L&D success: Is an enjoyable training experience an accurate measure of learning?

On the contrary, a more effective approach could be *spaced learning*—an approach that spaces out training over time. This form of learning uses the spacing effect, a cognitive bias that demonstrates that learning is more effective when spaced out instead of crammed into one session. Capitalizing on the spacing effect can help L&D interventions shine brighter for longer, enabling not just immediate satisfaction but sustained knowledge growth. Consistency is more important than intensity. Thirty minutes of learning every day leads to much better results than a single, three-hour learning sprint every week. Knowledge, like money, can compound, making one more and more aware of the world in which they live.

Moreover, organizations often operate on a reactive basis, offering generic training programs that aim to prepare employees for all eventualities, rather than tailoring learning to the specific and immediate needs of their roles. This just-in-case approach to learning often results in siloed knowledge, which can hinder cross-departmental collaboration and slow down the overall speed of employee development. Instead, a just-in-time learning approach emphasizes delivering relevant knowledge when it's most needed. That this could prove more effective is something we've seen in the dsm-firmenich case.

Lastly, many organizations maintain a predominantly results-focused mindset, emphasizing immediate results over long-term learning, which can discourage employees from fully engaging with L&D opportunities. Providing the right incentives that promote a learning-focused culture can help foster an environment conducive to sustained employee development. Again, an excellent example is the dsm-firmenich case, where the activation rate of employees skyrocketed when their learning library was expanded beyond the usual technical and business topics. Making learning fun is a worthy mission to pursue, not only because it makes your organization more human-centric but also because it incentivizes learning and professional development!

Having acknowledged the limitations with traditional approaches to L&D in the face of organizational change, it's important to recognize these as opportunities rather than impasses. These challenges bring us to the juncture where we introduce a new perspective on enhancing L&D through a behavior-driven approach. It's worth clarifying that the goal here is not a total reinvention of your L&D initiatives. As in the other chapters, we aim to augment your existing programs with targeted interventions. These interventions concentrate on prioritizing, habitualizing, and systemizing learning and development during organizational changes, which will encourage employees to seize the opportunity to learn and grow amid change.

On Biases in Learning and Development

When it comes to L&D, especially in the face of organizational change, there are various cognitive biases that can affect both the attitude toward learning in times of change and the learning process itself. Some examples of biases related to L&D are:

- **Spacing Effect:** This bias highlights how learning is more effective when study or training sessions are spaced out over time. In the context of employee development, it suggests that continuous, spaced learning often leads to better retention and application of new knowledge and skills. As such, it could be beneficial to design learning and development initiatives that are not one-off events but rather spaced over a longer period.
- **Outcome Bias:** This is the tendency to judge a decision based on its outcome rather than the quality of the decision at the time it was made. When leaders overly focus on the outcome of change initiatives, they may inadvertently impede learning by prioritizing results over the development of their employees.
- **Availability Heuristic:** This heuristic is our natural inclination to rely on immediate information. In siloed organizations, employees may fail to learn and innovate because they only work with what is readily available within their own silos. This restricts their ability to draw from a broader knowledge base.
- **Confirmation Bias:** This is our tendency to search for, interpret, and remember information in a way that confirms our preexisting beliefs or hypotheses. Within organizational silos, confirmation bias can cause stakeholders to become convinced that their way is the best, thereby discouraging them from considering broader perspectives that could help them learn new approaches or ideas.

Now that you're introduced to some of the relevant biases, let's go over some evidence-based interventions that are designed to complement your current L&D strategies. By embedding these in your existing L&D approaches, you can blend change management and L&D in a way that is guided by behavioral science. This approach aims to empower employees to thrive within an evolving workplace, leveraging change as a springboard for development.

Enhancing Learning Agility Amid Change with a Growth Mindset

Let's start by exploring an approach that can help your organization embrace experimenting, making mistakes, and learning in the face of change: cultivating a growth mindset, pioneered by Stanford psychologist Carol Dweck. Beginning her research in this area in the 1970s,[1] Dweck popularized the concept of a **growth mindset**—the belief that abilities can be developed over time—in her book *Mindset: The New Psychology of Success*.[2] Her studies suggest that with perseverance, dedication, and effective strategies, individuals can nurture and enhance their capabilities. Put simply, if you believe growth through effort is possible, it becomes achievable. A growth mindset contrasts with a fixed mindset, where individuals perceive abilities as innate and unchangeable traits. If you believe you cannot grow through effort, why try?

Before we move on, it's important to note that the concept of growth mindset has become a subject of debate in the scientific community at the time of writing this book. On one hand, Dweck's research and that of her contemporaries has suggested its significant impact on learning and performance. However, other studies contradict these findings, presenting no clear evidence of growth mindset's effectiveness.[3] This discrepancy in research results poses a challenge in validating and applying the concept in various settings.

It's important to consider these results with some nuance. It's typical for isolated applied behavioral science interventions, such as growth mindset and nudging (as discussed in Chapter 2), to have a small to moderate effect. This is to be expected given the complexities of human behavior, especially when applied in real-world settings like teams, organizations, and societies. Such environments are far more dynamic and unpredictable than the controlled setting of a lab.

Practitioners should never expect a "silver bullet" intervention strategy when it comes to changing behavior. In line with the goal of this book's philosophy, the goal should be to experiment with a broad spectrum of interventions and assess whether their collective effect contributes meaningfully to tackling real-world challenges.

Concerns regarding the replication of growth mindset's effects are not unique and are common in psychology and behavioral science. For instance, a similar debate arose in 2022 about the effectiveness of nudging.[4] When faced with such issues, it's crucial to approach with caution, but we should also avoid disregarding its potential practical value entirely. After all, it's not like nudge units all over the world were disbanded after some disappointing findings.

We learned about the many aspects of the growth mindset and their versatility in practice firsthand, as part of our collaboration with a leading energy provider. We worked to integrate a growth mindset within their organization to foster resilience amid disruptive changes brought about by the energy transition. One primary challenge was the organization's result-driven culture, which often hindered learning agility and innovation. Misaligned KPIs further diluted focus, and the prevailing "busy equals good" mindset promoted inflexibility.

In response to these challenges, we proposed an intervention that focused on fostering a growth mindset across the organization. We started by defining and operationalizing a growth mindset per business unit, promoting this shared belief as part of every job description and performance evaluation. Furthermore, we encouraged the inclusion of a growth mindset in the hiring process, ensuring new hires are aligned with the organization's focus on continuous learning and development.

The implementation of a growth mindset required strong leadership buy-in and clear top-down communication about its strategic importance. However, it also necessitated grassroots adoption, with teams and team managers embodying the growth mindset in day-to-day behaviors. By nurturing this mindset at all levels, the organization could equip itself better for the continuous change the energy transition would bring. (See Figure 10.1.)

In the scenario of organizational transformation, a growth mindset can be an important, pivotal asset. It prepares employees to adapt to novel roles, acquire new skills, collaborate across various teams, and

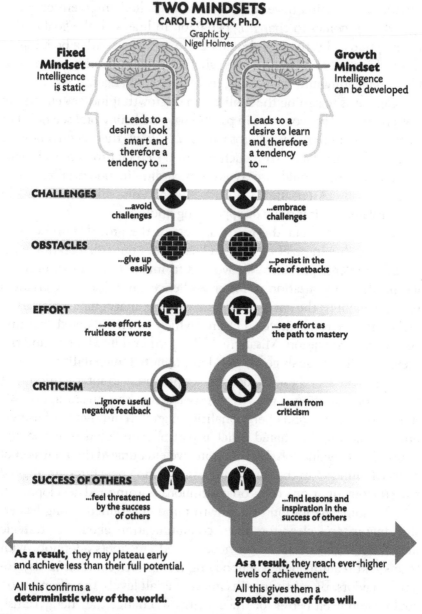

Figure 10.1   Growth mindset versus fixed mindset.

foster innovation—all of which are vital for navigating and thriving amid change. Change facilitators and managers can harness this mindset to cultivate an environment where learning is perceived as a journey, errors are viewed as opportunities for learning, and resilience is fostered in the face of adversity.

Look at Microsoft, for example, a beacon of cultural change, leveraging the power of a growth mindset on an organizational scale. It all started with CEO Satya Nadella's vision to pivot from a culture of "know-it-alls" to "learn-it-alls," stirring a wave of continuous learning across the tech giant.[5] The company dived deep, engaging leaders to champion a growth mindset, initiating awareness campaigns and developing systems to monitor this mindset's adoption. They designed interactive modules, conversations guides, and even celebrated growth-mindset oriented triumphs. Moreover, they interwove the principles of the growth mindset into their HR processes, and in talent reviews and succession planning.

As you see, the spectrum of growth mindset interventions is vast. Whole books can be written on how organizations can harness their potential. However, we're going to start with a simple intervention aimed at creating a growth mindset language toolkit that supports learning amid change. A growth mindset language toolkit consists of language patterns, phrases, and cues designed to evoke a growth mindset. For example, instead of using static feedback like "You're a natural," the toolkit encourages dynamic feedback such as "You're a great learner." It emphasizes phrases that highlight the potential for development and the value of effort.

Implementing this toolkit involves integrating growth mindset language into various aspects of organizational communication. For instance, during feedback sessions, instead of focusing on fixed traits, the toolkit encourages feedback that emphasizes efforts, strategies, and growth potential. Rather than saying, "You're not good at this," a growth-oriented feedback approach would be to say, "You haven't mastered this yet." These examples demonstrate how a growth mindset language can reshape the way feedback is delivered, promoting a belief in the capacity for growth and improvement.

Behavioral Break: Growth Mindset Language Intervention

1. **Create a customized language toolkit:** Begin by identifying language patterns, phrases, and cues that encourage a growth mindset, such as emphasizing the potential for development, an effort's value, and abilities' fluidity. Your toolkit should match the unique vocabulary and conversation style of your organization. It should not feel artificial or forced, and phrases like "You're growing in this area," or "Your efforts are paying off," should come off as genuine and organic. We saw an example of growth mindset language in Marco Mullers's story earlier in this chapter as well: "learn to love to learn together."

2. **Promote constructive feedback:** Shift feedback toward highlighting efforts, strategies, and growth potential rather than fixed traits. For instance, rather than saying, "You're not good at this," try a growth-oriented approach such as, "I can see you're working hard on this, and with continued effort and the right strategies, your skills will improve."

3. **Incorporate language toolkit into daily conversations:** Encourage the adoption of growth-oriented words such as "yet," "learn," and "grow" in day-to-day exchanges. All employees should be encouraged to embrace this shift in language, but in a way that feels natural and authentic to their and the organization's communication style.

4. **Foster open conversations:** Cultivate an environment that encourages open discussions about the growth mindset, reinforcing the desired language patterns. Create spaces like workshops, team meetings, or online platforms to facilitate these discussions, share examples, and reinforce growth mindset language.

> **5. Expand the toolkit's reach:** Get leadership buy-in to model growth mindset language in their communications. Integrate the language toolkit into HR processes and training programs to ensure a wider reach. Recognize and celebrate instances where growth language leads to learning and improvement.

It is important to note that the language we use significantly shapes our perspective and our actions. Small modifications in our vocabulary, like those facilitated by a growth mindset language toolkit, can cause vast improvements in learning agility across an organization when adopted at scale. For the successful evaluation and application of this intervention, it is smart to start where communication plays a pivotal role. Feedback sessions, team meetings, training workshops, or leadership communications are ideal places to initiate. Carefully observe and evaluate how the new language patterns affect discussions, decision-making, and employees' openness to learning and change.

However, these changes must be implemented with subtlety and tact. A forced change in vocabulary may come across as artificial and could potentially throw off employees. The change must be integrated thoughtfully into the organization's natural style of communication. Finally, growth mindset language's success depends on its adoption by role models in the organization. When leaders and influencers within the company use growth mindset language, it provides a powerful example for others. (To help stakeholders make a habit of using the growth mindset language, check out the behavioral break on if-then plans in Chapter 7.)

Going to the Gemba

During periods of organizational change, learning and development can serve as pivotal drivers for success. However, two common barriers often impede their integration: organizational silos and a lack of empathy. Silos manifest as isolated departments or groups, each with their unique cultures, processes, and methods, which often inhibit the free flow of knowledge and communication throughout the organization.

Similarly, empathy—or rather the lack thereof—can significantly impact the success of organizational change. Empathy is the ability to understand and share the feelings of others. In the context of change, a lack of empathy can make it difficult for stakeholders to understand and appreciate what their colleagues in other departments are experiencing. Without this mutual understanding, opportunities for collective learning and innovation may go unnoticed.

Consider an HR transformation as an example. HR staff might be learning to work with a new human resource management system, while team leads are adapting to a new way of evaluating and rewarding their team members. Each group is engaged in a different aspect of the change, and yet they remain unaware of the others' experiences, creating a missed opportunity for shared learning and collective innovation.

Several cognitive biases often underpin these challenges. **Availability heuristic** can cause stakeholders to focus disproportionately on information readily available in their department, thus overlooking valuable insights from other parts of the organization. **Confirmation bias** can lead to stakeholders seeking information that confirms their preexisting views or practices, discouraging exploration and adoption of innovative practices from elsewhere in the organization.

To be able to promote learning and development during organizational changes, teams and departments need to work cross-departmentally to actually be able to learn something from each other; it's essential to actively remove any barriers to make this happen. One way to do this is by adopting the Go-to-Gemba strategy. The term *gemba* is a Japanese concept meaning "the actual place" where value is created—whether that is the factory floor, office space, or sales desk.

Originally derived from Lean manufacturing and developed by Taiichi Ohno,[6] widely considered as the father of the Toyota Production System, the Go-to-Gemba strategy encourages managers, leaders, and employees to step out of their comfort zones and immerse themselves in the places where work gets done. In the context of change management, Go-to-Gemba provides an invaluable tool for fostering open communication, breaking down silos, and nurturing an environment conducive to shared learning and growth through empathy. Jim Womack discusses this in detail in his work *Gemba Walks*.[7]

By "going to the Gemba," all stakeholders can gain firsthand insight into the processes, challenges, and opportunities in different areas of the organization. They witness the impact of changes, understand the nuances that reports might not capture, and directly engage with those experiencing the change.

Implementing a Go-to-Gemba approach across multiple levels of the organization encourages a culture of empathy, understanding, and shared learning. Seeing firsthand the effects of change on their colleagues in different departments fosters empathy, which in turn can help to dismantle organizational silos, enhance communication, and drive innovation.

The benefits of this approach extend beyond change implementation. It fosters a culture of continuous learning, where every team and department is seen as a source of knowledge and innovation. It instills an environment where learning and development are not just tied to individual or departmental growth, but are seen as integral to the overall success of the organization. In essence, Go-to-Gemba can nurture an organization-wide learning mindset, a vital attribute during significant periods of change. However, since it's quite an unusual approach, it can be tough to implement, especially the first time. These are the steps you can take to start experimenting.

Behavioral Break: Go-to-Gemba Intervention

1. **Set the scene for empathy:** Highlight the need for empathy in facilitating effective organizational change. Bring awareness to existing silos and explain how these hinder innovation and shared learning.

2. **Introduce Go-to-Gemba:** Introduce the concept of Go-to-Gemba as a tool to bridge the silos, foster understanding, increase empathy, and build connections. Explain how it works in the context of change management.

(continued)

(*continued*)

3. **Choose an issue or process:** Identify a process or issue that's central to the ongoing organizational change, which will benefit from a Go-to-Gemba visit. It should be a process that affects multiple departments or a problem area that's been particularly challenging.

4. **Organize a cross-functional team:** Assemble a diverse team composed of stakeholders from various departments. This cross-functional team should ideally include people directly involved in the chosen issue or process, as well as those indirectly affected by it.

5. **Go to the Gemba:** Take the team to the place where the work is done. The goal is to observe the process or issue firsthand, understand the challenges, and explore potential solutions. Encourage the team to ask questions, engage with the work, and empathize with the people doing it. Many templates are available that can provide structure.

   For example: During a company-wide digital transformation, the marketing department struggles to adopt the new data analytics tool. Organizing a Gemba visit, the IT department shares their knowledge of the tool while the marketing team provides insight into their daily tasks and challenges. This collaboration fosters mutual understanding, resulting in more efficient problem-solving and tool usage.

6. **Reflect and ideate:** Following the visit, hold a reflection session for the team to discuss observations and insights, leading to a brainstorming on potential improvements or solutions.

7. **Implement and evaluate:** Put the devised solutions into action and observe their effects over time. Monitor process improvements, interdepartmental understanding, and signs of enhanced empathy.

> **8. Repeat:** After experiencing the benefits, plan for more Go-to-Gemba interventions. This practice helps embed continuous learning into the organizational culture, fostering adaptability and resilience during change.

Applying Go-to-Gembas at scale in large organizations requires strategic planning. Aimed at fostering empathy, collaboration, and innovation, these interventions should be integral to the organizational change journey, not one-off events. To successfully implement them, consider structuring a program with regular schedules, clear objectives, and inclusive participation rules. Embed this program within your change management strategy, linking it to your overarching goals. Go-to-Gembas are more than just problem-solving exercises; they facilitate learning, empathy, and the bridging of organizational silos. Therefore, encourage participants to understand and appreciate the perspectives of their colleagues in different departments.

Integrating Developmental KPIs: A Learning-Driven Approach

In considering how best to facilitate learning and development, leadership commitment is a significant factor. If L&D is not prioritized and incentivized across the organization, employees may find themselves too caught up in a whirlwind of immediate concerns to invest time in reflection, learning, and growth. As discussed in Chapter 4, lack of prioritization forms a barrier for cultivating the behaviors and habits needed for learning and gets in the way of setting up organizational systems that support these behaviors.

Traditionally, key performance indicators (KPIs) within organizations lean heavily toward outcome-oriented metrics. As long as the job gets done, leadership is satisfied. This approach, however, may not always deliver long-term results, nor is it particularly stimulating for employees to develop themselves in preparation for higher KPIs, especially in today's rapidly evolving work environment. Since the well-being and continuous development of employees play a pivotal role in organizational performance and resilience, let's see which insights we can borrow from behavioral science to move the needle here.

This is where the paradigm shift toward developmental KPIs comes into play. While performance metrics remain essential to clarify required results, a balanced focus on developmental KPIs can create an environment conducive to continuous learning and development. These new KPIs could encompass aspects like "percentage of employees who attended upskilling workshops," "average time spent on personal development activities per week," or "rate of improvement in identified skills over a quarter."

By incorporating developmental KPIs into your organizational strategy, you challenge cognitive biases like the **outcome bias**, which places disproportionate emphasis on results, often neglecting the process, effort, and learning opportunities that accompany it. Balancing performance with developmental KPIs encourages a culture that values the journey as much as the destination and places importance on continuous learning.

We can see this style of KPIs at work at McKinsey, a pioneer in strategic consulting and organizational practices. They champion the integration of developmental KPIs as part of a broader learning and development strategy and advise clients to focus on what they call "learning excellence."[8] This approach measures the impact of L&D initiatives using three key performance indicators—business excellence, learning excellence, and operational excellence, with learning excellence evaluating the effectiveness of L&D interventions in modifying people's behavior and performance. By promoting a balanced approach that includes developmental KPIs, you can foster a culture that values and emphasizes learning and development, as well as business performance.

Although this shift in performance assessments presents challenges, it is necessary to set the stage for a dynamic learning environment in which employees embrace change and use it as an opportunity for growth. The following behavioral break shows what development KPIs could look like in practice.

Behavioral Break: Developmental KPIs Intervention

1. **Engage stakeholders:** Begin by seeking input from key stakeholders to find out whether integrating developmental KPIs is something they would benefit from. Aim to understand their perspective and needs before attempting to be understood.

2. **Construct the narrative:** Demonstrate the need for the shift toward developmental KPIs in the context of your organization. Leverage data and anecdotal evidence to show the limits of traditional, result-oriented KPIs and how they can lead to burnout, diminished innovation, or stagnation. Reinforce that an emphasis on learning and growth is a competitive advantage. Leverage the evidence-based interventions in Chapter 6 to construct a persuasive narrative.

3. **Secure leadership support:** Engage top management to secure their buy-in. Craft a compelling case on why this shift is beneficial, not just for employee growth, but for the long-term success of the organization. Highlight case studies of companies that have successfully integrated developmental KPIs into their performance management systems, like Google. (Chapter 7 is full of actionable strategies to help you realize this.)

4. **Co-create with HR and leadership:** Collaborate with your HR team and leadership to design suitable developmental KPIs. Ensure these KPIs align with the overall strategic objectives and values of the organization. Integrate these into the existing performance management systems, with clear guidelines on how they will be measured. Remember, the goal is not to completely replace performance KPIs, but to balance them with developmental KPIs.

(continued)

(continued)

5. **Enable managers and team leads:** Managers and team leads play a critical role in driving this change. Conduct workshops to help them understand and embrace these new KPIs. Equip them with the necessary skills and tools to encourage a culture of continuous learning within their teams.

6. **Plan a pilot:** Before a company-wide rollout, consider a pilot implementation to gauge the new KPIs' effectiveness in one team or department. This experimental step underscores the importance of testing and learning.

7. **Communicate and implement:** Announce the new developmental KPIs company-wide. Ensure the communication is clear, emphasizing the importance and benefits of these KPIs. Once communicated, begin implementing the new KPIs into your performance management process.

8. **Monitor and review:** Regularly monitor and review the impact of these new KPIs on individual, team, and organizational performance. Collect feedback from employees at all levels to understand the effectiveness of these KPIs and make necessary adjustments.

9. **Continuously refine:** The work doesn't stop once you've implemented these new KPIs. Continually refine and adjust them as necessary to keep pace with the changing needs of your organization and workforce. Keep the dialogue open and encourage feedback to ensure your developmental KPIs remain relevant, beneficial, and motivating.

Integrating developmental KPIs into your L&D strategy sends a clear signal to your employees: learning and development are not just encouraged—they're essential. It communicates the commitment of the organization to the continuous growth of its people and reinforces that this growth is a valued component of overall performance.

Conclusion

Even though L&D may not be the most immediate change area, it forms the backbone of any successful transformation, especially in the long term. Done well, L&D initiatives empower employees to adopt the novel processes, roles, and technologies that an organizational change might bring. This chapter covered some challenges you might experience when incorporating L&D into organizational change, underlying biases and barriers, and interventions to foster an environment conducive to continuous learning and improvement.

You've learned that when you invest in your people and invest in their learning and development, you can set up your organization to grow and thrive amid change.

Revisiting the underlying framework from Chapter 4 one final time, you can see that actively prioritizing growth mindset is a precondition for L&D in organizational change. Furthermore, getting into the habit of learning from other teams and departments by practicing Go-to-Gemba embeds this priority in behavior. Finally, aligning organizational goals with learning by balancing performance KPIs with developmental KPIs tweaks the systems in such a way that it further reinforces these behaviors.

Conclusion: Toward Behaviorally Informed Organizations

BEHAVIORALLY INFORMED CHANGE management (BICM) is about more than harnessing the insights of behavioral science or applying them to change management. It's about bridging these two fields and moving toward more human-centric organizations. In that spirit, this behavioral business tale is not the end of the journey, but the beginning to transforming how we transform our organizations. It is a quest that motivates thousands of people across the world. How can we truly empower organizations with the value of behavioral science? That is, how can we make organizations more effective and human-centric in an evidence-based way? Nobody knows yet what this looks like in practice, but people are busy chiseling away at the core. One book that does exactly this is *The Behaviorally Informed Organization*,[1] published in 2020. Dilip Soman, whom we had the honor of meeting during our writing process, and Catherine Yeung edited this book, which is filled with real-life case studies and analyses contributed by a broad range of behavioral scientists and business professionals on how behavioral science can and should enrich organizational processes. This book follows the premise that, in the words of Professor Dilip Soman, "while we've made great progress in establishing behavioral economics as a field, we don't have great science on how to implement the science," which it then continues to provide the backbone for. This important work is worth reading for any (future) leader, even if only for the chapter on "Why Organizations That Need to Be Behaviorally Informed Resist It."

Another even more recent attempt is the Behavioral Insights Team's (BIT) manifesto for applying behavioral science led by Michael Hallsworth (discussed in Chapter 2), in which he lays out a roadmap for the future of behavioral insights. The manifesto analyzes the biggest challenges facing this field and offers ten proposals to address them, extending the scope not only to behavioral practitioners but to clients, academics, and funders of research. We found that Hallsworth, whom we also interviewed for this book, has captured the current and ideal relationship between BeSci and organizations in a beautifully illustrative metaphor in his article "Rewiring Organizations for Behavioral Science":[2]

> Think about it this way: how we've historically talked about setting up behavioral science teams is a bit like designating one room in an office building "the nudge room." Perhaps we've redecorated and refurbished it so that more people will go there when they want advice. But if a new CEO comes in and decides they want the room to do something else (like data science), then little will remain.
>
> In contrast, my proposal is more akin to deciding to upgrade the wiring or heating of the building. If behavioral science is baked into the core structures of the organization, perhaps in less prominent ways, then it will continue to produce benefits, regardless of the leadership's decorative preferences.

The ideas in this book build on this movement of creating more behaviorally informed organizations and aim to rewire how organizational change is managed. Given its psychological nature, OCM might be more behaviorally informed than many other organizational areas, but its effectiveness and sustainability can still be significantly improved by embedding it with behavioral science as we found in both our consulting work and interviewing people for this book.

Perhaps more importantly, OCM is the perfect tool and partner to make organizations themselves more behaviorally informed. Every time an organization's change practitioners support business managers in a change initiative, there are at least two opportunities to make the organization more behaviorally informed. One is by sharing BeSci insights and facilitating evidence-based interventions, leading to a more behaviorally informed workforce. The other is by experimenting with directly embedding BeSci principles into organizational processes, thereby making the organization more human-centric.

Professor Soman provided an enlightening analogy to illustrate the potential adoption of behavioral science in organizations, linking it to electricity.[3] He pointed out that electricity took over 40 years for widespread adoption: "We need to leverage behavioral science beyond quick wins and do more than just change messaging." Soman stressed the importance of pursuing a diverse portfolio of initiatives and concluded with a vision where behavioral science, like electricity, becomes integral to the organizational foundation, even if it isn't always consciously acknowledged. In his words, "Success is when you don't need a center of expertise."

This book builds on this movement. We aspire not just to introduce behavioral science into OCM but to help you embed it deep within. The ambition is to make behavioral science intrinsic to an organization's wiring, just as electricity is integral to modern living. With this, we aim to cultivate organizations that are behaviorally informed, not just at the surface but also at their core.

The real work begins now. You are now equipped with a fresh perspective and a broader toolkit. You have gained a wide variety of behavioral insights, evidence-based interventions, and insights from people at the top of their field. The next step is to put this knowledge into action. Through hands-on application and experimentation you can discover how BICM can add value to your organization and, more importantly, to your people.

If you read this entire book and have not yet started experimenting, today is the day.

Notes

Preface

1. Richard H. Thaler and Cass R. Sunstein, *Nudge: Improving Decisions About Health, Wealth, and Happiness* (New Haven, CT: Yale University Press, 2008).
2. Daniel Kahneman, *Thinking, Fast and Slow* (New York: Farrar, Straus and Giroux, 2011).
3. Robert Grossman and Eduardo Salas, "Training Transfer: An Integrative Literature Review," *Human Resource Development Review* 6, no. 3 (September 2007): 263–296.

Introduction

1. Department for Work and Pensions (DWP), "Automatic Enrolment Evaluation Report 2019," 2019.
2. Angelica LaVito and Lauren Feiner, "Facebook Says Apple's iOS Privacy Change Will Cost $10 Billion This Year," CNBC, February 2, 2022, www.cnbc.com/2022/02/02/facebook-says-apple-ios-privacy-change-will-cost-10-billion-this-year.html.

Chapter 1

1. Kurt Lewin, "Field Theory in Social Science: Selected Theoretical Papers," Dorwin Cartwright, ed. (New York: Harpers, 1951).

2. Elisabeth Kübler-Ross, *On Death and Dying* (London: Routledge, 1969).

3. Everett M. Rogers, *Diffusion of Innovations*, 5th ed. (New York: Simon and Schuster, 2003).

4. Robert H. Waterman, Thomas J. Peters, and Julian R. Phillips, "Structure Is Not Organization," *Business Horizons* 23, no. 3 (1980): 14–26.

5. Tessa Basford and Bill Schaninger, "The Four Building Blocks of Change," McKinsey & Company, April 11, 2016, www.mckinsey.com/capabilities/people-and-organizational-performance/our-insights/the-four-building-blocks--of-change.

6. Peter M. Senge, *The Fifth Discipline* (New York: Doubleday/Currency, 1990).

7. William Bridges, *Managing Transitions: Making the Most of Change* (Reading, MA: Addison-Wesley, 1991).

8. Daryl Conner, *Managing at the Speed of Change* (New York: Villard Books, 1993).

9. Homayoun Hatami and Liz Hilton Segel, "What Matters Most? Six Priorities for CEOs in Turbulent Times," McKinsey & Company, November 17, 2022, www.mckinsey.com/capabilities/strategy-and-corporate-finance/our-insights/what-matters-most-six-priorities-for-ceos-in-turbulent-times.

10. John Kotter, "Leading Change," *Harvard Business Review*, March–April 1995.

11. Dean Anderson and Linda Ackerman, *Beyond Change Management* (San Francisco: Jossey-Bass/Pfeiffer, 2001).

12. Gibbons, Paul, *The Science of Organizational Change: How Leaders Set Strategy, Change Behavior, and Create an Agile Culture*, illustrated ed. (Phronesis Media, 2019), 30.

Chapter 2

1. Herbert A. Simon, *Models of Man: Social and Rational* (New York: John Wiley & Sons, 1957).

2. Daniel Kahneman and Amos Tversky, "Prospect Theory: An Analysis of Decision Under Risk," *Econometrica* 47, no. 2 (1979): 263–291.

3. Richard H. Thaler, "Mental Accounting and Consumer Choice," *Marketing Science* 4, no. 3 (1985): 199–214.

4. Richard H. Thaler and Cass R. Sunstein, *Nudge: Improving Decisions About Health, Wealth, and Happiness* (New Haven, CT: Yale University Press, 2008).

5. Daniel Kahneman, *Thinking, Fast and Slow* (New York: Farrar, Straus and Giroux, 2011).

6. Charles T. Munger, "The Psychology of Human Misjudgment," in *Poor Charlie's Almanack: The Wit and Wisdom of Charles T. Munger*, Peter D. Kaufman, ed. (Virginia Beach, VA: Donning Company Publishers, 2005).

7. Michael Hallsworth, "Let's Talk Less About 'Irrationality,'" *Behavioral Scientist*, March 27, 2023, https://behavioralscientist.org/lets-talk-less-about-irrationality/.

8. Michael Hallsworth, "A Manifesto for Applying Behavioural Science," *Nature Human Behaviour* 7, no. 3 (2023): 310–322.

9. Susan Michie, Lou Atkins, and Robert West, *The Behaviour Change Wheel: A Guide to Designing Interventions* (London: Silverback Publishing, 2014).

10. Paul Dolan, Michael Hallsworth, David Halpern, Dominic King, and Ivo Vlaev, *MINDSPACE: Influencing Behaviour Through Public Policy* (London: Institute for Government and Cabinet Office, 2010).

11. Donella H. Meadows, *Thinking in Systems* (White River Junction, VT: Chelsea Green Publishing, 2015).

12. Daniel H. Kim, *Introduction to Systems Thinking*, vol. 16 (Waltham, MA: Pegasus Communications, 1999).

13. Matt Wallaert, "Applied Behavioral Science: A Four-Part Model," Behavioral Design Hub, May 5, 2021, https://medium.com/behavior-design-hub/applied-behavioral-science-a-four-part-model-48acde17b25f.

Chapter 3

1. Tim Creasey, "Enough Is Enough: Tips for Avoiding Change Saturation," Prosci. Accessed August 1, 2023, www.prosci.com/blog/tips-for-avoiding-change-saturation.

2. Joan C. Williams, *Bias Interrupted: Creating Inclusion for Real and for Good* (Harvard Business Publishing, 2021).

3. David L. Cooperrider, and Suresh Srivastva, "Appreciative Inquiry in Organizational Life." In *Research in Organizational Change and Development*, vol. 1, R. Woodman and W. A. Pasmore, eds. (JAI Press, 1987), 129–169.

Chapter 4

1. Isabel B. Myers, *The Myers-Briggs Type Indicator: Manual* (Consulting Psychologists Press, 1962).
2. "Insights Discovery," Insights Group Limited, accessed August 1, 2023, www.insights.com/products/insights-discovery.
3. Lewis R. Goldberg, "The Structure of Phenotypic Personality Traits," *American Psychologist* 48, no. 1 (1993): 26–34.
4. Jeffrey M. Hiatt, *ADKAR: A Model for Change in Business, Government and Our Community* (Loveland, CO: Prosci Learning Center Publications, 2006).
5. R. H. Waterman, T. J. Peters, and J. R. Phillips, "Structure Is Not Organization," *Business Horizons*, 23, no. 3 (1980): 14–26.
6. John Kotter, "Leading Change," *Harvard Business Review*, March–April 1995.
7. Ben Tiggelaar, *De Ladder: Waarom veranderen zo moeilijk is én. . .welke 3 stappen wel werken* (Tyler Roland Press, 2018).

Chapter 5

1. Ilaria Grasso Macola, "Berlin Brandenburg Airport: A Construction Timeline," *Airport Technology*, February 9, 2021, www.airport-technology.com/features/berlin-brandenburg-construction-timeline/.
2. Michael Bloch, Sven Blumberg, and Jürgen Laartz, "Delivering Large-Scale IT Projects on Time, on Budget, and on Value," McKinsey & Company, 2012, www.mckinsey.com/~/media/mckinsey/dotcom/client_service/corporate%20finance/mof/pdf%20issues/pdfs%20issue%2045/final/mof45_largescaleit.ashx.
3. Olivier Sibony, *You're About to Make a Terrible Mistake! How Biases Distort Decision-Making and What You Can Do to Fight Them* (London: Swift Press, 2020), 60.
4. Gary Klein, "Performing a Project Premortem," *Harvard Business Review* 85, no. 9 (2007): 18–19.
5. Dan Lovallo and Daniel Kahneman, "Delusions of Success," *Harvard Business Review* 81, no. 7 (2003): 56–63.
6. J. Park, "Curbing Cost Overruns in Infrastructure Investment: Has Reference Class Forecasting Delivered Its Promised Success?" *European Journal of Transport and Infrastructure Research* 21, no. 2 (2021): 120–136.

7. Marvin Weisbord and Sandra Janoff, *Future Search: Getting the Whole System in the Room for Vision, Commitment, and Action*, 3rd ed. (Berrett-Koehler Publishers, 2010).
8. Raaijmakers Mirea and Nikki Isarin, "How ING Uses Nudging to Mitigate Risk," *Financial Regulatory Forum* (Reuters), November 30, 2020, updated November 30, 2023, www.reuters.com/article/bc-finreg-ing-behavioral-risk-management/column-how-ing-uses-nudging-to-mitigate-risk-idUSKBN28A1WK.

Chapter 6

1. Jeff Boudens, Rodgers Palmer, and Brooke Weddle, "Mobilize Your Organization with a Powerful Change Story," Organization Blog, McKinsey & Company, October 28, 2019, www.mckinsey.com/capabilities/people-and-organizational-performance/our-insights/the-organization-blog/mobilize-your-organization-with-a-powerful-change-story.
2. Marshall Ganz, "Public Narrative, Collective Action, and Power," in *Accountability Through Public Opinion: From Inertia to Public Action*, Sina Odugbemi and Taeku Lee, eds. (Washington, D.C: World Bank, 2011), 273–289.
3. "Public Narrative: Leadership, Storytelling, and Action," Executive Education, Harvard Kennedy School, accessed August 2, 2023, www.hks.harvard.edu/educational-programs/executive-education/public-narrative-leadership-storytelling-and-action.
4. Paul Dolan, Michael Hallsworth, David Halpern, Dominic King, and Ivo Vlaev, *MINDSPACE: Influencing Behaviour Through Public Policy* (London: Institute for Government and Cabinet Office, 2010).

Chapter 7

1. Peter M. Gollwitzer, "Implementation Intentions: Strong Effects of Simple Plans," *American Psychologist* 54, no. 7 (1999): 493.
2. Dan Lovallo and Olivier Sibony, "Re-anchor Your Next Budget Meeting," *Harvard Business Review*, 2012, accessed August 2, 2023, https://hbr.org/2012/03/can-you-re-anchor-your-next-bu.
3. Olivier Sibony, *You're About to Make a Terrible Mistake! How Biases Distort Decision-Making and What You Can Do to Fight Them* (London: Swift Press, 2020), 225.

Chapter 8

1. Amy C. Edmondson, *The Fearless Organization: Creating Psychological Safety in the Workplace for Learning, Innovation, and Growth* (Hoboken, NJ: John Wiley & Sons, 2018).
2. "Creating Psychological Safety in the Workplace," HBR IdeaCast, episode 666, interview with Amy Edmondson, January 22, 2019, https://hbr.org/podcast/2019/01/creating-psychological-safety-in-the-workplace.
3. "Fearless Organization Scan Team Survey," Fearless Organization, accessed August 7, 2023, https://fearlessorganization.com/engage/fearless-organization-scan-team-survey.
4. Amy Edmondson, "Psychological Safety and Learning Behavior in Work Teams," *Administrative Science Quarterly* 44, no. 2 (1999): 350–383.
5. "Organizational Network Analysis," Deloitte Insights, accessed August 1, 2023, www2.deloitte.com/us/en/pages/human-capital/articles/organizational-network-analysis.html.
6. N. Tichy and C. Fombrun, "Network Analysis in Organizational Settings," *Human Relations* 32, no. 11 (1979): 923–965.
7. Gibbons, Paul, *The Science of Organizational Change: How Leaders Set Strategy, Change Behavior, and Create an Agile Culture*, illustrated ed. (Phronesis Media, 2019), 301.
8. Ibid., 309.
9. Micah Zenko, *Red Team: How to Succeed by Thinking Like the Enemy* (Basic Books, 2015).

Chapter 9

1. G. H. Litwin and R. A. Stringer Jr., *Motivation and Organizational Climate* (Harvard University, Graduate School of Business, 1968).
2. Olivier Sibony, *You're About to Make a Terrible Mistake!: How Biases Distort Decision-Making and What You Can Do to Fight Them* (London: Swift Press, 2020), 206.
3. Robert West and Ashley Gould, "Improving Health and Wellbeing: A Guide to Using Behavioural Science in Policy and Practice," *Public Health Wales* (NHS Trust, 2022), 35.

Chapter 10

1. Carol S. Dweck, "The Role of Expectations and Attributions in the Alleviation of Learned Helplessness," *Journal of Personality and Social Psychology* 31, no. 4 (1975): 674.
2. Carol S. Dweck, *Mindset: The New Psychology of Success* (New York: Random House, 2006).
3. Harry Fletcher-Wood, "Is Growth Mindset Real? New Evidence, New Conclusions," Blog post, March 6, 2022, https://improvingteaching.co.uk/2022/03/06/is-growth-mindset-real-new-evidence-new-conclusions/.
4. Michael Hallsworth, "Making Sense of the 'Do Nudges Work?' Debate," *Behavioral Scientist*, August 2, 2022, https://behavioralscientist.org/making-sense-of-the-do-nudges-work-debate/.
5. Jo Sweales, "How to Introduce a Learn-It-All Culture in Your Business: 3 Steps to Success," Microsoft UK Blog, October 1, 2019, www.microsoft.com/en-gb/industry/blog/cross-industry/2019/10/01/introduce-learn-it-all-culture/.
6. Taiichi Ōno, and Norman Bodek, *Toyota Production System: Beyond Large-Scale Production* (CRC Press/Taylor & Francis Group, 1988).
7. Jim Womack, *Gemba Walks* (Lean Enterprise Institute, 2011).
8. Jacqueline Brassey, Lisa Christensen, and Nick van Dam, "The Essential Components of a Successful L&D Strategy," McKinsey & Company, February 13, 2019, www.mckinsey.com/capabilities/people-and-organizational-performance/our-insights/the-essential-components-of-a-successful-l-and-d-strategy.

Conclusion

1. Dilip Soman and Catherine Yeung, eds., *The Behaviorally Informed Organization* (Toronto: University of Toronto Press, 2020).
2. Michael Hallsworth, "Rewiring Organizations for Behavioral Science," *Behavioral Scientist*, April 3, 2023, https://behavioralscientist.org/rewiring-organizations-for-behavioral-science/.
3. Michelle DiMartino and Pradnaya Pathak, "Four Perspectives on Embedding Behavioural Insights into Companies," *Behavioral Insights Team*, June 29, 2023, www.bi.team/blogs/four-perspectives-on-embedding-behavioral-insights-into-companies/.

About the Authors

Philip Jordanov is the Dutch-Bulgarian lead behavioral scientist at Neurofied. With a background in cognitive psychology and neuroscience at the University of Amsterdam, he is passionate about applying this knowledge to tackle challenges in business and society and contribute to positive change. Having played music for over 20 years, Philip can regularly be found playing gypsy jazz guitar with his brother on stage or, with the same stage passion, guest lecturing at universities in the Netherlands.

Beirem Ben Barrah is the Dutch-Tunisian Founder and CEO of Neurofied. He studied international business administration at the Free University Amsterdam (and Kansai Gaidai University), but his true education has been a combination of world-class martial arts training and fighting as well as independently building businesses since he was 18. He consumes dozens of books a year on topics ranging from entrepreneurship and behavioral science to technology and science fiction in order to find underlying patterns across disciplines. His other current passions include Wing Chun kung fu, running, coding, and VR.

Together they run **Neurofied**, the premier specialized consultancy for applying behavioral psychology and neuroscience to organizational change management in Europe. As a behavioral science company, they help organizations change, develop, grow, and innovate with scientific insights and evidence-based interventions. With their team of talented scientists and practitioners, they lead behavioral change projects in both the public and private sectors, ranging from change management and leadership development to public health and well-being in the built environment. Since 2018, they have been on a mission to democratize behavioral insights and translate them into practical, real-life solutions for positive change. Learn more at neurofied.com.

Index